WORK FOR WAGES IN SOUTH ASIA

SOUTH ASIA INSTITUTE, NEW DELHI BRANCH
HEIDELBERG UNIVERSITY
SOUTH ASIAN STUDIES NO. XIX

WORK FOR WAGES IN SOUTH ASIA

edited by
MARK HOLMSTRÖM

MANOHAR
1990

ISBN 81-85054-87-8

First Published 1990

Published by
Ramesh Jain
Manohar Publications
2/6 Ansari Road, Darya Ganj
New Delhi 110002

Phototypeset by
Spantech Publishers Pvt. Ltd.
5/58 Shankar Road, New Delhi 110060

Printed at
P.L. Printers
C3/19 Rana Pratap Bagh
Delhi 110009

Contents

Introduction

MARK HOLMSTRÖM

I sell my work for a wage. So, most probably, do you, unless you are a student and expect to do so later. If you are unemployed or look after children, you have worked for wages and may do so again. This is so whether you are a south Asian, a westerner like me, or whoever else is likely to read this book; even if, like me, you earn a wage which allows you to live while doing the work you would choose to do anyway, or if you work for a self-managed group like a co-operative.

Not only that, but I and probably you hope to build a *career*: to move into more responsible, more interesting and better paid jobs with the same employer or another. One job should be a preparation for the next and lead on to it in some intelligible way, though there are also accidents in the plot.

This book is about the development in south Asia, since the late nineteenth century, of the idea and practice of selling work as a commodity to an employer: whether by the hour or day, for a casual labourer (or a highly paid consultant); by the month or year, for a permanently employed industrial or office worker, who aims to build a career with the steady prospect of better things to come; even for years together, in the case of indentured labourers, or a whole lifetime's work as in a big Japanese company.

The terms of the contract, the social reality and expectations behind it, and the balance of power between the buyer and seller of labour, all vary enormously. We are in a very different position from low-caste casual labourers, even if in flights of political fancy we see ourselves as members of an academic proletariat. I belong to a registered trade union of university teachers. Our worries about academic freedom, as well as pay and conditions, are real and serious. But let us keep a sense of proportion.

The chapters in this book were originally papers presented to the section of industry and labour at the Ninth European Conference on Modern

South Asian Studies, held at Wilhelmsfeld near Heidelberg in July 1986.[1] These conferences, at three-year intervals, bring together historians, anthropologists, economists and others working in European universities—many of them south Asians themselves—and invited scholars from south Asia and elsewhere. Inevitably there is an emphasis on India, as the central and largest country in the region (though no one now speaks of 'the Indian subcontinent', unlike eurocentric writers who still call west Asia 'the Middle East'). Of the six chapters in the book, four are on what is now India, one on Indian migrant labourers in India and Sri Lanka, and one on Bangladesh.

Since so many papers were presented at the conference, on a wide range of topics, the organizer Dietmar Rothermund asked the convenors of some sections to select and edit papers for publication in short volumes on specific themes, each likely to interest a particular readership; rather than publishing all the papers as the conference 'Proceedings'—a volume or set of volumes which, he said, would be 'a gravestone', lying unread or seldom read in some distant library. I hope to justify his confidence by presenting, not an epitaph on the grave of south Asian labour studies, but a composite biography of the south Asian waged worker, a connected story traced from the transient agricultural labour of the nineteenth century to recent developments among sophisticated ambitious industrial workers.

Like any good biography, this should combine an outsider's view of what happened to the subject and why—for example, the economic pressures that formed the labour market—with the subject's own story: his or her experiences and ideas and choices. An economist alone, or an anthropologist or historian, can and should try to match the views from outside and from inside; but they are more likely to get the balance right if they collaborate and criticize each other's work as they did at this conference. Besides the usual arrangement by which each paper is introduced by a discussant—some by the writers of other papers, others by Pramit Chaudhuri and Peter Zingel—a rigorous malthusian policy of limiting both the number of papers and the time allowed to any speaker left time for others to take part in an animated discussion and to make connexions between the papers. Thus some of the rewritten papers are very different from the originals. Only Jacques Pouchepadass' paper was not discussed, as he was prevented at the last moment from attending. However, this paper makes such a good starting point that I have included it.

An editor's introduction often includes, or wholly consists of, a summary of each chapter, to allow the reader to choose the chapter or chapters most worth reading; or even to save the trouble of reading any of them (life is

[1] I am grateful to the British Council and the University of East Anglia, who paid for me to attend the conference.

short). I shall not do you this service. Instead I shall comment on the story as a whole, the biography of waged labour in south Asia, pointing up only some of the insights contained in particular chapters and, I hope, inspiring you to read them all.

The order of chapters is more or less chronological. Jacques Pouchepadass does not begin the story of the emergence of a market for agricultural wage labour—that was already under way—but he takes it up from 1860 onwards, in north Bihar. One can see some market forces at work within what was still a largely traditional system of relations between labourers and farmers. This explains the simultaneous shortage and excess of labour in the same areas. Yet the notion of 'segmented' or 'imperfect' labour markets does not advance our understanding much in a situation where the people themselves, labourers or masters, lack a capitalist definition of work and cannot think of it merely or mainly as a commodity bought and sold. In other words (mine, not Pouchepadass') we are not limited to explaining social relations in terms of the people's own categories (even if we assume—as we seldom can—that people in different positions agree about definitions and rules) yet we cannot ignore their ideas. At some point we must build a bridge between our categories and those which the people use to make sense of their social experience, on penalty of distorting that experience and fitting everything into universal explanations that explain nothing in particular.

Michel Cartier approaches the same problem in his introduction to a recent collection of studies, by historians and anthropologists, of representations of work in non-industrial societies (Cartier 1984, cf. Holmström 1987). His starting point is the observation that some societies but not others have a separate category of productive work, an activity by which man creates use-values: i.e. some version of the labour theory of value. Our political economy, derived from Adam Smith and Karl Marx, leads us to assume that capitalism has laid bare the true nature of work and of class, which had been hidden behind ideas of status and duty; and that we can only understand production and relations of production in ancient or primitive societies by describing them in terms the people themselves would not understand or, if they did, would deny. Cartier says we cannot dismiss the people's ideas so easily. The presence or absence of a category of 'work', generating use-values, reveals profound truths about the society. Analysis of each society's 'discourse about work' (discours sur la travail), or about production, gives us a privileged means to decode the underlying economic logic (pp. 12–3).

Pouchepadass, in his chapter here, is reasonably careful not to go beyond the recorded facts about his period. Yet his analysis implies recent departure from a baseline, a time before rapid change began: a time when labour was not bought and sold as a commodity, nor did people think of it in this way; a 'traditional' division of labour which in India took the form of the jajmāni system—the long-term exchange of work and prestations between clients and patrons, and an ideology of interdependence between specialized castes which was not too far from reality.

Edmund Leach follows Gandhi and W.H. Wiser (1936) in taking this ideology of interdependence as a true description of the situation in a not-too-distant past—the baseline, the time before rapid change:

> In a class society the 'people at the bottom' are those who have been forced there by the ruthless processes of economic competition; their counterparts in a caste society are members of some closely organized kinship group who regard it as their privileged right to carry out a task from which all other members of the total society are rigorously excluded.... The low castes suffer economically not because they are low *castes* but because present conditions have turned them into an unemployed working-*class*. (Leach 1962:6).

Yet there is evidence, from precolonial and early colonial times, of a large class of landless labourers, of migrant or urban wage workers, and craftsmen working for one-off payments in cash or kind (Kumar 1965, Das Gupta 1976, Meillassoux 1973, Holmström 1984:32–6).

If we simply contrast a modern economy where wage employment is the norm—in 'industry' and agriculture—with a preindustrial rural system of long-term patron-client relations (the *jajmāni* system), then we are not comparing like with like but ignoring the mixture of arrangements under which some people worked for others, both in towns and in the country, and the alternatives that existed for some people long before capitalism came to south Asia.

In other words, there is no baseline except an imaginary one: a time when castes served each other in the village community, joint families lived together in harmony and so forth. Yet the idea of departure from a baseline is still important, for two reasons. First, because there is some truth in it: especially since the beginning of this century, there has been a major shift from long-term relationships, including forms of tied labour rationalized as jajmāni, towards wage employment. Secondly, because the people themselves understand their present situation in terms of contrasts with, and survivals from, a past age of rustic harmony and stability, whether such an age ever existed or not. Their ideas are continuous with, though not the same as, the concepts used by anthropologists, sociologists, historians and political theorists: status and contract, community and individualism, the articulation of feudal and capitalist modes of production, and the rest.

If the chapters in this book have a common theme, it is the attempt to show how this 'discourse about work'—a debate, not a consensus, about production as it is and ought to be organized—has taken new turns in response to changing economic constraints and opportunities: the growth of capitalist industry and agriculture; the development of regional, national and even international labour markets, with railways and better communications; demands for migrant labour, for a seasonal or a settled work force, for a nucleus of highly-skilled workers, and so on. Pouchepadass takes up the debate at a point when several of these things were beginning to happen together; followed by Dick Kooiman and Colin Simmons who describe ideas about work and careers and relations between employers and workers, formed in the new environments of capitalist plantations and mines.

The idea of work as a commodity bought and sold, in a strictly limited contract between individual employers and employees, is not new in India (nor are traditions of economic or moral individualism); but capitalist employers and their employees now developed the logic of this idea more thoroughly and systematically *when it suited them*, depending on their bargaining power. At other times—like employers and workers in other industrial countries—they tended towards new forms of collectivism or corporatism: formal or informal agreements between, on one side, a big company or group of companies, or the state; and on the other side, a group of workers recruited by a jobber who may have exploited them but also spoke for them and defended them, or a trade union, or the settled residents of a factory township. The terms of the contract were constantly redefined and adjusted.

What we know about the changing terms of the contract in the past, about the supply of labour and working conditions, comes mainly from employers; also from government reports (Royal Commission on Labour in India 1931), social workers, and the middle class leaders of early trade unions. What is harder to get is the authentic voice of wage workers themselves. Oral labour history began late in south Asia (but see Perlin 1979). Anthropologists like Ramaswamy and Heuzé (in this book, and see Ramaswamy 1977) who write about the situation now, and some journalists, have the advantage that they can bring back full and largely verifiable accounts of how wage workers live, what the work means to them, and how they plan to survive and live better.

Dick Kooiman (in this book) takes up from Pouchepadass the story of male migrant labourers. These people travelled much greater distances to do more unfamiliar work, in the Ceylon coffee estates and Bombay cotton mills. Some did not survive the journey. The contract between worker and employer was mediated by *kanganies* or jobbers. The money which some workers sent back, or which stuck to the jobbers' fingers, enriched a few families and allowed the next generation to build solid middle class careers. In other cases the money enabled families to eke out a living from the land, or it was swallowed up in a black hole of debt.

Colin Simmons writes about a different relation between employers and workers. The classical male migrant worker—as in the Bombay cotton mills—made his own bargain with a jobber, who in turn made his with the mill manager (who made *his* bargain with the managing agency: a complication I shall not pursue here). Managers constantly complained of an unstable, uncommitted and undisciplined work force; but as Morris (1965) shows, most of these complaints were self-interested nonsense, entirely the managements' own fault—as the managements themselves came to see after about 1930. A few employers, like Tata at Jamshedpur (*ibid.*) or the Kolar Gold Fields (Simmons, in this book) designed stability into the work relation from the start, attaching the (male) worker to the company by a direct contract of employment, some prospects of advancement in a career (modified by the management's prejudices about the capabilities of different communities and races), and by providing a township for workers to live in with their families. Simmons insists this was not done from benevolence or paternalism, but out of sound economic logic. It was also meant to keep the unions out.

Now this type of relationship—job security, individual contract, often tied housing—set a pattern which became more common after Independence, both in some multinational or large Indian companies and especially in the public sector (it is one fault of this book that there is nothing on the public sector, which is important both because of its size and as an example to other employers and workers). Often it led to a kind of dualism in employment: permanently employed workers with unions to defend them, and 'temporary' or casual or contract workers with less pay and no security. This development could have led to a Japanese style of management, a firm expectation on both sides that the workers and the company are bound to each other: a lifetime's loyalty for a lifetime's security (Dore [1973:274–5], calls this 'welfare corporatism' rather than paternalism). Yet this never happened in India, except perhaps in rare cases. A few employers like Tata tried to build up such a relationship with their workers, but failed. Many more employers talk paternalism and practice chicanery. Workers and their unions want secure employment; but workers and managers generally expect that anyone who gets a chance to further his career elsewhere will do so. A discontented work force is simply a bad investment. Good conditions, some respect for the workers, and a well-equipped township are ways of making it rational for the worker to stay rather than go, and to learn to work better—when, and only when, it suits the employer to have a stable work force. In India, and probably in other south Asian countries, it is just not possible to build up the emotional loyalty to the company which the Japanese take for granted. Managers, workers and unions play the game according to market rules, each trying to turn the rules to their advantage.

The last three chapters—by an economist and two social anthropologists—bring the story up to date. It suited the Kolar Gold Fields management to have a stable work force; but the oil states of the Persian Gulf want temporary migrants only, and pay them much more than they could earn at home. Migrants' savings, whether spent on consumer goods, housing or productive investment, have transformed the economy of places like Kerala. Dick Kooiman described the long-term effects of migrants' savings and remittances on their own careers and their families. Béatrice Knerr (in this book) considers whether the spending decisions of migrants back from the Gulf—with far more to spend than Kooiman's earlier migrants—improved the long-term prospects for the desperately poor economy of Bangladesh. Her answer is: very little, and when the oil boom is over the chance will be lost.

Most south Asian manufacturing companies now find it most profitable to have both a stable core work force, and a fringe of workers—often women—who can easily be laid off without trouble. In this respect they follow the Japanese example. The difference is that the full Japanese option is not open to them. They cannot get a permanent work force with the same moral and emotional commitment to the firm for life; nor are they willing to pay the price, which is a job for life. The simplest way for employers to combine productivity with flexibility is to keep a sharp distinction between a core of permanent workers, and a disposable temporary labour force, including many skilled (but cheaper) workers. In practice this does not work, or no longer works. Permanent workers may work hard and well but they are difficult to control, constantly looking for ways to improve their position by joint action or by finding another job. Temporary or casual workers, with a foothold in the factory, find ways of becoming permanent in spite of the management's intentions (Holmström 1984:175–6, 224–7). E.A. Ramaswamy (in this book) describes the twists and turns by which managements try desperately to regain control of the work force. One way is to reduce the number of permanent manual workers—whom managements see as the most threatening and unpredictable element—not just by the old method of employing 'temporary' or contract labour, but by reclassifying some skilled workers as lower management staff in an attempt to divide and weaken their organization. 'Management' staff may even be cheaper, and easier to get rid of, than unionized permanent workers.

Another way is to meet the union head on: to reduce the complex issues of rights and career prospects and industrial relations to a straight bargain between two corporate groups: the management which gets control over work allocation, and the union which gets more money for its members. Managements emphasize that manning standards are fixed not arbitrarily but 'scientifically', by taylorist industrial engineers: an argument that middle-class union leaders can accept. The company and the union become mirror images of each other: hierarchically structured, under hardheaded leaders who believe they are competent to take decisions on behalf of the less qualified people below them. They can do business with each other, and they assume that most issues can be reduced to money. Working conditions, security, dignity and rights, all have their price.

We could leave it there, if industrial workers were really the ill-informed disorganized mass that some managers and some union leaders take them to be. But over the last few years—at least in India—two developments have undermined this cosy corporatism. The boundary wall between permanent and temporary workers has been eroded—sometimes faster than the employers could rebuild it—with the spread of unions among insecure workers employed both in large and small firms; and union members have become more sophisticated, clearer about their monetary and other goals, and more realistic about what unions can and cannot do for them. As Pouchepadass in his chapter says, 'With shopfloor activists as the vanguard, workers have begun to hem in their leaders and constrain them to function agreeably'. Either the dissatisfied members can change their leaders—something that was harder when the unions' democratic constitutions remained a dead letter—or they join another union, usually linked to another political party. They may move as individuals, or as a factory-based union branch which transfers its allegiance. The political links matter only for a few activists: the point is that the other union, and especially its leader, have shown an ability to stand up to management and to deliver the specific goods to which the workers attach most importance: usually pay rises, or job security, or both. The group of workers in a particular plant, sometimes a larger group bound together by ethnic or local loyalties, may or may not still have some solidarity. The relation between the union and the worker, or a united block of workers, becomes instrumental, contractual: the union must deliver within a limited time or the members will take their custom elsewhere.

The high point of this non-ideological, instrumental trade unionism is the recent 'Samant wave' of strikes in the Bombay area, as workers in factory after factory, in all kinds of industries, transferred their allegiance to Dr Samant, a leader who had shown great skill in pushing employers to the limit by aggressive bargaining and industrial action, while judging shrewdly their ability to pay in the end without going out of business or laying off too many workers. When Dr Samant lost his touch and miscalculated, when the losses began to outweigh the gains for many of his clients, the Samant wave broke. The initiative shifted back to activists working on the shopfloor. Gérard Heuzé in his chapter shows how this new attitude among industrial workers—their rejection of paternalism both at the place of work and in the union, their new realism about the rewards and costs of industrial work—is rapidly achieving what neither the market nor decades of theorizing about and exhortation to management could do: a rationalization of the work process bringing about a quick improvement in productivity and quality, as the only way the demands for higher wages can be met. Labour, rather than management, gives the push towards what Heuzé calls 'indigenous fordism' and sets the pace; seeing this as the price to be paid for the higher living standards which are now within industrial workers' grasp and which workers in other industrializing countries of Asia already enjoy. First things first: give us higher pay, job security and better prospects—the priorities vary; then there will be time to think about alienation, about the quality of life at work as well as at home.

To the extent that this move towards indigenous fordism or taylorism has taken place—and so far it has touched only a small though strategically important part of the work force—it has at least cleared some paternalist and corporatist lumber out of the way. The terms of the bargain, the relative strengths of the parties, are clearer than before. This could lead to an economic war of all against all, an atomized society where individuals attach themselves to unstable groups only for as long as this gives them some competitive advantage in the economic and political market place. But I suggest we should see it rather as a swing of the pendulum, a stage in the debate. For one thing, fordism quickly reaches its limits. 'Stable demand for large numbers of standard products is the cornerstone of Fordism . . . Fordism . . . is a method for the efficient production of one thing. It presumes that, once production goals are established, a set of routines and specialized machines can be devised to achieve them at minimum cost' (Sabel 1982:195, 210). Now this stable demand for industrial products is harder and harder to find. Besides the purely economic limitations of fordism, people simply will not put up with it for very long, especially once they know of alternative ways of organizing work: this has happened in one area after another—America, Japan, Europe, now perhaps in the 'newly industrialized countries' of southeast Asia. It becomes technically inefficient, and humanly intolerable, to take the separation of brain work and hand work beyond a certain point: the trend is in the other direction.

Besides, south Asian waged workers are not social atoms at all. Traditional loyalties to kin and community, new ideological loyalties, even the genuine appeal of equality—social, economic and sexual—all these things pull the other way. As the shopfloor activists—often politicized, sometimes idealistic—set the pace, and as new forms of labour organization emerge among the 'unorganized', we may be seeing a revival of ideological trade unionism with political and social concerns going beyond the interests of the individual plant or group of workers (see Holmström 1984:287–309 for some evidence).

This book, then, displays some of the terms on which labour has been employed, now and in the past, and how the parties to the contract have seen their relationship and acted in consequence. It is the history of the debate or discourse about work brought up to date. We leave you in the middle of the debate. Read the newspapers to discover what happens next.

REFERENCES

Cartier, Michel (ed.). 1984. *Le travail et ses représentations.* Paris: Éditions des Archives Contemporaines.

Das Gupta, Ranajit. 1976. 'Factory labour in eastern India: Sources of supply, 1855–1946'. *Ind. Econ. and Soc. Hist. Review* XIII, 3, 277–329.

Dore, Ronald. 1973. *British factory—Japanese factory: The origins of national diversity in industrial relations.* London: Allen and Unwin.

Holmström, Mark. 1984. *Industry and inequality: The social anthropology of Indian labour.* Cambridge: University Press; and 1976, Hyderabad: Orient Longman.

——— 1987. Review of M. Cartier, *Le travail et ses représentations. Man* (N.S.) 22, 1.

Kumar, Dharma. 1965. *Land and caste in south India.* Cambridge: University Press.

Leach, E.R. (ed.) and intro. 1962. *Aspects of caste.* Cambridge: University Press.

Meillassoux, Claude. 1973. 'Are there castes in India?' *Economy and Society* 2, 89.

Morris, M.D. 1965. *The emergence of an industrial labour force in India: A study of the Bombay cotton mills, 1854–1947.* Berkeley: University of California Press.

Perlin, Enid. 1979. 'Ragi, rice and four-yard dhoties: Indian mill workers as historical sources' in *Asie du sud: traditions et changements*, 451–7. Colloques Internationaux du Centre National de la Recherche Scientifique (intro. M. Gaborieau and A. Thorner). Paris: Éditions du CNRS.

Ramaswamy, E.A. 1977. *The worker and his union: A study in south India.* New Delhi: Allied.

Royal Commission on Labour in India. 1931. *Report.* Calcutta: Govt of India, Central Publication Branch.

Sabel, C.F. 1984. *Work and politics: The division of labour in industry.* Cambridge: University Press.

Wiser, W.H. 1936. *The Hindu jajmani system.* Lucknow Publishing House. Reprinted 1958.

The Market for Agricultural Labour in Colonial North Bihar 1860–1920

JACQUES POUCHEPADASS

The agricultural labour market in late nineteenth and early twentieth century North Bihar exhibited two apparently contradictory features. On the one hand, there is evidence that, in normal times, there was under-utilization of the agricultural labour force on a considerable scale in most districts as early as the last decades of the nineteenth century, a point which has been convincingly elaborated by Colin Fisher in his study of European indigo plantations in this region (Fisher 1976:228–37). The facts of the case are the chronic unemployment of the field labourers at certain periods of the year, as well as the early development of streams of temporary or semi-permanent labour migration from the crowded Gangetic areas to the less densely occupied sub-Himalayan fringe of North Bihar, not to speak of the long-distance migration flows to Bengal and Assam, which gain momentum from the 1880s onwards. The situation worsened as the years went by, and the Royal Commission on Agriculture in India unambiguously asserted in 1928 that in Bihar (as in the whole of Eastern India) 'the problem is definitely one of the superfluity of agricultural labour (even after allowance is made for the intense seasonal demand at seed time and harvest)' (*Report of the Royal Commission on Agriculture in India* [hereafter *R.C.A.I.*], para. 506). Yet during the same period, one often comes across equally sweeping assertions made by qualified observers which convey an entirely opposite point of view. A Muzaffarpur sugarcane planter, in his evidence before the very same Royal Commission on Agriculture, laments the fact that 'shortage of agricultural labour prevails everywhere', thus confirming the Bihar Census Report of 1921 which states that 'complaints under this head are universal'. F.H.B.

Skrine, reporting on the condition of the lower classes in Bengal thirty years earlier had already observed that 'in North Bihar, the demand for labour exceeds the supply'. The indigo planters, during the second half of the nineteenth century, had to induce Oraon tribals from Chota Nagpur (locally called Dhangars) to settle in their villages in order to ensure a minimum supply of manpower in times of need. All indigo factories also gave rent-free houses and rent-free plots of land to coolies on the understanding that the factory, in its capacity as *thikedar* or *mukarraridar* (tenure-holder, and representative of the zamindar) of the village, had a first call on their services whenever wanted. The competition for labour in the indigo villages was a constant cause of tension between planters and the local peasant élite. The various ways of binding labourers to which the landlords usually resorted, as well as the frequent employment of children on supposedly light work such as weeding in times of urgency, also point to a situation of recurring scarcity of labour.[1]

In order to explain these apparent inconsistencies, one would have to present a full-length examination of the agricultural system, demographic evolution and sociological structure of each North Bihar district. For example, one obviously important factor is the distribution of peak periods in the agricultural year in subsistence agriculture as well as in the commercial crops (opium, indigo and sugarcane) grown by the local peasantry and planters. The differential impact of the vagaries of the climate on dry and wet agriculture, and on heavy and light soils, also bears heavily on the rate of employment in each region and season. An equally essential factor was of course the density of the settled population. The agricultural employment situation was altogether different in districts which were sparsely populated, being either insalubrious or risk-prone or both, such as North Champaran, North Darbhanga or Purnea, and in densely settled areas such as Saran or the greater part of Muzaffarpur district. The situation also varied from village to village within each region according to facts of social structure, such as the caste composition of the agricultural population and the size of the poor and landless low-caste communities. Competition with child and female

[1] *R.C.A.I.*, vol. 13, *Evidence taken in Bihar-and-Orissa*, p. 40; Skrine 1892, para. 161. On Dhangars, see Inglis 1878: 380–1. On the competition for labour in indigo villages, India Office Records (hereafter I.O.R.), Bengal, General (Miscellaneous), August 1873, nos. 37–8. On the special conditions granted by indigo factories to coolies, Bettiah Raj Archives (Bihar), English correspondence, basta 1918–9, collection I, file 11.

labour may have aggravated unemployment. Coolies were often allowed by their employers to bring their wives and sons to work; and in the slack season, it was not uncommon for whole families to travel in search of work from village to village. The common practice of mutual aid may similarly have had a depressing effect on the labour market. In Champaran district in the 1880s, a large part of the land was tilled and sown, transplanted and weeded, without any wage labour. A cultivator beginning his cultivation obtained the use of his neighbour's plough. He helped him in weeding or transplanting his field, and was helped in return, etc. In Saran district, mutual aid was the rule for threshing, as the Settlement Officer reported: 'One cultivator lends his bullocks one day to his neighbour and gets his neighbour's bullocks the next day, the one condition being that the bullocks shall not be muzzled, that is to say, the man whose crop is being threshed feeds the bullocks as long as he uses them.'[2]

A detailed examination of the push and pull factors which constitute the main determinants of short-term and long-term labour migrations would also be necessary, as well as a study of the customary and economic factors which regulated the entry of women and children into the labour market. I cannot attempt to draw here the outlines of this complex and varied picture, which would be a long task even for a single district. The purpose of this paper is more limited. It focuses not on the ecological, demographic or economic determinants of the *size* of the supply and demand of agricultural labour, but on the *mode of operation* of the labour market as seen from two major standpoints, labour mobility on the one hand, and wage formation on the other. In the 'perfect' market model, there is no dichotomy between these two aspects: labour flows and the determination of wages are two facets of the same process of adjustment of supply and demand. But, of course, all labour markets are imperfect (and the labour market in colonial Bihar very much so), and both aspects are relatively independent of each other.

To begin with mobility, it is clear that the coexistence of under-utilization of labour and chronic labour shortage in rural North Bihar was largely due to the fact that the existing labour supply was not freely accessible to all

[2] Champaran Collectorate Record-Room (hereafter C.C.R.R.), General Department, basta 1888–9, collection II, file 5, 'Report on the economic condition of the lower classes of the rural population'; *Final report on the survey and settlement operations* (hereafter *S.R.*) *in the District of Saran (1893–1901)*, Patna, 1903, para. 595.

potential employers, on account of the heterogeneous and segmented nature of the labour market. It was of course segmented socially, not only according to age and sex as all labour markets are, but also according to caste status. The four highest castes in the countryside (Brahmans, Rajputs, Bhumihars and Kayasthas) did not as a rule cultivate land themselves, and very seldom performed manual labour for others; even the poor among them refrained from hiring themselves out unless distress compelled them to do so.[3] The percentage of workers of these castes who declared themselves as agricultural labourers oscillated around 2 per cent in Bihar as a whole in 1911 and 1931 (the real percentages may be a little higher) (*Census of India* [hereafter *Census*], *1911*:576–8; *Census 1931*:210). Similarly, small cultivators of respectable castes, even when under-employed, were reluctant to work for others unless at exceptional rates. The overwhelming majority of field labourers belonged to the low and untouchable castes such as Chamars, Ahirs, Dosadhs and Musahars: so much so that the percentage of agricultural labourers in the total working force of each district varied to a large extent in proportion to the percentage of these low and untouchable castes in the total population.

More importantly, most agricultural labourers were subject to constraints which prevented them from seeking employment freely when and where they wished. The basic distinction between free (mostly casual) and unfree (attached or bonded) labour is of course of relevance here, but there is no clear-cut demarcation between the two categories. It is true that the seasonal character of agricultural operations implied that the demand for agricultural labour was predominantly for casual hire, as the maintenance of permanent labour would be unprofitable for most farmers. But even where the labourers were not formally attached to their employers, there were often links of an implicit nature between them (Jha 1970:64). Traditional ties of long standing frequently existed between families of labourers and individual landowning families, which might be strengthened by credit and accommodation facilities offered by these employers. Moreover, as long as most of the opportunities for alternative employment had to be sought within the confines of the village, the independence enjoyed by the casual worker was necessarily more symbolic than real. Finally, there was a great variety of categories of free labour, from short-term contracts for a single day's work or a particular agricultural operation to arrangements lasting an entire crop season, or a whole year or more, based mostly on oral understanding in a context of personal relationships, and involving side-stipulations which shaded off into unfree labour. Then there was the social distance between employer and employee, as shown for instance by the

[3] I.O.R., Bengal, Financial, May 1892, A, 'District Census Report, Champaran', p. 210.

manner in which the untouchable labourer bowed to receive his wages at the end of the day, and by many other forms of ritually significant behaviour, which manifested the symbolic domination of the master over the low-caste casual farmhand. All things considered, it seems that the agricultural labourer was hardly ever able to hire himself out on a purely economic and objective contractual basis.

According to the Agricultural Labour Enquiry of the early 1950s, 97.7 per cent of agricultural labour families in Bihar were casual workers' families (*Report on intensive survey of agricultural labour* [hereafter *R.I.S.A.L.*]: 49). This percentage, as I said, cannot be taken as the actual figure for free labour. But in any case, before the vast increase of the number of landless agricultural workers which set in during the 1920s and 1930s, the situation was altogether different. The pressing need to ensure an adequate supply of labour during peak periods was a strong incitement to attach labour in the form of permanent servants, or to hypothecate labour services through interlinked land-labour or credit-labour contracts, particularly in areas where the proportion of high-caste peasants was high. The Collector of Saran District reported in 1879 that 'there is a large class of middle class farmers whose caste or pride restrains them from working, and who are prepared to devote all their influence and much of their substance to keep the really poor in the district, [so that] all schemes for diminishing the population by emigration infallibly fail' (*General administration report of Patna Division* [hereafter *A.R.P.D.*], *1878–9*: para. 35). Servile relations in agriculture existed in Bihar during the Mughal period, and were still observed by Francis Buchanan around 1810.[4] Actual slavery had disappeared in North Bihar in the second half of the nineteenth century (though the semi-servile *kamiauti* system remained in full force in Purnea District and in South Bihar), but debt bondage was common everywhere.[5] About 50 per cent of the agricultural labour force of the Patna Division was tied labour in 1888. As late as 1919, the Subdivisional Officer of Bettiah (Champaran) said that to impose the principle of free labour in his district would revolutionize the villages (*Report of the committee on the agrarian conditions in Champaran* (hereafter *R.C.A.C.*), II: 33; Fisher 1976:248–52).

Bonded labourers in North Bihar were known as *halwahas* (literally ploughmen, but it seems the name had come to designate the whole category of unfree agricultural labourers). A halwaha received a loan from his

[4] Buchanan 1928: 162; Buchanan 1934: 166. See also *Bihar Research Society Journal*, vol. XXXII (1946), pp. 98–105, and vol. XLIV (1958), pp. 50–1.

[5] As it was in Bengal proper: see Chaudhuri 1969: 243–5. On former forms of slavery, see *Bengal district gazetteers* (hereafter *B.D.G.*), *Bhagalpur*, p. 112. On the kamiyas, see *B.D.G., Monghyr*, pp. 129–30, *Purnea*, p. 110, etc.

employer, on the understanding that he would have to work for the employer until the debt was repaid with interest. It often happened that the sum, though actually quite small, was too large for the labourer to return, and he remained in perpetual bondage. He had to be at his master's beck and call all year round, and was allowed to seek employment elsewhere only when there was no work to be done on the farm. He might be given a piece of land rent-free as a house site. He usually got food and grain wages on working days. A plot of arable land could also be allotted to him for his subsistence on *batai* (share-tenancy), a tie-in arrangement which in fact aggravated his debt-bondage. His day's work was often longer than that of the casual labourer, and he often had to do household work or run errands for his master in addition. On the other hand, he enjoyed a greater security of employment than most casual labourers. But the frequency of court procedures instituted by the employers to secure the return of their halwahas was sufficient proof of the hardships many of these unfree workers endured.[6]

Another form of unfree labour was *begari*, or forced labour, which the zamindars or tenure-holders demanded from their tenants as a customary right. The origin of begari may be traced to the personal service which all subjects, in the traditional kingdom, were expected to render to the king in return for the right to reside and work on the land, and which local chiefs and magnates exacted on their own account as a normal corollary of power (Galey 1983). Begari as outright unpaid corvée, being forbidden as an illegal cess and punishable under the law, seems to have been declining in North Bihar by the end of the nineteenth century. An authorized representative of the North Bihar indigo planters declared in his evidence to the Indian Industrial Commission of 1918 that it had disappeared from the districts of Tirhut Division, at least in the indigo villages (*Report of the Indian Industrial Commission* [hereafter *R.I.I.C.*], *Evidence*, I: 421). Yet other witnesses expressed opposite opinions before the same commission (*R.I.I.C.*, *Evidence*, I: 1030); and complaints relating to unpaid labour, though not always well founded, were often received around the same time by the district or settlement authorities from the tenants of Indian zamindars as well as of certain European tenure-holders (*S.R. Champaran* [1922]: para 78). The Village Notes drawn up by the settlement staff in the late nineteenth and early twentieth century settlement operations in North Bihar also occasionally mention local landlords who illegally claimed begari from their raiyats.

[6] See the evidence given by the Subdivisional Officer of Bettiah (Champaran) in *R.C.A.C.*, vol. II. The condition of the Bihari halwahas in 1950, as described by Govt. of India, *Agricultural wages in India* (hereafter *A.W.I.*), pp. 68–9, was still very similar to what it had been half a century earlier.

In any case, even if unpaid begari had become less widespread, the recruitment of compulsory labour at nominal wages by local landlords remained common everywhere. By village custom the landlords were generally entitled, in rotation, to use each tenant's plough for one or a few days each year to cultivate their private (*ziraat*) lands. Each raiyat had to give one or two ploughs, usually with bullocks and drivers, to his master (*malik*) on the day or days chosen by the latter.[7] This service was generally paid for, but at a low rate, and begari remained the popular term by which it was called. European tenure-holders were as keen as Indian landlords to exert this right fully. It was of course extremely distasteful to the raiyats, all the more as they were not free to choose the days on which they were to do the landlord's work. The settlement officials were surprised to find that ziraat lands were sometimes let out to them at rates enormously in excess of the current village rates. The tenants agreed to these rates in order to avoid the begari they should have to render if the lands were not let out (*S.R. Champaran* [1922]: para. 78). In the same way, the landlords (or tenure-holders) could requisition their tenants' carts for transport. For threshing the landlord's crops, a tenant had to lend his bullocks, and got little in return except their feed, and perhaps a meal for himself if he assisted personally (*Bihar-and-Orissa district gazetteers* [hereafter *B.O.D.G.*], *Saran*: 80).

These obligations fell on the tenants. But the field workers were equally subject to the arbitrary will of their landlords, who had first call on the services of all labourers available in their villages whenever they needed them, and who often paid them less than the local average rate. This was one of the privileges which landlords and tenure-holders enjoyed as local power-holders, and which the indigo planters labelled 'zamindari influence'. A Champaran planter stated in court in 1876:

> By zamindari influence, I mean that a zamindar takes carts and employs labourers for his own use without paying for them, or paying too little for them; he makes his ryots attend his weddings; he collects the rent from them, takes salamis on various occasions. These are matters of custom.... If an outsider offers 8 annas to a cartman, and the factory 4 annas or 5 annas, he would prefer the outsider's offer if he is allowed to do so. An outsider would not be in a position to offer 8 annas in opposition to the factory influence, because the factory servants in the dihat would not allow him. They will probably abuse him and in some other way put him out of the place.[8]

This prior right of the Bihar landlords to employ the labour force of their

[7] The detailed conditions for particular villages are often mentioned in the Village Notes compiled during the settlement operations, which are kept in the revenue records of each District Collectorate in Bihar.

[8] I.O.R., Bengal, Judicial, June 1877, A, no. 13.

villages at abnormally low wage rates was still prevalent in the 1920s (*R.C.A.I.*, XIII: 269).

Since the labour market was segmented socially, by age, sex and caste differences, and politically, owing to considerations of power, the role of market forces was inevitably limited, and the mobility of the workers was reduced. It was in this context that labour migrations took place. The second half of the nineteenth century was a period of improvement and extension of road, river, and above all railway transport. The new railways, in particular, were largely used by the labouring population of North Bihar, as the statistics of passenger traffic showed (*Census 1921*:4, 109), at a time when the high demographic pressure on the land, and the low level of wages in the area (Bihar wage rates being the lowest in the whole Bengal Presidency) induced an increasing number of agricultural workers to seek employment beyond the immediate neighbourhood, and sometimes far afield. The Census of 1901 enumerated 245 000 emigrants from Saran district, and about half this number from Muzaffarpur, Darbhanga and Bhagalpur (while the two other districts of North Bihar, Champaran and Purnea, were predominantly immigration areas). The figures were a little higher in 1911, then fell slightly in 1921 (*Census 1911*:162; *Census 1921*:77). These emigrants were to an appreciable extent agricultural labourers (*Census 1911*:166–73; *Census 1921*:109–11). About half were long-distance migrants, i.e. migrants to non-contiguous districts, most of them temporary. Permanent long-distance migrants nowhere accounted for more than 10 per cent of the total number of migrants.

There were however strong limiting factors to this migratory activity. Essential among these was the fact that a high percentage of labourers combined self-employment with wage employment, which partly explains why most emigrant workers wished to go home during the busy season. In the districts of Patna Division at the end of the nineteenth century, about two-thirds of agricultural labourers had some land of their own to cultivate (*S.R. Muzaffarpur*, para. 922; *S.R. Champaran* [1900], paras. 70, 590; Skrine 1892, para. 161). It often happened that officially landless resident labourers had small unassessed plots cultivated adjoining their houses (which was really a case of trespass, and rendered them liable to ejection by their zamindars) (*S.R. Champaran* (1922), para. 91). To own or lease in a parcel of land, however small, which the labourer cultivated intensively with the help of family labour, was an important guarantee in the absence of assured and continuous employment, whatever it may have cost in mobility.

Even the mobility that existed was not synonymous with an integrated labour market. In most cases the decision to emigrate was not a result of competition between alternative employment opportunities, but a way to avoid slack season unemployment. There was little emigration from May till the end of October or even November, that is to say during the busy agricultural season. Most temporary migration occurred in the cold season, between the reaping of the winter and spring crops. Only in the districts where the spring crops were not cultivated on a large scale and could be reaped by those who remained behind, the labourer often stayed away all through the hot weather until the rains came. This movement of labour was usually unguided and haphazard, owing to the lack of proper information on employment opportunities. The emigrants often had no definite promise of work when they set out, but only the knowledge, derived from past experience or hearsay, of place where work was likely to be available, and they wandered about from village to village hiring themselves out when occasion arose. Those who sought work outside the agricultural sector, as earth-workers on public works, miners, mill-hands, factory workers, railway coolies, deckers, domestic servants, cartmen, palki-bearers, chaprasis etc., did so in the same haphazard way, or under some kind of jobber system which lured them into yet another form of unfree labour (*Census 1911*:166–73; *Census 1921*:109–11). When the labourer returned to his village, he resumed his place in the local power structure, which he had been allowed to leave temporarily while his services were not required. Lastly, the demand for labour was itself extremely fragmented. The employers naturally tended to recruit their labourers, especially on long-term contracts, in their own villages or in the immediate vicinity, even when lower wages prevailed outside, because their own influence was purely local, and because they put a premium on the character and dependability of the workers they employed. All this leads to the conclusion that though some degree of mobility of labour existed, the labour market remained fundamentally unorganized and spatially segmented. A clear sign of this lack of integration was the fact that agricultural wages varied not only from district to district, but even from village to village. For instance, daily grain wages in the Dhaka thana of Champaran district during the revisional survey of 1913–9 varied in neighbouring villages from 2½ to 5 kachcha seers of 46 tolas, i.e. up to twice as much.[9] We must now turn to this essential question.

Most agricultural wages were paid in kind. Even though the wage census reports of the early twentieth century seemed to imply that grain wages in Bihar were already gradually dying out, there is ample evidence that it was only in towns and bazars, in indigo and other factories, and on public works, that money wages were paid. In towns and factories, the employers preferred cash payments because they were easier to administer, and

[9] C.C.R.R., Revenue Department, Village Notes (revisional survey), Thana Dhaka.

because, in a situation of rising prices and wages lagging behind prices, they provided a bigger share in real terms. But agricultural wages were nevertheless paid in kind in nearly all cases. Even in the 1950s, a high proportion of casual labourers in Bihar were paid wholly or partly in kind, and the wages for certain agricultural operations such as reaping and threshing still consisted everywhere of a specified share of the produce.[10]

The systems of payment in kind differed from place to place and even from employer to employer. The labourer got a fixed allowance of grain for each working day or agricultural operation. This formed the basic element of his pay, and was usually uniform within the village limits. The type of grain given was invariably the cheapest and coarsest kind of cereal or pulse available on the market, except when the wages consisted of a certain percentage of the crop, or in areas specialized in paddy cultivation such as North Champaran, where rice was usually given. Casual labourers also received their midday meal free, consisting of fried cereal or pulse, *sattu* (ground parched grain) etc. The remuneration of attached farm servants was more complex. In addition to their regular ration of grain and free meals, they were entitled to various perquisites at different times of the year. They could be given one or more dhotis in the year, one blanket in the cold weather, advances or small gifts to meet ceremonial expenses such as marriage, festival gifts, free housing, small plots of rent-free land, domestic fuel and vegetables, grass stalks as fodder, thatching grass, plus an occasional small cash wage, etc. These perquisites were neither uniform nor systematic. They varied in value and quantity from village to village, and were often given only irregularly. They entailed no loss to the employers. Free meals given on the spot allowed employers to get more work from their coolies than if the coolies had been permitted to leave work to take their food. Though permanent servants received perquisites, their grain allowance on working days was usually somewhat lower than that of casual labourers (a 'security discount' which they accepted as the price of guaranteed year-round employment). In any case, the employers were willing to pay a little extra in order to be assured of an adequate supply of labour at peak periods.[11]

Both casual and attached labourers received specific rates of payment for

[10] I.O.R., Bengal, Revenue (Agriculture), May 1908, A, no. 7–8, 'Report on the First Wage Census of Bengal' (1908), p. 4; *Report on the Second Wage Census of Bengal taken in April 1911* (hereafter *S.W.C.*); *Report on the administration of the Lower Provinces of Bengal* (hereafter *R.A.B.*), *1896–7*, p. 130; *R.C.A.C.*, II, p. 32; Bettiah Raj Archives, English correspondence, basta 1918–9, collection I, file 11; *A.R.P.D., 1881–2*, para. 14; *S.R. Saran*, para. 590–5; *R.I.S.A.L.*, p. 18.

[11] I.O.R., Bihar-and-Orissa, Financial (Commercial), January 1920, A, nos. 14–31, Deputy Collector, Muzaffarpur, to Commissioner, Tirhut, R–3293, 13.9.1919.

certain agricultural operations. For harvesting and treading out or threshing the gathered crop, payment almost always consisted of a share of the produce. In harvesting, the labourer usually got one sheaf out of every sixteen cut and deposited at the owner's yard. A smart worker could earn in this way about eight sheaves (roughly 5 seers) a day. The state of the weather had so much to do with the progress of the work that this, from the employer's point of view, was the only fair method of payment. In threshing, the workers were similarly entitled to 1 seer out of every 16 threshed.[12] The customary rates varied when the pressure of market forces was too compelling. In the great rice-cultivating area of North Champaran in the 1870s, the labour supply being particularly scarce and largely dependent upon seasonal immigration, the reapers received two out of every sixteen bundles reaped, with an occasional bundle thrown in, a mode of remuneration so much more advantageous to the labourers that it was difficult to induce them to accept any money wages during harvest time (Hunter 1877:280). On the other hand, in Saran district at the end of the 1920s, owing to the excess supply of labour and to the rising trend of prices, the labourers, though still paid in kind for these operations, were only given one out of 21 bundles cut or seers threshed (*B.O.D.G., Saran*: 80). This of course did not mean that non-market influences were then totally ruled out: in South Bihar, almost at the same time, a reaper was usually paid with the largest sheaf out of a certain number, which varied according to his status.[13] The mode of remuneration of ploughmen was also specific, and probably more complex than that of any other category of labourers. The constituents of the salary were of necessity the same as those of other labourers (including payment in advance, a share of the produce, grant of rent-free land, clothing etc.), but the system of extras was more elaborate, as the relationship of a ploughman to his employer was often a lifelong connection (*S.W.C.*: 20).

Such complicated patterns of payment present a difficult problem to the economic historian whenever he tries to find out how and why they varied, and to what extent they were amenable to market forces. The main difficulty is that these wages are practically impossible to convert into money terms. Grain payments are very difficult to evaluate in cash terms because of the wide diversity of the kinds and varieties of foodgrains and pulses used;

[12] *A.R.P.D., 1876–7*, para. 25, and *1881–2*, para. 14; Hunter 1877, p. 108; Harrison 1890, p. 277; I.O.R., India, Revenue and Agriculture (Famine), December 1888, A, 'Report on the condition of the lower classes of people in Bengal', enclosure, report by J. Boxwell, Commissioner of the Patna Division, para. 23; *S.R. Saran*, para. 590–5; *S.R. Darbhanga*, para. 479.

[13] I.O.R., Bihar-and-Orissa, Financial (Commercial), January 1920, A, nos. 14–31, Secretary to Govt. of Bihar-and-Orissa, Financial Dept., to Secretary to Govt. of India, Dept. of Revenue and Agriculture, 4868–Com., 8.12.1919.

because of the variability of grain prices from season to season and from place to place (according to the cropping system, the difficulty of communication with centres of trade etc.); and because of the problems of identifying correctly the units employed to measure out the wages. Moreover, how is one to calculate the value of gleanings (which halwahas were normally allowed to collect) or of grain left on the threshing floor, which formed part of the remuneration of certain categories of labourers? The quality and value of meals provided by the employers also varied considerably. A rent-free house, clothes, shoes, bundles of straw or domestic fuel are equally difficult to convert into money with any precision (Atchi Reddy 1978 and 1979). Finally, time comparisons would have to be made for each agricultural operation (ploughing, embanking, harrowing, manuring, sowing, transplanting, weeding, irrigating, reaping, threshing etc.), since the wage rates, and the combinations of cash and kind payments, were more or less different in each case (*A.W.I.*: 20).

The impression one gets from the official sources of the period under study is that the wages of agricultural labour remained remarkably stable in spite of the steeply rising trend of agricultural prices. One can read everywhere in the reports and correspondence of the colonial administration of North Bihar during the last decades of the nineteenth century that wages in the villages were primarily regulated by custom, and that for this reason they were basically stable, whatever the fluctuations in the supply and demand of labour or in the price of food.[14] These assertions were largely based on the half-yearly district returns of wages collected from 1873 and published in the official provincial Gazettes and, in condensed form, in the *Prices and wages in India*. This series was discontinued around 1908 and replaced, as far as Bihar was concerned, by a quinquennial wage census, the fourth and last of which was taken in 1924. For earlier periods, only scattered and haphazard wage quotations are available. It would seem for instance from these figures that the average daily wage of an unskilled agricultural labourer in Muzaffarpur district had remained close to 1½ anna from 1814 down to *c.* 1900, and had risen to 2 As only by 1910. The average remuneration in Champaran (a district where labour was scarce) oscillated between 1½ and 2 As around 1870, rose to 2 As around 1900, and to 2½ As around 1915; and so on.[15]

Prices and wages in India has been so often and competently criticized

[14] Such comments are of almost yearly occurrence in the *A.R.P.D.* and the *R.A.B.* between the 1870s and the end of the century. See also *B.D.G., Darbhanga*, pp. 84–5; etc.

[15] See particularly, among innumerable official statements, *A.R.P.D., 1872–3*, app. I, and *1876–7*, app. A; *S.R. Muzaffarpur*, para. 895; *B.D.G., Champaran*, p. 93; *S.W.C.*, p. 7; wage censuses of 1916 and 1924 quoted in *Bihar statistical handbook, 1950*, p. 117.

right from the beginning of this century (notably in 1904 by W.H. Moreland in his capacity of Director of Land Records and Agriculture, United Provinces, then by K.L. Dutta in his *Enquiry into the rise of prices in India* [1914], etc.) that there is no need to draw up a new indictment against it here.[16] These figures were simple arithmetical averages of agricultural wages which varied considerably according to place, agricultural operation, employment conditions etc.; they lacked comparability in time, as they were not collected under the requisite systematic conditions; and above all they were only money equivalents of grain payments and perquisites, which means, for the reasons given above, that they were at best hypothetical. Moreover the figures collected by the local agencies were often corrected by district authorities, on the basis of their own impressionistic assessment of the movement of wages. These corrections probably tended to flatten out short-term variations. The demand for unskilled labour created by railway and canal construction and other public works, or by the proximity of an indigo or sugar factory, led to increases in the price of unskilled labour in the neighbourhood, and this was well recognized. But these rises were purely local and (in the case of public works) temporary. Wages were also indisputably higher in the vicinity of towns, where the presence of a European civil or military population increased the demand for labour, but the interior of the districts remained unaffected by these trends. Urban and industrial development, in any case, was much too sluggish in Bihar to generate any general rise in wage levels (O'Connor 1886:3; *A.R.P.D., 1874–5*: para. 52, *1876–7*: para. 25, *1881–2*: paras. 12 and 14, *1882–3*: para. 24, *1884–5*: para. 43, etc.). So there was nothing to undermine the general belief in the fundamental stability of agricultural wages.

There is no question that grain wages were rigid, and not only because they were governed by custom. On the one hand, it was hardly possible for the employers to reduce them, because they were close to the minimum subsistence level (*R.A.B., 1876–7*:109). There were many reasons for this: the employers' generally low capacity to pay, the periodic excess supply of labour, the low output per labour unit etc. On the other hand, all-round wage rises were impossible to obtain, because of the frequent concentration of land control and power in the hands of a small village élite which kept wage rates at their base level; because of the indebtedness of the workers, which reduced their bargaining power; because of their low social status and lack of organization, etc. Yet one fact should not be lost sight of: this stability of nominal grain wage rates, given the vagaries of the monsoon

[16] See I.O.R., Chief Secretary to Govt. of United Provinces to Secretary to Govt. of India, Dept. of Revenue and Agriculture, no. 203 of 1905, 23.1.1905; Dutta 1914, I, pp. 198–202, 244–6. Among recent studies, see Kumar 1965, chap. IX; Bhattacharya 1965; Atchi Reddy 1978.

and the extreme irregularity of the crops, was synonymous with violent fluctuations in real terms. This fact, of course, was not as significant then as it would be today, since the village economy was little monetized and only a minor part of the foodgrain crops found its way to the market, most of it being destined for subsistence consumption and exchange in kind (Pouchepadass 1984). Yet there are signs that even the customary grain wages were not totally immune to seasonal fluctuations. It had long been remarked that exceptional rates were paid in times of serious scarcity or famine (Geddes 1873:47). But it also appears that some wage variations did in fact occur as a result of seasonal crop irregularities, though in a disguised fashion. The kind of grain which was given as wages was at the employer's discretion, which permitted some adjustment of the actual wage rate when high prices ruled the market; in any case, the fact that grain payments were made in the coarsest qualities of grain, which were as a rule least affected by the market rises, limited the loss which the employer was liable to incur. The quantity of food allotted to the workers for their midday meal could also be a little reduced in times of strain: this was often the case before the summer crop. On the other hand, the labourers were more liberally treated when crops were abundant (*A.R.P.D., 1881–2*: para. 14). But the excess payments were given in the form of extras, the traditional rate remaining officially unchanged. In this way, custom always tended to bring the wage level back to the accepted standard, though the transient prosperity of favourable seasons did materially affect the rate of remuneration.[17] On the whole, wages in kind did vary to some extent with short-term fluctuations in the availability of grain.

In all likelihood, wages also varied in consequence of the long-term rise in agricultural prices in our period. This was of course a very slow and irregular process. S.R. Bose, in his statistical survey of foodgrain prices in Bihar and Orissa from 1861 to 1934, found that it was only when there was a long-term trend for the price level to increase or decrease, and when this increase or decrease was considerable, i.e. 20 per cent or over, that wages moved, frequently with a time-lag of several years (Bose 1938:30). Of all categories of wages, moreover, agricultural wages were the slowest to move. Of course the fall in nominal grain wages may have long been negligible in the areas where the commercialization of food crops remained on the whole a marginal phenomenon. But at the beginning of the twentieth century, it was obvious in many parts of North Bihar that peasant employers tended to reduce grain allowances or to shift to money payments whenever market prices rose.[18] The labourers were of course very much

[17] I.O.R., Bihar-and-Orissa, Financial (Commercial), January 1920, A, nos. 14–31.

[18] See I.O.R, Bengal, Revenue (Agriculture), May 1908, A, nos. 7–8, 'Report on the First

against the conversion of grain payments into cash in these circumstances. They occasionally went on strike to oppose their employers on this account, as for instance in the Bettiah subdivision of Champaran in 1908. In Bhagalpur district the following year, they migrated to Bengal rather than accept an unfavourable wage rate (*R.A.B., 1909–10*:5). But it became gradually easier for the employers to impose their own terms after the First World War, as the labour supply began to rise swiftly, and little remained of whatever small bargaining power the labourers may have formerly enjoyed.

There is evidence, then, that both the supply/demand ratio and the availability and price of grain, which remained the main medium of payment, increasingly influenced the terms of remuneration of agricultural labourers in early twentieth century North Bihar. Yet one cannot say that the logic of competition was the only or even the main factor in the working of the agricultural labour market. The heterogeneous and segmented nature of the market reduced the mobility of the workers and limited the influence of market forces, as we have seen in the first part of this paper, and the wage level remained partly dependent on customary criteria. In a rural society still structured in terms of caste and clientèle, it is natural that labour transactions should still be affected by considerations of status and power. In the context of the face-to-face village society, the relationship between employer and labourer was heavily conditioned by social distance and the distribution of power, and in no way resembled the theoretically impersonal, standardized and competitive model of capitalist labour relations. To argue in terms of 'imperfect' or 'dual' labour markets is rather unhelpful here. Not only are all labour markets more or less imperfect, but there is no clear-cut demarcation, in the agricultural labour market of North Bihar, between traditional and modern: market forces do play a role, as we have just seen, within the framework of 'traditional' labour relations (Breman 1976). Such terms, moreover, may be misleading if they have any teleological implications, as is often the case. It might be more useful to probe into the meaning attached to work in the peasant society of North Bihar. The capitalist definition of work as a distinct category of human behaviour and action, with its own economic rationality and autonomous institutional set-up, seems inappropriate here. The agricultural labourer in colonial North Bihar lives in a world where labour relations are but a component part of a hierarchical and redistributive social system. This world is by no means impervious to market influences. But a crucial factor in shaping any labour system is the

Wage Census of Bengal'; I.O.R., Bihar-and-Orissa, Financial (Commercial), January 1920, A, nos. 14–31, District Magistrate, Bhagalpur, to Commissioner, Bhagalpur, no. 4836G, 18.9.1919.

conception employers and labourers have of their own condition, rights and duties; and this, in colonial North Bihar, often had little in common with what is known as the 'market mentality'.

REFERENCES

Official Publications

Bengal District Gazetteers, Bhagalpur, Calcutta, 1911.

Bengal District Gazetteers, Champaran, Calcutta, 1907.

Bengal District Gazetteers, Darbhanga, Calcutta, 1907.

Bengal District Gazetteers, Monghyr, Calcutta, 1909.

Bengal District Gazetteers, Purnea, Calcutta, 1911.

Bihar and Orissa District Gazetteers, Saran, Patna, 1930.

Bihar Statistical Handbook, 1950, Gulzarbagh, 1951.

Census of India, 1911, vol. v, *Bengal, Bihar-and-Orissa and Sikkim.* pt. 1, *Report*, Calcutta, 1913.

Census of India, 1921, vol. vii, *Bihar-and-Orissa*, pt. 1, *Report*, Patna, 1923.

Census of India, 1931, vol. vii, *Bihar-and-Orissa* , pt. 1, *Report*, Patna, 1933.

Dutta, K.L. 1914. *Report of the enquiry into the rise of prices in India*, Calcutta, 5 vols.

Final report on the survey and settlement operations in the district of Champaran, 1892–1899, Calcutta, 1900.

Final report on the survey and settlement (revision) operations in the district of Champaran, 1913–1919, Patna, 1922.

Final report on the survey and settlement operations in the district of Darbhanga, 1896–1903, Calcutta, 1904.

Final Report on the survey and settlement operations in the district of Muzaffarpur, 1892–1899, Calcutta, 1901.

Final report on the survey and settlement operations in the district of Saran, 1893–1901, Patna, 1903.

General administration report of Patna Division (annual).

Goverment of Bengal, *The crops of 1865–66 for comparison with those of 1873–74: Extracts from official papers*, compiled by J.C. Geddes, Calcutta, 1873.

Government of India, Ministry of Labour, Agricultural Labour Enquiry, *Agricultural Wages in India*, Delhi, 1952.

Government of India, Ministry of Labour, Agricultural Labour Enquiry, *Report on intensive survey of agricultural labour (employment, underemployment and levels of living)*, vol. iii, *East India*, Simla, 1955.

Hunter, W.W. 1877. *A statistical account of Bengal*, London, vol. xiii, *Tirhut and Champaran.*

O'Connor, J.E. 1866. *Prices and wages in India*, Calcutta.

Report of the Committee on the Agrarian Conditions in Champaran, Patna, 1917, vol. i, *Report,* vol. ii, *Evidence.*

Report of the Indian Industrial Commission, 1916–18, Minutes of Evidence, vol. I, in *Parliamentary Papers*, 1919, vol. XVII.

Royal Commission on Agriculture in India, *Report*, London, 1928, and *Evidence*, vols. I–XIII, London, 1927–8.

Report on the administration of the Lower Provinces of Bengal (annual), 1870–1910.

Skrine, F.H.B. 1892. *Memorandum on the material condition of the lower orders in Bengal during the ten years from 1881–82 to 1891–92*, Calcutta.

SECONDARY WORKS

Atchi Reddy, M. 1978. 'Official data on agricultural wages in the Madras Presidency from 1873', *Indian Economic and Social History Review*, 15, 4.

——— 1979. 'Wage data from private agricultural accounts, Nellore District, 1893–1974', *Indian Economic and Social History Review*, 16, 3.

Bhattacharya, D. 1965. 'Trend of wages in India (1873–1900)', *Artha Vijnana*, 7, 3.

Bose, S.R. 1938. *A statistical survey of food grain prices in Bihar-and-Orissa*, Patna.

Breman, J. 1976. 'A dualistic labour system? A critique of the "informal sector" concept', *Economic and Political Weekly*, 11:18–50, 27 Nov., 4 and 11 Dec. 1976.

Buchanan, F. 1928. *An account of the District of Purnea (1809–10)*, Patna.

Buchanan, F. *An account of the District of Shahabad (1812–13)*, Patna, 1934.

Chaudhuri, B.B. 1969. 'Rural credit relations in Bengal, 1859–1885', *Indian Economic and Social History Review*, 6, 3.

Fisher, C. 1976. *Indigo plantations and agrarian society in North Bihar in the nineteenth and early twentieth centuries* (unpubl. Ph.D. diss., Univ. of Cambridge).

Galey, J.C. 1983. 'Creditor, king and death. Bonded labour in the Garhwal Himalayas', in C. Malamoud (ed.), *Debt and debtors*, Delhi.

Harrison, F.C. 1890. 'The Behar ryot at home', *Calcutta Review*, 92.

Inglis, J. 1878. *Sport and work on the Nepal frontier*, London.

Jha, D. 1970. 'Structure, employment and earnings of agricultural labour in Champaran District in Bihar', *Indian Journal of Agricultural Economics*, 25, 3.

Kumar, D. 1965. *Land and caste in South India: Agricultural labour in the Madras Presidency during the nineteenth century*, Cambridge.

Pouchepadass, J. 1984. 'Peasant economy and the market system in early twentieth century Bihar', in K. Ballhatchet and D. Taylor (eds.), *Changing South Asia: Economy and society—papers presented to the Seventh European Conference on Modern South Asian Studies*, Hong Kong.

Questions of Money: A Comparative Analysis of Ceylon Coffee Estates and Bombay Cotton Mills

DICK KOOIMAN

Most South Asian studies take for granted the coexistence of a capitalist mode of production, based on wage labour and geared to a world market, and a non-capitalist mode of production, held together by personal relations and kinship ties, and operating within the confines of a more local market. This study is no exception to that rule. The same paradigm implies that both modes of production should not be viewed as watertight compartments, as there is a large amount of interaction and, in fact, subordination of the second to the first. In this paper I make an exploratory analysis of the function of debt relations and financial remittances in the articulation between these two modes of production in South Asia.

As Das Gupta (1981:1783ff.) has pointed out, the labour market in colonial South Asia was rigged and essentially unfree. Pouchepadass argues the same for the agricultural labour market in Bihar (see this volume). To a large extent, labour migration was determined by non-economic factors like compulsion, government intervention and debt bondage, while mobility remained restricted to a movement from certain 'catchment areas' to some economic centres, and the preservation of existing social relationships within those centres. Following the same line of argument Omvedt (1980:200) refers to 'the relative immobility of peasant migrants who kept their family and village ties and their debt bondage'. Therefore in the first part of this paper I will investigate the function of debt relations, old and new, in the recruitment of labour in the colonial period.

According to Omvedt, the lack of a family wage[1] was a dominant characteristic of the colonial labour market. Wages in the capitalist mode were just sufficient for the worker's subsistence, but in case of illness or old age and for the maintenance of his family members he was relegated to his village of origin. And as far as there were any financial remittances from the capitalist centre to village society—in the form of advances, transfers or savings—they are assumed to have been insubstantial (Omvedt 1980:195). So a second question will be whether there were financial remittances from the workers involved in the capitalist mode of production to their places of origin and, if so, the amount of these remittances.

These questions will be analysed from a comparative perspective by focusing on two cases: the coffee plantations in Ceylon in the nineteenth century, and the Bombay cotton mills at the end of the nineteenth and the beginning of the twentieth century.

The first coffee plantation in Ceylon was opened in 1824. From the 1830s onwards the culture of coffee made spectacular progress and substantial profits were made. The necessary labour came from the rural, Tamil-speaking districts of south India. Systematic recruitment started round about 1840 and in the 1850s the coffee plantations used 70 000–80 000 workers at harvest time. In 1867 more than 1.5 million Indian emigrants had crossed the sea to Ceylon. In the 1870s, however, leaf disease destroyed most of the shrubs and planters shifted to tea or other cash crops.

In 1856 the Bombay Spinning and Weaving Company started its first cotton mill. Many others followed suit and in 1875 Bombay had 27 and in 1900 even 82 cotton mills, making textiles the leading sector of the urban economy. The majority of the mill workers came from the surrounding countryside, especially from the southern district of Ratnagiri. In 1921 the Bombay mill-industry employed 147 000 and in 1931, 136 000 workers. In other words, about 12 per cent of the city's inhabitants, almost one quarter of the working population, depended for their livelihood on the cotton mills.

I am acquainted with the situation in Bombay through previous research on the emergence of trade unions in that city. Labour relations in Ceylon came within my ken during my present research on the position of the Untouchables in nineteenth century Travancore. This paper is a comparative analysis of both cases, partly based on research findings that have already been published elsewhere.

For the study of the Ceylon case I could make use of recent publications

[1] Radha Kumar (1983:82) makes the critical comment that the concept of the 'family wage' was introduced only around 1930 and with exclusive reference to the male worker, reducing women's wage labour to a supplementary status.

as well as contemporary sources, like planters' memoirs and planting directories. I also consulted some missionary archives for information on the plantation workers and their places of origin. For Bombay, apart from literature, there are several official reports of inquiry into labour matters, often supplemented by volumes of evidence that are very instructive. There is also a unique study by Harold Mann (1917) of a village that supplied labour to Bombay.

THE COFFEE ESTATES IN CEYLON

Recruitment and Debts

In the beginning Ceylon planters sent their own agents to south India to recruit the necessary labour. Within a short time, the workers began to migrate on their own, forming a gang with one of them as their leader. This leader or *kangany* first of all conducted his gang on the hazardous journey from south India to Ceylon, mainly along the 'North Road' via Mannar, where many fell victim to local robbers or fatal diseases. On the estates, the *kangany* negotiated wages and other employment conditions and eventually supervised his people at their daily work.

As the cultivation of coffee continued to grow, the demand for labour kept increasing. Therefore it remained necessary for many coffee planters to go in search of labour, which could take months. Sometimes a planter was lucky enough to run across a gang of coolies who stopped on the road to enable their *kangany* to start negotiations. That was a hopeful sign—one planter wrote in his memoirs—as usually they were already firmly bent on some destination, 'in which case they marched past, shouting out, as they did so, the name of the estate to which they were proceeding' (Millie 1878, ch. III).

About the middle of the nineteenth century the *kangany*'s function gradually changed. According to Millie *kanganies* and workers began to realize their own value when they saw the *durais* (Europeans) taking the trouble to leave for India to meet their growing demand for labour. The *kanganies* were said to have offered to take over that role from the planters.

Other sources confirm this picture, albeit without mention of white superintendents hunting for labour in south India. In the 1850s a new and more enterprising class of *kanganies* emerged. Instead of the chosen gang-leader of the first period, the *kangany* increasingly became a planters' agent in charge of recruitment (Roberts 1966:12ff.; Samaraweera 1981:138). It was still possible for a worker to be appointed *kangany* in exchange for the supply of 'a large fine gang of able-bodied men' (Ferguson 1868:126). In most cases, however, a planter would choose the *kanganies* himself from among his most reliable men who had a long service-record and a clean crime-sheet. Later, there also appeared *kanganies* who were exclusively engaged in recruitment and never set foot on the estate.

In that way the position of the *kangany* became more firmly established, but at the same time his dealings grew more business-like and even ruthless. For every worker he brought in the *kangany* received a small amount of 'head money' from the estate.

Loans or coast advances became a major instrument in the recruitment of labour. The *kangany* left for India with a certain sum of cash to be paid to prospective workers as a portion of wages and by way of inducement. These advances could be used for a farewell party in the village, travelling expenses to Ceylon or the support of family members left behind (Tinker 1974:133; Samaraweera 1981:138). Other sources suggest that these advances were primarily meant to free potential migrants from existing debt relationships. In that case their financial dependence on local landlords and moneylenders merely shifted to the labour contracting *kangany* (Omvedt 1980:197–8; Das Gupta 1981:1787–8).

The point is that plantation workers ran into debt right from the moment of their recruitment in India. On arrival in Ceylon, a planter wrote, they were already 'deeply indebted to the Estate' (Ferguson 1868:121) and soon after that they had to contract further loans to cover their living costs for the first month. All these loans had to be repaid from the wages received. And even if planters may not have charged interest on the advances paid, *kanganies* were not always of that mild disposition.

The planters used to place unlimited faith in their *kanganies*. Many contemporaries, however, held a more critical view and asserted that *kanganies* greatly abused their power and appropriated considerable part of their people's earnings. For instance, they made every effort to save on travelling expenses and to pocket the money thus saved. By raising the pace of march, the average travelling time and thus the required amount of food could be reduced, but migrants who could not keep up with the main group died of exhaustion by the roadside (Roberts 1966:117; Tinker 1974:172–3, 179).

The costs of travel, ferry included, ranged from Rs 2 to Rs 3. Therefore the amount of the coast advance was mainly determined by the amount of money a worker wanted to use for other purposes. According to Millie (1874, ch. III) an advance of Rs 4–5 per head was sufficient to get the necessary labour. Roberts (1966:118), speaking of the 1860s, takes Rs 5–7.5 to be the usual average, while in 1868 a planter wrote: 'Mootoosami [meaning the Tamil coolie], however much he may like his old estate, yet will not (I believe in many instances, cannot) return to it from his country without some rupees—eight or ten, in advance' (in Ferguson 1868:121). This means that the average advance did not surpass or hardly surpassed the average monthly wage (Rs 9).

Higher advances per head were not considered to be safe, even by a planter like Millie. Sometimes *kanganies*, after receiving the coast advances, vanished without leaving a trace and workers could run away without repaying their debts. To minimize these risks a part of a *kangany*'s gang remained on the estate to guarantee his return and in many cases the whole gang was held responsible for the financial obligations of individual members.

Wages and Remittances

In the introduction the question was raised as to the extent village society benefited from its supply of labour to the capitalist mode of production. Several research scholars claim that the migrant labourers received just enough to keep body and soul together for the period of their employment, and that financial remittances were insignificant or non-existent. But most of these views are of a general nature or derived from preconceived theories, not based on detailed analysis. It remains to be seen, however, whether it is possible to reach final conclusions from the available source material.

Most studies agree that work on a Ceylon coffee estate was much better paid than comparable employment in south India. So migrant labour was not only pushed by poverty, famine or unemployment at home, but also pulled by the prospect of better earnings on the plantations. In the 1860s casual labour in the Tamil districts of Travancore was paid Rs 4–5 per month (LMS Odds, Baylis 11.11.1864; Mateer in LMS Chronicle 1869:135) as against Rs 7–9 on the Ceylon coffee plantations (Roberts 1966:118; Bandarage 1983:209, 218; Ferguson 1868:123). The crucial question, of course, is how much the plantation workers were able to save.

On most estates the workers received part of their wages in rice. Although Millie admits that this transaction was especially profitable to the plantation,[2] he nevertheless contends that 'a good man, after full work, on deducting his rice, would probably have a balance of 11s or 12s to receive', that is Rs 5.5–6 per month. He is probably referring to an early period. Roberts has made a computation for the 1860s. According to him, every worker needed about Rs 4 per month for living expenses. Adding Rs 0.5

[2] Bandarage (1983:211–2) makes the point that rice was supplied at a fixed rate generally below the retail market price. Nevertheless, this was more advantageous to the planters than raising wages.

for extra expenses, this means that every male worker had an average monthly surplus of Rs 2.5–4.5; for females it was one or two rupees less. Families, though not numerous in this kind of seasonal labour, had higher expenses, but usually women and children were also gainfully employed. The surplus could be used to purchase clothing and toddy or to repay the advances. Taking Rs 5–7.5 as the average advance, Roberts (1966:118–9) is of the opinion that a worker was able to repay the advance within three or four months. Following this line of reasoning, the planters' contradictory statements about their workers' debts and savings might be explained by their initial but passing state of indebtedness.

Roberts is aware that the picture he has given might be too rosy. Yet his calculations do not take account of continual hazards like illness, interruption of work, withholding of wages, new loans or payment of interest. All these factors reduced net wages and any surplus.

Returning to the main questions of this paper, it might be useful to emphasize that the advances paid by the coffee plantation already represented a financial remittance to village society, even if the money was not used for family subsistence but for debt clearance as Bandarage argues (1983:210). In the 1860s the advances, according to most estimates, amounted to Rs 5–10. After deducting Rs 2–3 for travelling costs, there remained Rs 3–7 for expenditure in the village, i.e. an average monthly income in south India. This income is even more significant when we remember that the peak period in coffee coincided with the slack season in south Indian agriculture.

There remains, of course, the question whether the financial remittances from the plantation economy to the south Indian rural districts deserve to be called 'substantial'. The government of Madras had no difficulty in answering this question and considered migration to Ceylon to be of obvious benefit to its citizens (De Silva 1961:115).[3] In the same vein, authors like Hardgrave (1969:53), Kumar (1965:141–2) and Wesumperuma (1978:12) mention sizable sums of money brought home by the Tamil migrants used for the purchase of land or shops in south India. As a more indirect benefit they refer to the spread of a reform-minded and enterprising mentality as well as the outlet which Ceylon offered to the most depressed in times of crisis.

Since there were Christian missionaries working among the families of

[3] Later official reports held the same view. In 1931 the Census Commissioner of Madras reported that 'on several occasions [he] had pointed out to one a house differing markedly from its neighbours as being that of someone who had been to Malaya or Ceylon', *Census of India* 1931, Madras, XIV:I, p. 93. The Ceylon Census Report of 1901 noted, that in Ceylon the Indian estate workers were better fed, clothed and housed than their fellow villagers in south India (quoted in Rote 1986:77).

plantation workers in Ceylon and south India, it might be interesting to see whether their reports contain any information on this subject. Although these reports mainly deal with Christian workers, in socio-economic terms this small group may be seen as representative of the larger working force. We start from the assumption that financial remittances from the plantation economy to the church in south India should be considered a financial benefit to village society.

From the 1840s missionaries of the London Missionary Society (LMS) in south Travancore frequently reported that local Christians were lured away to Ceylon because of better paid employment on the estates. Several pupils of LMS boarding schools and the Nagercoil Seminary managed to get *kangany* positions and recruited their own friends and family members, which led to a growing orientation of native Christians to plantation economy. Further inspiration was received from famous success stories like those of Devasagayam and Paul who, after a career as *kangany* in Ceylon, settled in Travancore as well-to-do coffee planters and supported the Christian community with handsome donations (Kooiman 1984:199). Although only a small number of returned migrants succeeded in starting their own plantation, the names of many Christian *kanganies*, conductors, clerks and coolies regularly appeared in the LMS donation lists. Nevertheless, the coffee boom was no unmixed blessing and in 1872 the missionary in Nagercoil complained that 'thoughts about property, money and coffee estates bulk much more largely in the minds of many native pastors and teachers' than he feared to be good (LMS Odds, Duthie 20.2.1872).

From 1855 to 1862 Hobbs served the Tamil Cooly Mission in Ceylon. His reports confirm that Christian plantation workers could save money and send remittances home, perhaps partly because they spent less on liquor. In one of his letters Hobbs mentioned that 'a large proportion of Tamil Christians on the Estates are connected with the London Mission and send their contributions in aid of it to Nagercoil' (CMS Hobbs, Letter 24.11.1859).[4]

THE COTTON MILLS IN BOMBAY

Recruitment and Debts

Right from the beginning the recruitment of labour for the Bombay cotton mills was entrusted to jobbers. These jobbers had the same socio-economic

[4] De Silva (1965 ch. IX) accuses the missionaries of ignoring the grave social problems on the estates, as they were interested in the plantation workers only as potential converts. Hobbs, however, realizing 'that it would have been . . . criminal to keep silence', criticized the treatment of the workers on different occasions, risking his mission which depended heavily on the goodwill of the planters (CMS Hobbs, Journal 13.7.1859, Letter 24.11.1859).

background as the workers, but as labour contractors, foremen and supervisors they were able to build up positions of considerable power. In the 1930s, however, they began to lose influence in consequence of technological change, rationalization and the institution of independent labour officers.

In the early period many jobbers went up-country to collect the necessary labour for their mill department. They seem to have pictured urban factory life in bright colours, but went no further than advancing travel expenses as additional inducement. In cases of labour scarcity the jobbers did receive a premium for bringing in labour, but there is no evidence that this money was handed over to potential recruits by way of advance. (Labour Commission 1931 Report, pp. 22–4; Burnett-Hurst 1925:47).

Within a short time it was no longer necessary to recruit labour in the countryside. A migration movement started and the field of recruitment shifted from country to city. There the jobber lived amongst his relatives and friends and by acting as adviser and moneylender he was able to wield sufficient influence over these people to staff his department (Burnett-Hurst 1925:46–7; Edwardes 1909–10, vol. I: 493–4).

The provision of loans by the jobber could be one of his instruments to gain control of his men. But usually it was the job-seeking migrant who contacted the jobber and asked him for work and a loan. First of all, migrant labourers arriving in Bombay possessed little hard cash. Generally they did not find work overnight, but somehow they had to eke out a livelihood. Apart from that they were expected to pay the jobber some *dasturi* (fee or commission) as the price of engagement. And even if a job was secured, it did not solve the urgent problem of lack of cash. Cotton mills used to pay the first wage only after two months and kept regular wages in arrears. The end result was that in most cases engagement by a cotton mill coincided with entering into a debt relationship. Special circumstances like marriage, illness or death created the need for fresh loans, while fines or the obligation to buy spoiled cloth could increase indebtedness beyond redemption (Kooiman 1978:41).

The jobber played an important part in arranging these loans. Sometimes he acted as a moneylender himself. But as his means were limited, the jobber usually introduced his men to other moneylenders, like mill-officers, grain dealers or *marwari* merchants, and stood security for them (Kooiman 1983:143). At the beginning of the 1920s the average annual interest amounted to 75 per cent, but evidence from the 1180s suggests a rate of 100–300 per cent (Factory Commission 1185, pp. 112, 122). In the countryside the interest was considerably lower. Harold Mann (1976:96–7) noted that in 1916 the average interest in a village near Poona was 19.5 per cent.

No wonder, in 1908 a Factory Inspector reported that the majority of mill-workers were indebted to their jobber and that 'some mill hands were so greatly in debt that they would never be free' (Labour Commission 1908 II, p. 52). Such a debt relationship need not be entirely to the worker's disadvantage. He could also derive some security from it, since his chance of employment was guaranteed as long as his debt to the jobber was not cleared. Therefore in some mills the jobber was officially forbidden to lend money, as very inefficient workers managed to enter the mills through that channel (*ibid.*, p. 106). But the dependence was mutual and so was the risk. If a labourer left before the debt was cleared, the jobber had to bear the loss.

The chief function of the debt relationship seems to have been to tie workers to the mill. Late payment of wages was a deliberate management policy to reduce the threat of high labour turnover, while the consequent dependence on loans enabled the jobbers to strengthen their control over the men. Lokhande, a labour sympathizer who tried to organize Bombay labour in the 1880s, considered earlier payment of wages the most urgent necessity. In 1884 he presented the President of the Factory Commission with a petition, signed by 5500 mill workers, requesting 'that payment of wages be made not later than the 15th of the month following that for which they have been earned' (Factory Commission 1885, p. 230). In 1890 he even advocated weekly payments (Labour Commission 1892, pp. 168, 172). His efforts remained fruitless and the 1929 Royal Commission on Labour had a clinching explanation for this: a belated monthly payment served the interests of moneylenders and jobbers, 'whose anxiety not to relax any hold over the workers is greater than that of the employers [and who] are not likely to favour any step which tends to make the workers more independent' (Labour Commission 1931 Report, pp. 239–40).

Wages and Remittances

Once again, any discussion of wages, costs of living and eventual remittances has to allow for a serious lack of reliable quantitative data. The researcher has to hew his way through a jungle of contradictory statements and mere impressionistic comments. Even if something can be said about the relation between wages and the costs of living, actual remittances remain unclear. A mill-worker might use a surplus for other purposes than the support of his family in the village. On the other hand, the occurrence of financial remittances cannot simply be taken as an indication of comparative prosperity. Several reports mention that workers had to contract fresh loans in order to send money home (Labour Commission 1908 II, p. 97).

Before World War I the mill-owners used to defend their wage policy by emphasizing the workers' 'extravagant habits' like drinking, gambling and other vices. In 1908 an employers' representative expressed the opinion that 'all the money they earned went to the graindealers and in sweetmeats and drink and no less than 10 per cent of them saved money. Very few sent money to their country' (*ibid.*, p. 66; see also p. 85). Sometimes this view was endorsed by government officials like the Collector of Bombay, who declared shortly after World War I that 'he was informed by the Excise Staff that at least 70 per cent of the Bombay working men were drinkers. Excessive drinkers were less than 10 per cent' (*Times of India* 24.5.1923). Of course the question remains whether excessive drinking should be seen as an indication of abundance or as a mark of poverty.

Generally, however, the government held the view that the mill-workers as a thriving community yearly sent large sums home, which were partly invested in buying land (Labour Commission 1892, p. 174). The Gazetteer of Ratnagiri, the district that supplied almost half the textile labour force, also referred to large sums of money that were used for wedding-feasts and the purchase of land and jewellery (Gazetteer 1880:143).

The social worker Nare, who ran a night school privately for workers' children, acknowledged that many workers wasted their money on gambling and drinking. His estimate was that 50 per cent of the cotton mill-workers were in debt and that only 20 per cent had provided for old age and 'live[d] happily in their homes, generally in Ratnagiri District' (Labour Commission 1908 II, p. 116). More representative, probably, was the opinion of Lokhande who at the end of the nineteenth century had campaigned for earlier payment of wages. Time and again he pointed out that the workers could save no money at all and that most of them were burdened by debts. He denied resolutely that the workers were a thriving community and attributed their addiction to drink to their misery and ignorance. 'Any independent and unprejudiced judge going round the mills on a pay day can immediately form an opinion whether the operatives really accumulate money or whether their means are insufficient to keep them in a safe position' (Factory Commission 1885, p. 112, also pp. 123, 230–1; Labour Commission 1892, p. 169).

After World War I the government set up the Bombay Labour Office to examine in a scientific and exact manner the real conditions of work and wages. In 1922–23 it conducted one of its first and most frequently quoted inquiries on working class budgets in Bombay. This inquiry, based on about 3000 budgets of families and single men, nearly 50 per cent of which were mill-workers' budgets, disclosed monthly remittances of considerable sums, from Rs 1–11–1 in the case of families to Rs 11–7–1 in the case of single men. But at the same time it concluded that half the mill population was in debt—to the extent of Rs 50 on average at an interest of 75 per cent per annum—and that every worker earning less than Rs 30 per month added one rupee to his burden every month (Labour Office 1923).

As might have been expected, this report in no way solved the dispute. The mill-owners missed no opportunity to quote the remittances, whereas labour sympathizers kept referring to the existence of mass indebtedness (Kooiman 1983:137–8).

There were, however, some fundamental weaknesses in the report as has been shown very competently by the Bombay Textile Labour Union (Tariff Board 1927 III, pp. 443–7; Labour Commission 1931 I, 1, pp. 344–5). First of all, the finding that the textile worker's average earnings were Rs 30–10–1 per month was very misleading, as the salaries of highly paid mill officials (masters, store-keepers, jobbers) were included in the calculations. Equally erroneous was the report's failure to take account of the many deductions from wages in the form of fines, interest or *dasturi*. It was also unmistakably clear from the report's own pages that remittances were sent in spite of the excess of expenditure over income, resulting in increasing indebtedness. This suggests, again, that remittances cannot be regarded as an accurate index of the workers' economic position.

Harold Mann is one of the very few who at that time did research at the receiving end of the remittances, a small village in Poona district. In 1917 nine families and eleven single men were absent from this village because of employment elsewhere, mainly in Bombay. Using local information, from the Post Office for instance, he estimated that these people sent a total of Rs 900 a year to their village by way of money order or savings brought home; this figure, he says, is 'guess work, though not far from the truth' (Mann & Kanitkar 1921:110–1). This sum of Rs 900 is considerably less than the Rs 1700 that might have been expected from nine families and eleven individuals on the basis of the 1923 Labour Office Report, but we have to bear in mind that in summer 1917 monthly wages in the Bombay mills averaged Rs 16–6–3 (Tariff Board 1927 I, pp. 109, 111). The estimate of Rs 900 to Rs 1700 agrees remarkably well with the average monthly wages of Rs 16–6–3 in 1917 and Rs 30–10–1 in 1923, lending additional support to the findings of the Labour Office inquiry.

Another calculation shows that the yearly remittance of Rs 900 works out to Rs 3–12–0 per month per migrant family or single man. That information is interesting, as Mann reports that the average monthly income in his village of research was Rs 14 per family or Rs 2–12–0 per head (Mann and Kanitkar 1921:116). Mann concludes that financial remittances to the village were much smaller than was often supposed. But compared to the average income in the village these remittances were far from negligible.

One of the most significant findings of the Labour Office inquiry might well be that industrial workers consumed less cereals than the diet prescribed by the Bombay Jail Manual, although 57 per cent of their income was spent on food. That means that if remittances were sent home, it must have been to the detriment of the workers' health, the recovery of which was a cost to the same village society.

SUMMARY AND CONCLUSION

Plantation *versus* Industry

In Ceylon as well as Bombay, debts played a prominent part in labour recruitment and employment. By entering into a debt relationship the worker was tied to the estate or mill or to its representatives, and restricted in his mobility. This loss of freedom (how free was he before?) was mitigated but not compensated for by a guarantee of employment.

A notable difference, however, was that the plantation workers ran into debt before or right from their departure for Ceylon, whereas workers bound for the Bombay cotton mills incurred their debts only after getting a job in the mill or at least after their arrival in the city. Another difference was that the advances paid through the *kanganies* were in fact paid by the estate, whereas in Bombay loans were supplied by independent moneylenders not formally associated with the mill.

Further investigation shows that this applies not only to the difference between Ceylon and Bombay. *Sardars* from the tea plantations in Assam, *maistries* from the coffee plantations in south India and labour contractors from the coal fields in Bihar and Bengal paid advances in the same way to induce potential recruits to follow them to plantation or mine (Das Gupta 1981:1787–8; Manickam 1977:80; Chatterjee and Das Gupta 1981:1862–3). In the Calcutta jute mills and the Kanpur cotton mills, however, the situation was like that in Bombay: most labourers migrated to the city on their own, waited for a job at the mill gate and tried to tide over the period without income by borrowing money from shopkeepers or professional moneylenders through *sardars, maistris* etc. (Das Gupta 1981:1791; Joshi 1981:1829; Mitra 1981:1839). This immediately raises another question: why was there this difference between plantations and mines on the one hand and cotton and jute mills on the other?

A first thing to note is the geographical location of the new capitalist enterprises. The plantations and mines were in less accessible and more thinly populated areas. The cotton and jute mills, on the other hand, could only be found in big cities that were centres of densely populated regions. Therefore the urban industry could recruit its labour force from surrounding districts, and between Bombay and a more remote district like Ratnagiri there was a direct sea link by coastal vessels. But a journey to Ceylon or

Assam was a much more troublesome and even dangerous affair that could last several days if not weeks, and left many dead by the roadside as victims of disease or exhaustion.[5]

Here we probably touch on the heart of the matter: in the plantations and coalfields labour was in great demand, whereas in urban industry the supply of labour was sufficient. Contemporary reports from Ceylon frequently refer to labour shortage, crimping of workers and *kangany* rivalry, and especially in the picking season planters were virtually left to the tender mercies of their *kanganies* (De Silva 1961:107; Samaraweera 1981:146; Lewis 1926:52). For Bombay, Morris has convincingly demonstrated that the cotton industry, if there were no exceptional circumstances like epidemic or war, could always command a sufficient number of hands. This difference becomes manifest in that the *kangany* was paid head-money by the plantation for every worker he brought in, whereas the jobber received his commission (*dasturi*) from the worker in return for employment.

What remains is the question whether the plantation workers of south India were more dependent on local landlords and moneylenders than were the cotton labourers of Maharashtra. That could explain why the former had to be bought off, or at least transferred to another debt relationship, much more often than the latter. For a more definite answer we need more information about the economic situation in the villages of origin. That information is as yet inadequate, even with authors like Omvedt who take local debts as the starting point of their argument.

Poverty and Inequality

It is still very difficult to ascertain whether remittances from the capitalist mode of production to village society were substantial or not. There is a great lack of reliable data, and it is not clear what exactly should be meant by 'substantial'.

As I have shown, the advances received by estate labour in Ceylon in the 1860s ranged from Rs 2.5 to Rs 7.5 (travelling costs not included), i.e. more than an average monthly wage in south India. It is not clear to what extent this money was spent on behalf of the family or used to repay loans, as Omvedt and Das Gupta suggest. In view of the seasonal character of the coffee culture and the fact that family members stayed behind, repayment of loans does not seem to have been an urgent priority. Apart from that, the amount of debt cannot have been onerous, if one advance was sufficient to

[5] In 1849 the *Colombo Observer* estimated the mortality rate among the Indian immigrants at 25 per cent (De Silva 1961:120). Hobbs wrote in 1859 that 'out of 120,000 immigrants last year, I think 10,000 at least died . . .' (CMS Hobbs, Journal 13.7.1859).

pay it off. Therefore Omvedt's remarks may well be more relevant to the tea estates which came up after 1880 and required a more permanent labour force.

How much money the plantation workers themselves brought home from Ceylon remains impossible to determine. In some cases it must have been substantial, considering that they were able to invest in land, as in Travancore.

As for Bombay it was found in 1917 that a village received about Rs 3–12–0 per family or single man working in the city. In 1923 a family in Bombay might send Rs 1–11–1 and a single man Rs 11–7–1 to their home village. Remember that in 1917 the average monthly income in a village was about Rs 14 per family, as against Rs 16–6–3 per head in a cotton mill. And in 1923 nearly half the mill labour force had an average debt of Rs 50 per head.

Omvedt holds the view that village society was impoverished by the production and reproduction of labour for plantations and factories. She refers to districts as Tanjore and Ratnagiri that were chief suppliers of labour to Ceylon and Bombay but nevertheless still remain among the most backward regions of India. The only reply can be that in the nineteenth century these regions were already seriously overpopulated and economically stagnant. The poorer classes were fighting a desperate struggle for subsistence and it might well be that the crumbs that fell to them from the capitalist table, and the refuge it offered in times of crisis, enabled them to survive. One should also make a distinction between the material improvement of private households from external sources (however small) and the economic growth potential of an entire district. Over the past years Kerala has supplied labour to the Gulf countries on a large scale and, as local newspapers testify, these workers return home with heavily-packed suitcases and full purses. But that does not necessarily mean that Kerala state, which was noted until recently for its high birth-rate and low income per head, will derive any long-lasting economic benefit from this labour migration.[6] In the same way, as Béatrice Knerr observes in her contribution to this volume, labour migration from Bangladesh to the Gulf does bring a higher standard of living for the poor, but will have no long-term growth effects for the country as a whole.

Another of Omvedt's conclusions is that, as far as there was any inflow

[6] From 1837 to 1877 more than £3 million were paid in wages to immigrant workers from south India, according to the *Planting Directory* (1879:86). Today India is among the largest beneficiaries of migrant remittances and in 1980 it received no less than $3000 million from that source (World Economic Survey 1983, provisional figures, *Economic and Political Weekly* 1984:536).

of remittances, it only increased existing inequality within village society. The local dominant classes pocketed most of the profits, since their representatives held the better paid positions in capitalist enterprises and even the meagre earnings of the workers largely came into their hands through debt clearance (Omvedt 1980:207). Tinker (1974:60) and Standing (1981:195–6) are of the opinion that, though some migrants did make material progress, the majority merely changed one form of poverty and dependence for another. Speaking of Ceylon, Roberts (1966:121) refers to the *kanganies* as those who profited most from the plantation economy; but generally the migrants to Ceylon are supposed to have made less socio-economic progress than their counterparts in Mauritius, Fiji or the Caribbean.

It is quite right that the biased, often officially fed view of labour migration as a wealth-creating mechanism should be unmasked as just another myth. In many cases the identification of labour migrants with itinerant merchants or members of the professional classes has further strengthened this misconception. The crucial question, however, is whether there is a model of economic development that guarantees material progress to all classes at the same time. If there is no such model, then the most important thing is to determine who does and who does not benefit from this type of development.

In south Travancore *kanganies* were the main group able to benefit from coffee growing. The local dominant castes had inhibitions about selling their labour to estates and no compelling reasons to do so; therefore the *kanganies* came almost exclusively from the lower rungs of society, especially the untouchable *Shanars* (*Nadars*). Their earnings from the plantation (with monthly wages of about Rs 50) and investments in land (partly planted with coffee) did not increase existing inequalities, but offered an unprecedented opportunity to these poor people to free themselves from exploitation and oppression. These benefits did not remain confined to the *kanganies,* but also affected—to a much lesser extent, of course—friends and relatives whom they recruited. An LMS missionary wrote from Neyoor in 1875 that 'a great deal of money is circulating among the people from their connexion with the Coffee Estates in which many are employed as overseers, contractors and coolies . . .' (LMS Odds, Baylis 14.7.1875). The same source indicates an unmistakable relationship between the results of the coffee crop and the amount of church contributions collected from native planters, *kanganies* and coolies (LMS Reports, Tittuvilei 1878 and Santhapuram 1880). The improved position of many *Shanars*, Christian and Hindu, can also be seen from their claim to high status attributes, like two-storeyed houses, breast cloth, ornaments etc., which provoked violent reactions from the caste Hindus.

The Bombay jobbers, who like the workers came from the lower classes of Maharashtra, also derived considerable profit from their position in the mill hierarchy. Some of them wasted their money on drink; others invested their earnings in shops, houses or ferries that plied along the coast to Ratnagiri, or rose to prominence in the emerging trade union movement. If this information is to be trusted, we may assume that returning jobbers were able to use their surplus for productive purposes in their home villages. Information on this is hard to come by, but seems to offer a promising way of research.

Most studies of migration in contemporary South Asia accept the existence of a large flow of remittances as an established fact and merely deal with its spread and spending in the migrants' place of origin (see e.g. Oberai and Manmohan Singh 1983). Our study of the Ceylon plantations and Bombay mills leads to the conclusion that in the nineteenth century remittances may have been smaller but were not altogether absent. This seems to suggest that the historian should also shift the main emphasis of his research to the migrants' villages and investigate the local effects of remittances, however small that trickle may have been.

REFERENCES

Bandarage, Asoka. 1983. *Colonialism in Sri Lanka: The political economy of the Kandyan Highlands, 1833–1886.* Berlin: Mouton.

Burnett-Hurst, A.R. 1925. *Labour and Housing in Bombay: A study in the economic conditions of the wage-earning classes in Bombay.* London: P.S. King.

Chatterjee, S. and Ratan Das Gupta. 1981. 'Tea Labour in Assam: Recruitment and government policy, 1840–80.' *Econ. & Pol. Weekly* XVI, 44, 45, 46, special number, 1861–1868.

CMS. Church Missionary Society Archives for Travancore and Ceylon.

——— Letters, Journals, etc., from Rev. Septimus Hobbs, Missionary Tamil Cooly Mission, 1856–62, C Ce/O 70/1–84.

Das Gupta, Ranajit. 1981. 'Structure of the labour market in colonial India'. *Econ. & Pol. Weekly* XVI, 44, 45, 46, special number, 1781–1806.

De Silva, K.M. 1961. 'Indian immigration to Ceylon: The first phase, *c.* 1840–1855.' *Ceylon J. Hist. & Social Studies* IV, 106–137.

——— 1965. *Social policy and missionary organizations in Ceylon, 1840–1855.* London: Longmans, Green.

Economic & Political Weekly 1984. 'Migrant workers' remittances.' *Econ. & Pol. Weekly* XIX, 13, 536.

Edwardes, S.M. 1909–10. *Gazetteer of Bombay City & Islands*, 3 vols. Bombay: The Times Press.

Factory Commission 1885. *Report and proceedings of the Commission appointed to consider the working of factories in the Bombay Presidency.* Bombay: Govt. Central Press.

Ferguson, A.M. (ed.) 1868. *The Ceylon Directory calendar and compendium of useful information for 1866–68.* Colombo: Observer Press.

Gazetteer 1880. *Gazetteer of the Bombay Presidency*, vol. x (Ratnagiri and Savantvadi), Bombay.

Hardgrave, R.L. 1969. *The Nadars of Tamilnad: The political culture of a community in change.* Berkeley: University of California Press.

Joshi, Chitra. 1981. 'Kanpur textile labour: Some structural features of formative years'. *Econ. & Pol. Weekly* XVI, 44, 45, 46, special number, 1823–1838.

Kooiman, Dick. 1978. *Koppelbazen, kommunisten en ekonomische krisis: Arbeidersorganisatie in de textielindustrie van Bombay 1917–1937.* Amsterdam: Rodopi.

——— 1983. 'Rural labour in the Bombay textile industry and the articulation of modes of organization', in Peter Robb (ed.), *Rural South Asia: Linkages, change and development.* London: Curzon Press.

——— 1984. 'The gospel of coffee: Mission, education and employment in Travancore (19th century)', in Dick Kooiman, Otto van den Muyzenberg, Peter van der Veer (eds.), *Conversion, competition and conflict: Essays on the role of religion in Asia.* Anthropological Studies no. 6. Amsterdam: Free University Press.

Kumar, Dharma. 1965. *Land and caste in south India.* Cambridge: University Press.

Kumar, Radha. 1983. 'Family and factory: Women workers in the Bombay cotton textile industry, 1919–1939.' *Indian Economic and Social History Review* 20, 1, 81–110.

Labour Commission 1892. *Royal Commission on Labour: Foreign reports*, vol. II, the Colonies and the Indian Empire. Presented to both Houses of Parliament, June 1892.

Labour Commission 1908. *Report of the Indian Factory Labour Commission*, vol. I, *Report* and vol. II, *Evidence.* Simla.

Labour Commission 1931. Royal Commission on Labour in India, *Report.* Calcutta: Govt. of India, Central Publication Branch.

——— *Evidence*, vol. I, Bombay Presidency, London: HMSO.

Labour Office 1923. *Report on an enquiry into working class budgets in Bombay.* Bombay: Govt. Press.

Lewis, Fr. 1926. *Sixty-four years in Ceylon.* Colombo.

LMS. London Missionary Society Archives for Travancore.

——— Odds, Box 17, Travancore, reports, letters, papers, 1861/1899.

——— Reports, Box 2, Travancore 1873/1882.

——— Incoming letters, Box 5.

LMS Chronicle 1867ff. *Chronicle of the London Missionary Society.* London: Directors of the London Missionary Society.

Manickam, S. 1977. *The social setting of Christian conversion in south India: The impact of the Wesleyan methodist missionaries on the Trichy Tanjore diocese with special reference to the Harijan communities of the mass movement area 1820–1947.* Wiesbaden: Steiner.

Mann, Harold H. 1976. *The social framework of agriculture: India, Middle East, England.* Edited by Daniel Thorner. London: Cass.

Mann, Harold H. and Kanitkar, N.V. 1921. *Land and labour in a Deccan village.* Bombay: University of Bombay, Economic Series No. III.

Millie, P.D. 1878. *Thirty years ago, or reminiscences of the early days of coffee planting in Ceylon.* Colombo: A.M. and J. Ferguson.

Mitra, Ira. 1981. 'Growth of trade union consciousness among jute mill workers, 1920–40.' *Econ. & Pol. Weekly* XVI, 44, 45, 46, special number, 1839–1848.

Morris, M.D. 1965. *The emergence of an industrial labor force in India: A study of the Bombay cotton mills 1854–1947.* Berkeley: University of California Press.

Newman, Richard K. 1981. *Workers and unions in Bombay 1918–29: A study of organization in the cotton mills.* Canberra: Australian National University.

Oberai A.S. and Manmohan Singh H.K. 1983. *Causes and consequences of internal migration: A study in the Indian Punjab.* Delhi: Oxford University Press.

Omvedt, Gail. 1980. 'Migration in colonial India: The articulation of feudalism and capitalism by the colonial state.' *Journal of Peasant Studies* 7, 2, 185–212.

Planting Directory 1878. *The Planting Directory for India and Ceylon: With a list of coffee, tea, cinchona and other plantations in India and Ceylon etc.* Compiled by A.M. and J. Ferguson, Colombo.

Roberts, M.W. 1966. 'Indian estate labour in Ceylon during the coffee period (1830–1880).' *Indian Economic and Social History Review* 3, 1, 1–52 and 3, 2, 101–130.

Rote, Ron. 1986. *A taste of bitterness: The political economy of tea plantations in Sri Lanka.* Amsterdam: Free University Press.

Samaraweera, Vijaya. 1981. 'Masters and servants in Sri Lankan plantations: Labour laws and labour control in an emergent export economy.' *Indian Economic and Social History Review* 18, 2, 123–158.

Standing, Guy. 1981. 'Migration and modes of exploitation: Social origins of immobility and mobility.' *Journal of Peasant Studies* 8, 2, 173–211.

Tariff Board 1927. *Report of the Indian Tariff Board* (cotton textile industry enquiry), 4 vols., Calcutta: Govt. of India Central Publication Branch.

Tinker, H. 1974. *A new system of slavery: The export of Indian labour overseas 1830–1920.* London: Oxford University Press.

Wesumperuma, D. 1978. 'Unindentured Indian labour overseas: Plantation labour in British Ceylon.' 6th European conference on modern South Asian studies, Sèvres.

The Creation and Organization of a Proletarian Mining Labour Force in India: The Case of the Kolar Gold Fields, 1883–1955

COLIN SIMMONS[1]

1. INTRODUCTION: PROLETARIANS, PEASANTS AND THE LABOUR HISTORY OF THE THIRD WORLD

Preliminary Remarks and Argument

One aspect of the underdevelopment of that polyglottic inconvenience known as 'the Third World' is the undeveloped state of its labour history. Irrespective of whether we choose to consider its remit in the very widest or the very narrowest of terms, surely there can be little quarrel with the proposition that the subject area has yet to be properly established in all three of the worlds. By 'properly established' I am not specifically referring to either a corpus of professional academics in University departments and other teaching and research institutes who make regular contributions to a specialized literature, or to those—often gifted—amateur historians who, usually drawn from within the labour movement itself, have taken the responsibility to record selected parts of 'their' own past: although the existence of either or both can certainly help. No, what I principally have in

[1] I would like to thank Mr Robert Ward, Research Officer in the Department of Economics, University of Salford, for his invaluable assistance in helping to process many of the statistics which have been used for the long-term project on the development of the K.G.F. and for this paper in particular.

Mr Hugh Stapleton, formerly a senior employee of Messrs John Taylor & Sons Ltd (for the Mysore Gold Mining Co.) has also been kind enough to give me much time and valuable advice. However I am solely responsible for any errors.

mind is the general level of informed interest in and attention accorded to the subject—in short, what might be called its social consciousness. It is this which ultimately determines practicable things such as the commitment of public resources towards furthering its study and hopefully promoting a better understanding; the 'felt need' of those actors who have been directly involved in the workers' struggle to publicise their experiences; the receptivity of the population at large; and, in those anti-labour authoritarian states, the opportunity for free investigation and expression.

In my view one of the most obvious reasons for the apparent lack of this consciousness has been the acceptance of the all-pervasive eurocentric equation of 'labour' with organized working class proletarians mainly employed in factories, and predominantly urban-based. Now whilst this has made some sense in both the western capitalist countries and in the Soviet bloc, in the Third World—where rural peasantries continue to predominate in the population—there is a clear identification problem. Though they labour hard (but not necessarily for the market) such peasantries do not easily fall within the conventional categories of labour history; and they have seldom evolved either 'normal' union institutions analogous to those which have been the stock-in-trade of labour historians, or formal labour parties which have been the province of the political historians. Since the great bulk of the 'occupied' labour force is therefore outside the confines of traditional labour historiographical territory—and (courtesy of Chayanov) is thought to comprise a distinctive mode of production and now enjoys a thriving academic establishment of its own, witness publications like the *Journal of Peasant Studies* and *Peasant Studies*—this leaves only a minority to focus upon. Furthermore, if the rural non-agriculturist, handicraft, and the so-called unorganized sectors are omitted, then we are talking about a fractured minority in a three-dimensional sense!

Quite apart from the effect of reducing the perceived importance and significance of the greatly truncated segment of Third World labour, this eurocentrism has also affected the character of the limited historiography in a number of deleterious ways. Let me highlight just two. First, and directly following what has just been said, the basic bifurcation of the labour force between proletarian and peasant, each with their own separate histories, has made it exceedingly difficult for students (as well as political activists) to get a grasp of the overall process of labour articulation within and between Third World economies. Only where the former category has grown to a substantial size (relatively as well as absolutely), in other words where modern industrialization has taken a real hold, has the interface between the two been systematically examined. Thus the migrant labour system of South Africa has attracted a good deal of attention, but over the last century that unhappy Republic can hardly be considered a proper member of the Third World fraternity. Moreover, and in extension of this point, whereas it seems reasonable to think of the study of the various types of sub-categories of labour in the west (household, informal domestic service, artisan etc.) as heading towards some sort of convergence on account of the linkages and general sense of 'unity' within these economies, in the Third World, accounts of the acknowledged fragmentations and divisions seem to suggest divergence. Secondly, and related to the above, there is something of a paradox at the heart of Third World labour history. On the one hand, until comparatively recently a great majority of the few specialist studies of Third World labour could easily be fitted into the paradigms established by western and, to a much lesser extent, Soviet models. This applies to the boundaries of the subject, the theoretical underpinnings, the methodology and, most visibly, to the standard nomenclature. On the other hand, because capitalism (or socialism) was introduced to the Third World from outside and specifically through the medium of imperialism and, most directly, colonialism—and partly for that very reason has yet to fully establish itself as the dominant mode of production—the history of labour in general, and that of the proletariat in particular, has usually been deemed different from that operative in the west (and east). If neither the forces of production (such as modern technology) nor the relations of production (such as 'pure' wage labour) have been so highly developed, then the ensuing labour process must necessarily have followed a different course. Issues of race must also be considered here, since the colonial state (indirectly) and foreign traders and capitalists (directly) evolved an ideology towards native labour that in part involved their distinguishing between it and labour 'back home'. Thus, after the formal abolition of slavery (itself a powerful factor in the making of the ideology) there were innumerable instances of forced and semi-forced labour (into colonial armies, the building of public works and private housing, and other social and economic infrastructure), draconian labour laws, restrictions on movement and organization, and of the conscious rigging of labour markets. For many, the 'coolie' was an altogether different species of labour from that of even the most 'lazy' and 'bolshie' of European worker; and it is important to remind ourselves that this encounter with the world of native labour spawned much of the extant documentary archives (now our basic raw material) that are currently available and which, naturally enough, affects our present-day vision and colours our views. So the contradiction of using western (or Soviet) bags to wrap around and hold together Third World entities—differing quantitatively and qualitatively from their corresponding 'peer' groups in the west (Soviet Union)—becomes glaring. We next turn to a discussion of some of the causes of this unsatisfactory situation.

Causes

An important manifestation of the general correspondence between the degree of material advance in a given area over a specified period on the one hand, and the interest in, concern about and resources directed towards understanding key but problematic socio-economic issues on the other, is the close relationship connecting the level of industrialization with the extent and sophistication of purposeful investigation into the world of work, employment and labour markets. This has meant that quite irrespective of whether the students of the subject have been drawn from within or without the organized labour movement itself, and independent of the dominant ideological persuasion of the majority, both the quality and the quantity of the historiography on labour has been directed—overwhelmingly—towards the experience of the western capitalist economies. Starting with the classic 'craddle' case of the UK—and the pioneering work of Sidney and Beatrice Webb, John and Barbara Hammond, and G.D.H. and Margaret Cole—and subsequently fanning out to embrace much of the European Continent, the USA, the white-settled dominions (Canada, New Zealand), Australia, Japan, South Africa and, most recently of all, the so-called NICs (Newly Industrializing Countries), the diachrony of labour studies has tended to follow a predictably logical geographical pattern. As far as the group of countries subsumed under the Third World is concerned (and perhaps the Soviet bloc too, but in a different way) this tradition, like that of 'late starting' as a whole, offers some advantages to actual and future labour historians. There is, first, a body of theory—or rather of varying and competing theoretical perspectives—from which we can draw. This ranges from the insights thrown up by mainstream classical and neo-classical analysis through to institutionist, marxist and neo-marxist formulations. Secondly, since much thought has been given to a discussion of the respective merits of different research methodologies, the pros and cons of alternative techniques of enquiry, and the virtues of particular classificatory systems, the overall approach to the discipline is no longer as consciously narrow, partisan and descriptive as it once was; indeed with such initiatives as the *History workshop series* in mind[2] the old-style barriers and artificial intellectual frontiers have rapidly begun to crumble away. Finally, in addition to the weighty stock of empirical studies that have been compiled over the last three quarters of a century or so, new journals, new monographic series, and the proceedings of regional, national and international conferences and symposia are being published at a seemingly accelerating rate. Indeed, since the early 1970s the subject has grown at an extraordinary pace, and has put down deep roots at all

[2] *The history workshop series* is edited by Raphael Samuel and published by Routledge and Kegan Paul.

levels of the western educational establishment. Its dynamism has been partly attributed to the infusion of successive waves of new developments stemming from the enthusiasts for such diverse interests as oral history; computer applications; working class biographies (especially the work of John Saville); women's studies; culturalism (notably the contributions from the Contemporary Studies Unit at Birmingham); family history; community and even street-based history (Jerry White); the editing of working class diaries, journals, letters and notebooks; and, more generally of People's history. Taken together these trends represent an emancipation from the formalist, usually officially-sponsored and, more often than not, stultifying accounts of individual unions forever battling against the odds of worker indifference, an unsympathetic ruling class and unfair anti-labour legislation.

The advantages, actual and potential, of all this research are not, however, without countervailing dangers and costs as far as the Third World is concerned. The main problem, of course, lies in the difficulty of transplanting theory, method, factual narrative and interpretation from one major type of social environment, that of advanced capitalism, to other quite differnt ones—whatever the terms we may wish to characterize them by—traditional, pre-modern, less developed, underdeveloped, dependent, Asiatic, command-despotic, semi-feudal, neo-colonial, etc., etc. In fact the kind of theoretical framework which is chosen—explicitly or, more commonly, implicitly—to work within; the precise method of investigation which is opted for; and the applicability of those Western mores, institutions, ways of organization and case histories, are as much a matter of judgment as to the nature of the social formation (and which mode of production is deemed dominant) under question, as they are to the more usual considerations such as the perceived explanatory power of the concepts, and of sheer convenience. Moreover the very pace of change, the vigorous growth, and the new eclecticism of the subject in the west may well act as a disincentive for the pursuit of original lines of thinking in the periphery. After all, great names and reputations, well-trodden grooves, established criteria and accepted norms of procedure offer much emulative temptation, and the rewards of scholarly 'replication' are still high—hence, in another but related area, the mushrooming number of 'new economic histories' of railroads extending over the Third World.[3] There is no denying that in the past eurocentrism has proved to be a powerful factor in the creation of a special form of determinism—which then directly impinged upon the choice of political strategy. Thus in our

[3] For one of the latest attempts, see John Hurd's essay on the railways in D. Kumar and M. Desai (eds.), *The Cambridge economic history of India, vol. 2 c. 1757–1970* (Cambridge, 1983), ch. VIII, part 2.

particular context, the hard-line marxist notion that the factory proletariat was the only true vanguard of revolution, and the liberal reformist idea that democratic trade unionism and parliamentary representation were the most effectual channels open to the labour movement, have both, in their different ways, influenced several generations of Third World activists. Away from the political arena the determinism comes through in the preponderance of academic and quasi-academic attention devoted to the clearly recognisable and visible labour organizations, and to the modern industrial and largely urban-based working class—invariably at the expense of agriculturists and peasants, handicraft artisans, itinerant service workers, gangs of contract labourers, women and children in 'illegal' jobs, domestic servants, those engaged in the 'informal' sector, in family non-market occupations, in black-market activities, and so on. Perhaps it is also worth remarking that despite both Gunnar Myrdal's warnings to us in *Asian drama* of almost twenty years ago,[4] and the recent rethinking exercise being conducted in the west in the face of 'our having to live with' permanently high levels of unemployment most of the words, terms, conceptual categories and aggregations—such as work, employment, unemployment, collective bargaining, class consciousness, the occupied labour force, labour aristocracies, absenteeism etc.—continue to be in common currency in the Third World. The internationalization of one quite special version of the English language, particularly in terms of official government and civil service business, has quickened the transposition but seemingly without the necessary caution and essential qualifications; and unfortunately there seems no end in sight—however many TEFL (Teaching English as a Foreign Language) people are recruited to further the cause!

Character and Consequences

Although these advantages and disadvantages are not immediately translatable into specific strengths and weaknesses of the existing historiography on labour in the Third World, it is possible to identify a number of the more obvious and general ones. Before I do so, however, let me digress in order to put in a brief word of explanation and a strong disclaimer. The main purpose of this introduction is to place my particular area of research within its proper context, namely the labour history of the Indian sub-continent. But this in turn is difficult to approach without an appreciation of many broader concerns—one of which is clearly the labour history of the Third World. Now given that this grouping—besides being an unwieldy,

[4] G. Myrdal, *Asian drama: An inquiry into the poverty of nations* (London, 1968), esp. vol. 2, part 5, chs. 21–4.

rather cumbersome and often inappropriate unit of analysis—is both huge and fragmented, it is clearly well beyond the scope of these remarks to embark upon even a highly cursory review. Instead, using India as my major exemplifier and point of reference, and without claiming to present anything other than a crude sketch, I would make the following general observations on the state of the art.

1. ITS UNDERDEVELOPMENT

The labour history of much of the Third World—like its economic and social history—is still a highly undeveloped subject of scholarly research. This applies both within as well as without its geographical borders. For reasons we cannot pursue here (and which more properly belong to the sociology and financing of knowledge), it has commanded relatively little interest and few resources. This low priority and almost anonymous profile has meant that we have few real facts, few acceptable accounts and few reliable interpretations. Of course, in an absolute sense, and in purely national terms, a fair body of secondary writing on and around the subject has accumulated—especially if we feel inclined to take a very elastic view of what labour history properly consists of. But in my opinion, much of this stock written prior to the last dozen years or so is—with some obvious exceptions—of a depressingly poor standard, somewhat antiquarian, polemical, and of uncertain accuracy. This has begun to change, largely in response to the infusion of neo-marxist work, and particularly with respect to the more intensively developed and industrialized areas, but progress is still very slow and patchy and, because of the ideological undertones, is by no means acceptable to many.

2. ITS THEORETICAL AND METHODOLOGICAL PARASITISM

By and large it has been a borrower of theory and methodology from outside. It is my impression that Third World labour historians (or rather, since it is not yet an established discipline in its own right, those historians who work on labour for some of their time) tend to follow the intellectual currents and preoccupations underway in the west—in a lagged and often quite slavish manner.[5] Although we sometimes detect a sense of unease and disquiet over this 'follower' tendency, in my view there seem to be few seriously genuine attempts to break the mould—and this applies to both orthodox and (most) marxist contributors.

[5] Thus over the past decade or so the following orientations have percolated through to a rising—but admittedly still selected—number of Third World labour history projects: oral history, feminism, class consciousness, class differentiation, people's history, and the labour process debate since Braverman.

3. THE CONTEXTUAL VACUUM

There is a contextual vacuum operating at several levels, which badly weakens the subject. Whereas in the west there exists a tolerable set of studies covering the behaviour of firms, groups of firms, entrepreneurs, industries, sectors, regions, nations and even (in a selective way) the 'international' economy, there are great lacunae with respect to the Third World. The few general surveys which attempt to tackle the big peer themes of industrialization, economic growth and economic development in a long-run perspective, hardly come near to 'setting the scene';[6] and I would argue that this gap is simply another reflection of the underdevelopment of Third World history—and its consequences are analogous to that of our highly imperfect state of knowledge on the wider condition of underdevelopment.[7] This suggests that it is difficult to make meaningful and informed comparisons between and within particular Third World states, and also that even if we follow conventional neo-classical theory and reduce labour to being just another 'factor of production', we cannot readily articulate it with existing production and marketing processes as a whole.

4. THE COLONIAL IMPACT: A POTENTIAL STRENGTH?

Because of imperialism, the colonial impact and the associated question of foreign ownership and control, there has always been an added ingredient to studies of labour in the periphery. For contemporary commentators, and in the Indian case this encompasses the great official enquiries,[8] labour was perceived as something of an undifferentiated mass of natives (which could pose a threat to public order), very much as an 'object' and, most commonly, as a 'problem'. Centring around the idea of the 'lazy native', unfavourable epithets abounded—insufficient and irregular supply; migrant; uncommitted; unskilled; undisciplined; mentally and sometimes physically poorly endowed;

[6] Cf. P. Bairoch, 'International industrialization levels from 1750 to 1980', *J. Eur. Econ. Hist.* II, 2 (1982); T. Kemp, *Industrialization in the non-western world* (London, 1983); A.J.H. Latham, *The international economy and the undeveloped world* (London, 1981); L.J. Reynolds, 'The spread of economic growth to the Third World: 1850–1980', *J. Econ. Literature* 21, (1983); and his recent book *Economic growth in the Third World 1850–1980'* (Yale, 1985).

[7] I have attempted to argue this point with respect both to a particular experience, 'De-industrialisation, industrialisation and the Indian economy *c.* 1850–1947', *Mod. Asian Studies* 19, 3 (1985), and subsequently to a wider brief, 'Economic development and economic history' in B. Ingham and C. Simmons (eds.), *Development studies and colonial policy* (London, 1987), ch. 1.

[8] Culminating in the monumental *Report of the Royal Commission on Labour in India* (Cmnd. 3883, HMSO 1931).

irrational; bedevilled by tribal and caste prejudices; led on by outside agitators; spoilt; and so on. These allegations were legion and transcended industry, region and continent. In the formal organized sector—the factories, the plantations, the mines—capital in the shape of the entrepreneurial class typically demanded, and usually got, the direct and indirect assistance of the colonial state; and in order to avoid personal contact with the natives, relied upon extensive networks of intermediary contractors[9] who were made responsible for recruiting and managing the labour force (in India the Eurasian population was also used in this way). Nationalists, on the other hand, were everywhere keen to help organize labour into familiar union forms, and ultimately sought to win and maintain their political support. They then pressed for the repeal of restrictive legislative decrees and became interested in amelioration. Communist parties—everywhere weak at that time and generally proscribed—followed the Comintern in seeing the proletariat as the spearhead for the overthrow of not only the existing order, but also of international capitalism. All three of these pre-Independence positions provided serious legacies to the post-colonial period, and although there are no direct analogues we might trace them through as follows:

(A) Class conflict positions

Grouping 1: Foreign capital, some elements of the traditional indigenous capitalist class, and the 'apologists' of imperialism.
Charge: Capital suffers from truculent, unresponsive and low productivity labour forces.

Grouping 2: Radical
(a) Marxist
Charge: Labour suffer from capitalist exploitation; surplus value is extracted.
(b) Dependency
Charge: Identifies foreign ownership and control through the medium of multinational corporations as the new instruments of exploitation.
(c) Neo-marxist
Charge: There is a new world-wide division of labour and this breaks down the artificiality of national analysis of exploitation.
(d) Structural marxist
Charge: Migrant labour systems and peasantries act as the principal means of labour reproduction.

[9] The ubiquity of labour contracting and managerial sub-contracting extends to Europe (where it persisted until the late nineteenth century), the USA, Japan and parts of China. For a survey of the general literature see C.R. Littler, *The development of the labour process in capitalist societies* (London, 1982); for China see T. Wright, 'A method of evading management: Contract labour in Chinese coal mines before 1927', *Comp. Studies in Society & History* 23, 4 (1981); and for a valuable—and rare—comparative study see R.K. Newman, 'The recruitment of an industrial labour force through intermediaries: A comparative study of the cotton textile industry in Bombay and Shanghai' in C. Dewey (ed.), *Arrested development in India* (New Delhi & Riverdale, 1988).

(B) Class harmony and individual choice positions

Grouping 1: Nationalist politicians and some military juntas.
Advocacy: To unite against foreigners and hold the fabric of the society together, organized labour (especially its leadership) must be included as 'partners'. There should be 'fair' labour law and some measure of protective legislation.

Grouping 2: Enlightened domestic bourgeoisies (e.g. the Tata group).
Advocacy: In order to install modern technology there is a need to enhance skill levels; in order to have smooth production runs it is necessary to have a 'contented' labour force; in order to widen domestic markets wages should not only be regarded as costs but also as a feeder to the level of effective demand.

With further cross-country and even cross-continental research it might eventually be feasible to conceptualize the distinctiveness of Third World labour history. Certainly those—like the structural marxists[10]—that choose to emphasize the importance of the colonial encounter and its line of influence in the post-colonial period, seem to have more to offer than the historians who would only focus upon individual worker choice and the operation of particular labour markets.

5. THE PERENNIAL PROBLEM OF DATA SCARCITY

Finally, there is no escaping the paucity of traditional documentary materials pertaining to Third World labour forces. Virtually all labour historians complain about the absolute as well as the relative scarcity of material (vis-à-vis the West), especially that contributed by Third World labour itself.[11] To some extent this deficiency can be compensated for by an imaginative use of alternative sources (principally oral history)[12] but to my mind the scope is still quite limited, particularly the further back in time we wish to go. Similarly, when we turn to the records of firms, government departments (including the police), special commissions of enquiry, missionary papers, travelogues and the like, we tend to get a very one-dimensional, highly

[10] As far as the French structuralist school is concerned, the seminal article (at least in English) was contributed by Claude Meillassoux, 'From reproduction to production: A marxist approach to economic anthropology', *Economy & Society* 1, 1 (1972). P.P. Rey and E. Terray are two other prominent members of this traditon. Also important, but falling within a mere orthodox marxist line, was G. Arrighi's 'Labour supplies in historical perspective: A study of the proletarianization of the African peasants in Rhodesia', *Journal of Development Studies* 6 (1970).

[11] For an informed discussion of this problem as it relates to Africa see R. Cohen *et al.* (eds.), *African labour history* (Berkeley and London, 1978), introduction.

[12] Some of the techniques suggested in J. Vansira, *Oral tradition: A study in historical methodology* (2nd edn., London, 1985); P. Thompson, *The voice of the past: oral history* (Oxford, 1978); and the 'Special issue on using oral sources' in *Social Analysis* 4 (1980), are now standard practice for many Africanists.

biased and often paternalistic picture which can distort as much as enlighten. Jean Chesneaux has gone as far as to remark that 'whole sections of world history are known only by what oppressors have said or permitted to be said'.[13] Another common type of distortion which arose from the great racial and social barriers between owners, managers and their native work-forces was the lack of direct contact between them: household servants were perforce regarded as individuals and given pet names, but in the formal work situation, the 'lords of human kind'[14] only seemed to see row-upon-row of indistinguishable brown/black/yellow faces—all more or less perfect substitutes for each other. This impersonality could often lead to a curious kind of blindness: thus in the early 1920s one of the mining engineers on the Kolar Gold Fields admitted that 'hours of thought were given over to the current lubricating oil for some machine or motor, but in comparison, little thought was given to the amount of food a coolie needed'.[15] Again, assuming the survival of such archives and free access to them, it is possible to 'read' such material in a way that its writers certainly never intended, and this is perhaps what the editor of the *Subaltern studies* series had in mind when the first volume was launched in the early 1980s.[16] Nevertheless, it would be foolish to deny the existence of a real problem and dismiss talk of source pessimism as defeatist; on the other hand the very absence of 'obvious' data on the working and living conditions of millions of people should encourage us to seek out (where necessary) more unorthodox types of material.

If the labour history of the Third World as a whole and that of India in particular is to come of age we must find the ways, means and resources to lift this veil; and if it is difficult to reach consensus on the existing state of the art and upon the directives and priorities for future research agendas—and there seems little likelihood of that given the spread of opinion even as expressed over the last five or six years on India alone[17]—then at least we

[13] Quoted in R. Cohen *et al.* (eds.), *op. cit.* (1978), p. 23.

[14] The phrase comes from the title of victor Kiernan's study *The lords of humankind: European attitudes to the outside world in the imperial age* (London, 1972); also see A. Memmi, *The colonizer and the colonized* (New York, 1965).

[15] Mr Cooke's comment on J.A. Pringle's 'Efficiency and economy in the underground department' in the *Bulletin of the Kolar Gold Fields Mining & Metallurgical Soc.* 7 (Jan.-Mar. 1922), p. 143.

[16] R. Guha (ed.), *Subaltern studies: Writings on South Asian history and society* (Delhi, 1982), esp. ch. 1, 'On some aspects of the historiography of colonial India', pp. 1–18, by the editor. Three further volumes in this series have now been published.

[17] The recent clutch of publications which set out to survey generally or in some way to offer informed commentary upon the labour history of India include J. Pouchepadass' introduction to 'Labour history of pre-independent South Asia' in M. Gaborieau and A. Thorner (eds.), *Asie du sud: traditions et changements* (Paris, 1979), pp. 447–50; G. Omvedt, 'Migration

can agree on that to put aside our differences for the sake of acheiving wider recognition. After all one does not need to subscribe to any of the versions of the labour theory of value to recognize the importance of uncovering the 'lost' history of Third World working men and women, and as far as India is concerned, a number of scholars have started to take up the challenge.[18] Though this is obviously an encouraging development it should be emphasized that the subject is still in early infancy, and huge areas of the work force—even those in the organized modern sector—have yet to be properly examined let alone understood. In what follows an attempt is made to uncover some aspects of the history of those involved in the mining, conveying and treating of gold-bearing ore—an industry and a labour force which has received little scholarly attention.

2. THE KOLAR LABOUR FORCE: ITS RECRUITMENT STRUCTURE AND ORGANIZATION

If the study of the growth of 'modern' Indian industry during the colonial period is the poor relation of the economic and social history of the subcontinent,[19] then the mining industry is very much the Cinderella of the accounts of industrialization. Neither the mining sector as a whole nor the development

in colonial India: the articulation of feudalism and capitalism by the colonial state, *J. Peasant Studies* 7, 2 (1980); Ranajit Das Gupta, 'Structure of the labour market in colonial India', *Econ. & Pol. Weekly* special no., xvi, 44–6 (1981); D. Kumar and J. Krishnamurthy, 'The evolution of labour markets in India, 1857–1947', *Studies in employment and rural development* 72, World Bank (Sept. 1981); A.K. Bagchi, *The political economy of underdevelopment* (Cambridge, 1982), chs. 4 & 7; M.D. Morris. 'The growth of large-scale industry to 1947' in D. Kumar and M. Desai (eds.), *op. cit.* (1983), esp. pp. 642–68; A.N. Das, V. Nilakant and P.S. Dubey (eds.), *The worker and the working class*: Studies anthology (New Delhi 1984) ch. 8 pp. 3–24; S. Bose, 'Indian labour and its historiography in pre-independence period; Social Scientist 18, 4 (1984): R. Chandravarkar. Industralization in India better 1947 contributions approaches and alternative perspectives'. *Mod. Asian Studies* 19, 3 (1985) esp. pp. 661–4: and S.B. Datta. *Capital accumulation and workers' struggle in Indian industrialization: The case of Tata Iron & Steel Co. 1910–70* (Stockholm, 1986), esp. ch. 2.

[18] Mooris David Morris—an important catalyst in several fields of Indian economic history, was certainly instrumental in arousing interest in this area, and his pioneering study of the Bombay cotton mills is still an important point of deaparture: *The emergence of an industrial labour force in India: A study of the Bombay cotton mills, 1854–1947* (Berkeley, 1965). The new breed of 'labour historians' include—in no particular order and without any prĕtence as to full coverage—R. Das Gupta, D. Mazumdar, R. Newman, E. Murphy, E. Perlman, B. Misra, L. Chakravarty, J. Breman, P.S. Gupta, R. Chandravarkar, D. Kooiman, Shahid Amin, J. Krishnamurthy (by virtue of his work on the occupational structure) and Stephen Gourley (but not yet in published form).

[19] Which, in its turn, is the poor relation of political and constitutional history.

of any one of its constituent parts features in the major secondary interpretations in anything other than a cursory and offhand way. Professor Morris' regrettable decision to omit consideration of it altogether from his recent survey in the *Cambridge economic history*[20] is unfortunately typical, and bears testimony to the low level of scholarly priority it is accorded. One reason for this neglect is the modest relative contribution it made to the economy as a whole: less than 1 per cent of N.N.P. over 1890–1947; a mere 0.4 per cent of the total occupied labour force over 1881–1951; and a maximum of just 3 per cent of the total value of domestic exports.[21] But, like many other activities in the huge and densely populated subcontinent, this relativity disguises respectable rates of growth and impressive absolute magnitudes. Thus, at the time of Independence, the sector had become a substantial employer of labour—just under half a million people were involved in the Group 1 category of minerals,[22] and the value added to N.N.P. amounted to Rs 431 million (in constant 1938/39 prices).[23]

With a view to piecing together the career of the mining industry in order, *inter alia*, to place the history of labour within its proper context, work has commenced at two levels: first along a broad sector-wise front, and secondly the building up of a series of individual profiles of the different minerals. Coal mining, by virtue of its overriding role in the long-run development of the sector, was the first to receive detailed treatment;[24] and now attention has turned to gold, for long the second most important mining activity in

[20] M.D. Morris, 'The growth of large scale industry to 1947', *op. cit.*, pp. 553–675.

[21] These estimates have been derived from a variety of primary and secondary statistical sources: For detailed citation see my 'The economic growth of the Kolar Gold Fields, 1881–1955: Introduction, discovery and source materials', paper presented to the International Mining History Conference, University of Melbourne, August 1985 (and forthcoming in a collection of papers under the editorship of P. Richardson). The paper is also available in the *Salford papers in economics series*, nos. 85–7.

[22] This category simply refers to the mineral returns which were considered reasonably reliable and published by the *Records of the Geological Survey of India* between 1905 and 1947.

[23] Calculated on the basis of Alan Heston's national income estimates in the *Cambridge economic history of India* (*op. cit.*), vol. 2, table 4.3B, pp. 398f.

[24] As far as labour supply is concerned, see my 'Recruiting and organising an industrial labour force in colonial India: The case of the coal mining industry 1880–1939', *Ind. Econ. & Social History Rev.* XII, 4 (1976); 'Seasonal labour oscillations in the Indian coal mining industry before Independence' in M. Gaborieau and A. Thorner (eds.), *op. cit.*; 'Vertical integration and the Indian steel industry: The colliery establishment of TISCO 1907–50', *Mod. Asian Studies* 11, 1 (1976); and 'Imperial dictate: The effect of two world wars on the Indian coal industry', *World Development* 9, 8 (1981). For conditions see my 'Working conditions, accidents and "protective" labour legislation in the Indian coal mining industry in the pre-Independence period', *Bengal Past & Present* CV, 180 (1976); and 'Housing, health and educational facilities in the Indian coalfields during the colonial era', *S. Asia* 8 (1978).

the subcontinent,[25] and up to the early 1950s, far and away the leading 'organized' industry in Mysore State.[26] My research on the gold mining industry (which, for all intents and purposes can be reduced to the Kolar Gold Field, since it alone was responsible for no less than 97 per cent of all Indian gold production between 1885 and 1955),[27] is nearing the analytical stage. Most of the quantitative data covering the usual aspects of corporate behaviour and industrial performance have now been placed on computer file, and the bulk of the available qualitative material has been collected, collated and sifted through.[28] Now although there are some glaring gaps in the data base,[29] the reconstruction of the business history of the industry and of the respective component enterprises appears to be feasible.[30] When it comes to probing the history of the labour force, however, the lacunae multiply, and even from the restricted vista of the primary company-wise archives there is disappointingly little relevant documentation. Further, there does not appear to be any usable written records generated from within the ranks of labour itself. The position is somewhat rosier with respect to official and demi-official sources: but of course they too suffer the common problem of being composed from 'on high'. As a corrective, during the field-work, the standard oral history techniques were tried but, even here, little real progress was made, mainly because of the fuzzy recollection of pre-nationalization (1951) days by the few remaining survivers of that era. Like all activities based on a strictly limited supply of exhaustible natural resources, the Kolar Gold Field (which first began to experience diminishing returns during the First World War) has shrunk in importance: today the undertaking—though still staggering on at considerable financial loss[31]—

[25] Expressed as a percentage of the total value of mineral output, the gold mining industry ranked second to coal for most of the period 1890–1946: For details see 'The economic growth of the K.G.F. . . .' *op. cit.*, table 2, p. 36.

[26] See R.H. Elliot, *Gold, sport and coffee planting in Mysore* (London, 1894); C.H. Rao, *Mysore gazetteer* vol. III (Bangalore, 1929); R. Balakrishna, *Industrial development in India* (Bangalore, 1940); and B.N. Sathyan (ed.), *Mysore State gazetteers, Kolar* (Bangalore, 1968).

[27] See 'The economic growth of the K.G.F. . . .', *op. cit.*, table 1a, p. 35.

[28] For full information on sources refer *ibid.*, esp. pp. 9ff. and appendix, pp. 22–34.

[29] Notably the destruction of the London Office papers of the managing agents, and the inexplicable shredding (by the Public Record Office) of the Board of Trade file on the premier mining company, the Mysore G.M. Co. Ltd.

[30] In a paper presented to the conference on 'Enclave development' convened by the Development Studies Association in Easter 1983, at the University of Liverpool, entitled 'Golden imperialism: A study of the economic development of the K.G.F. undertaking, 1883–1951', I presented some preliminary findings. A revised version of this is currently being prepared for publication.

[31] Thus for 1975–6 the undertaking (now known as Bharat Gold Mines Ltd) was in the red to the tune of Rs 249.82 lakhs, even with the massive government subsidy of Rs 557.35

has been greatly run down.[32]. Fortunately for the local population, an alternative employer of labour (Bharat Earth Movers Ltd) has sprung up, and so Kolar has not suffered the fate of many other worked-out mining areas of the world.[33] This welcome diversification, however, has had the effect of reducing the power of both collective as well as individual memory, and the once great industry has all but faded from private memory and the public eye; and not even the elaborate pomp and ceremony marking the centenary of the undertaking (in 1983)[34] has done much to enhance its status. Notwithstanding these caveats, I believe that it is possible to identify some of the major features of the labour history of the Field, and to put it in the contextual setting of the industry's growth, and also the comparative experience of other mining and industrial communities.

The Industrial Context

Although members of the resident European community in the Bangalore cantonment had long known of the existence of auriferous lodes at Kolar, it took a combination of two major forces to bring about its purposeful exploitation in the early 1880s.[35] The first, on the demand side, was the rise in the international demand for gold consequent upon the accelerated development of the Gold Standard after 1871. This triggered off a fresh wave of exploration for payable deposits which, in turn, led to successive bouts of speculative frenzy and fraudulent scrip flotation. One of the first instances of these manias was the Wynad boom, which swept through the London Stock Exchange between December 1879 and June 1881. But once it was realized that this area (in present-day Kerala) contained no payable quartz, attention switched to nearby Kolar. Two dozen companies

lakhs included; see balance sheet included in the *Report of the Directors of the B.G.M. Ltd, 1976–77*, pp. 13f.

[32] In local regional, national and international terms, cf. Govt. of Karnataka, *Talukawise plan statistics, Kolar District* (Bangalore, 1976), tables 3, 5, 15 & 16; Govt. of Karnataka, *Statistical outline of the state* (Bangalore, 1977), tables 1.5, 9.1, 9.2, 9.3, 11.1 & 13.5; M. Ziauddin and S. Narayanaswami, *Gold resources of India* (Delhi, 1974); and R. Weston, *Gold: A world survey* (London, 1983), esp. table 16.1, pp. 212ff. Thus in 1982 the K.G.F. produced barely 1 00 000 troy ounces of gold, or 0.22 per cent of world output (it ranked 21st in the country-wise league table).

[33] See e.g. the study by D. Reid on *The miners of Decazeville: A genealogy of de-industrialisation* (Cambridge, Mass., 1986).

[34] No less a person than Indira Gandhi opened the celebrations, and the organizing committee also arranged for the attendance of two old (European) hands as well as the publication of the *Centenary souvenir volume of the K.G.F. undertaking 1883–1983* (Ooregum, 1983).

[35] For the full story of the discovery of the Field see 'The economic growth of the K.G.F. ...', *op. cit.*, pp. 11–21.

were floated by promoters and a perusal of their prospectuses[36] reveals an exaggerated optimism.[37] A mad scramble for prospecting licences and leasehold rights—obtainable from the Maharajah of the newly rendered Princely State of Mysore[38]—ensued, and much plant, machinery and stores were despatched to the District. But despite all this endeavour, only very limited quantities of gold were won between 1881 and 1883, and the future looked decidedly unpromising for the more rash and overcommitted of the shareholders. At this juncture the second consideration, this time on the supply-side, came into effect. Anxious about the capital already sunk and fearful of losing the entire value of their holdings, a consortia of influential shareholders brought in the well respected London-based firm of John Taylor & Sons to be the managing agents. This long-established and highly experienced house of mining engineers sent two of their most talented staff to Kolar, and by a combination of luck, informed geological survey and sound judgement, they were able to make the decisive strike (the Champion lode in the late summer of 1884).[39] The management's willingness to use the most up-to-date technology and their undoubted entrepreneurial acumen did the rest, and within a matter of two years the industry had become firmly established. By the turn of the century four spectacularly successful joint stock companies with a widely dispersed British shareholding had emerged[40]—all under the management of the Taylors—and this set the pattern for the following fifty years. The K.G.F. Undertaking, as it was collectively referred to, not only became the dominant power within the Kolar locality, but was a crucial force in the economy and polity of Mysore: indeed it could be argued that the direct and indirect effects which flowed from the mines—the first great capitalist venture of the area—was the essential condition for the creation of the model Mysore State under the direction of that extraordinary Dewan, Sir M. Visvesvaraya.[41]

[36] Which are now stored (partly on microfiche) in the Guildhall Library, London.

[37] All the companies painted an incredibly rosy picture of their prospects: the hyperbole is remarkable and even the language is unrestrained.

[38] It is one of the ironies of colonial history that the Rendition took place just three years prior to the establishment of the industry.

[39] One of the most graphic descriptions of the strike is in the *Prospectus* of the New Mysore Gold Mining Co. (29 Nov. 1884), an enterprise which quickly went into liquidation because none of its claim contained any gold!

[40] The four were the Mysore, the Ooregum, the Nundydroog (all founded in 1880) and the Champion Reef (1889) Gold Mining Companies. A fifth enterprise, the Balagat Gold Mines Ltd. (1880) which was also under the Taylor umbrella, had a chequered career before going into liquidation in 1931.

[41] In my view, neither of the two modern accounts of the state's history has given sufficient weight to the role of the K.G.F.; cf. J. Manor, *Political change in an Indian state: Mysore*

From the summary data presented in table 1, the bare bones of the growth and the fluctuating fortunes of the K.G.F. may be gleaned.[42] During its first three decades of operation the industry developed at an extraordinarily rapid pace;[43] and physical output reached an all-time peak in 1915. For the next fifteen years sales revenue declined in accordance with diminished production and reached a floor in 1930. Then came the 'kiss of life' in the shape of the abandonment of the Gold Standard in September 1931. The breaking of this 'golden constant' dramatically changed the fortunes of the industry, and though it proved impossible to arrest the fall in output volume and quality (as measured by d.w.t.) the rise in the money and real price of the commodity was so sharp[44]—as to more than compensate (the K.G.F. was of course a price-taker throughout). Naturally enough, the situation could not continue for very long because the payable reserves were being rapidly depleted, so that by 1946 output was down to just a quarter of its 1900 level. During and just after the war, a cascading number of new developments—perhaps the most important of which was the imposition of an unprecedented punitive tax regime within Mysore—reduced the attraction of the investment for the foreign shareholders and so ownership was rapidly transferred to Indian hands. But this era of private indigenous share domination was shortlived and in 1956 the State Government decided to nationalize the concern. By then, however, the Field was effectively exhausted; in fact the mines were the deepest in the world,[45] and after much struggle the state-owned Undertaking (still under Taylor's day-to-day management) had soon to be baled out by the central government (in 1962), and so the K.G.F. has the dubious distinction of being one of the few firms to be nationalized twice over. These trends are reflected in the changes in profitability and divided declarations.

A detailed investigation of the costs of production by company for each

1917–1955 (New Delhi, 1977); and B. Hettne, *The political economy of indirect rule: Mysore 1881–1947* (London, 1978). This verdict also applies to the more ambitious study of K. Puttaswamaiah, *Economic development of Karnataka: A treatise of continuity and change* (New Delhi, 1980), vol. 2.

[42] For more detailed figures see 'The economic growth of the K.G.F. . . . ', esp. tables 4 & 9; and 'Golden imperialism…' which will contain a comprehensive range of performance statistics.

[43] Though not quite so rapid as that of the Witwatersrand over the same period. See N. Levy, *The foundations of the South African cheap labour system* (London, 1982), esp. part 1.

[44] Within weeks the quoted piece of gold on the London bullion market went up from 84/- per fine oz. to 120/-. *Annual report of the Chief Inspector of Mines for Mysore, 1932–33*, (henceforth, A.R.C.I.M.M.), p. 6.

[45] In 1946 the workings had reached 9141 feet at Ooregum, 8794 at Champion Reef, 8138 at Mysore and 7175 at Nundydroog. A.R.C.I.M.M., 1946.

year between 1898 and 1946 has confirmed the *a priori* expectation that labour constituted the most important charge on working expenses. Indeed, over the period the annual wage bill averaged just over half of all variable costs. It was far and away the largest single item of mining costs—which itself was the major element of the total. This can be seen from the cost sample presented in table 2, and although quite crude, this measure gives an indication of the operation.

THE LEVEL AND TREND OF EMPLOYMENT AND LABOUR PRODUCTIVITY

The basic statistics on employment are presented in table 3—which shows the aggregate position over 1891–1951, and table 4, as broken down by mining company over the slightly different time-span, 1895–1946. Since the officially published figures provided by the Mysore Mines Inspectorate and the various Departments of State closely tally with those contained in the primary sources, it seems reasonable to accept their veracity.[46] In common with established practice in the subcontinent, prior to the Second World War the annual employment returns are measured by the 'average numbers at work daily throughout the year' (column 2 of table 3 and all of table 4). The choice of this particular criterion of standard was largely governed by the ubiquitously held and time-honoured assumption that absenteeism—thought to be specially pronounced during the peak seasons of the normal agricultural cycle—was rife.[47]

As a result of this procedure there is a downward bias in the data and the actual number of workers dependent upon an industry for the bulk of their (cash) livelihood is larger than otherwise might appear at face value. In the case of the K.G.F.—where there was certainly a considerable degree of absenteeism (but not in any way related to the demands of agriculture)—we can construct a crude estimate of the extent of understatement. This is made possible since, in addition to the usual category, we possess details of those

[46] I have cross-checked the official figures with those presented in the *Annual reports of Directors* (for each company), the *Annual reports of the Superintendents*, the anonymous publication, 'K.G.F.: Particulars and statistics from the commencement of operations to the 31.12.1925' and, where available, with extant muster rolls. The slight discrepancies that do exist in various years are probably attributable to some inaccurate contractor returns and to the fact that some members of the European staff were employed 'centrally' by John Taylor & Co. rather than by specific companies. It should also be noted that the 1946 Labour Investigation Committee and the 1941 Census survey produced figures for 1939, 1944 and 1941 respectively, which were marginally higher than the official numbers—but this is explained by their once-and-for all technique of measurement and sample.

[47] The classic statement of this appears in the *Report of the Royal Commission on Labour*, op. cit.

workers 'in service in the year' (column 4, table 3) for 1939–46 (and again for 1951). Now although this is only a short span of time, and perhaps an unrepresentative one at that, because of the Second World War, it does provide us with a useful indicator.

DIFFERENCE BETWEEN NUMBERS IN SERVICE (COLUMN 4, TABLE 3) AND AVERAGE DAILY NUMBERS AT WORK

	Actual numbers	*Percentage of numbers in service*
1939	3 935	13.89
1940	3 568	12.28
1941	3 799	13.26
1942	5 757	21.15
1943	4 098	16.57
1944	4 986	22.15
1945	4 782	22.56
1946	4 127	18.69
1951	3 818	16.70
average over 1939–46	4 256	17.56

SOURCES: See table 3 and footnote 46.

If the 17.5 per cent average difference is applied to the whole career of the industry—and there is some independent evidence which lends support to this[48]—then for each year column 2 is some 4 000–5 000 workers short of the 'true' number.

This absolute discrepancy, however, would not seriously affect the trend of change through time. Here, and not surprisingly in view of what has been stated earlier, the picture is one of broad correspondence with output volume until 1931 and with output value thereafter until the early part of World War II. From 1891, when reliable returns become available, to the early twentieth century, the labour force grew rapidly (faltering only in the plague and famine years of 1898 and 1899). Indeed for about a decade and a half its growth equalled that of coal mining—even though this was the period when the great Jharia field in Bihar was being opened up as a result of the penetration of the Bengal-Nagpur railway link.[49] In

[48] See M.A. Sreenivasan's *Report on socio-economic conditions of workers in the Kolar gold mines* (Bangalore, 1930) and reprinted as *Labour in India* (New Delhi, 1980, with a 'Foreword' contributed by me), ch. 3, pp. 6–10.

[49] Between 1891 and 1901 employment in coal mining tripled (from 34 827 to 95 318); but despite this rapid growth, the gold mining force roughly kept pace with it so that it amounted to 26.5 per cent of it in 1891 and 26.3 per cent in 1901.

1907 employment peaked at just under 35 000, and from that high point dropped gently over the next ten years in consonance with the payload equation. The War and the 1920s were difficult years for the mines and there was steady retrenchment of jobs as costs rose and the final price of gold remained fixed. Thus by 1930 the mines provided work for a daily average of just over 17 000 persons—or 10.6 per cent of coal mining and 5.4 per cent of all mining employment.[50] Thereafter, and thanks to the rise in gold prices, more labour was taken on, and so by 1940 there was a greater number employed than at any time since 1915. But the problems arising during the Second World War led to a loss of some 9 000 jobs, and although there was a temporary increase in employment opportunities towards the close of the 1940s the writing was on the wall, and no amount of politically-motivated subsidy for job support could prevent the decline as the known ore lodes became progressively exhausted.

The company-wise pattern of employment distribution revealed in table 4 is a reasonably faithful indicator of the relative profitability and importance of the different mines. After a brief period of being second to Champion Reef (between 1896 and 1901), the plumpest golden goose of the Undertaking, the Mysore Gold Mining Co. Ltd, was the largest employer of labour. Over the half-century ending in 1946, it was responsible for just over 30 per cent of all employment—followed by Champion Reef (with 23 per cent), Nundydroog (19 per cent) and Ooregum (18.2 per cent). Between them these four enterprises accounted for over 91 per cent of all employment—the residual mainly provided by the Balagat Company which, by an unhappy coincidence, had closed down (its assets were in fact transferred to Ooregum Co.) in the very month that Britain went off the Gold Standard. After the war the situation remained the same, except that in 1953 Ooregum was acquired by Champion Reef. Thus, at the time of the first nationalization in 1956 the Mysore Mine was still the largest employer (7 034) with Champion Reef (6 062) and Nundydroog (5 670) just behind.

Table 5 presents three measures of labour productivity—two in purely physical terms (columns 1 and 3) and one by value (in current prices, column 2).[51] By and large, the former move together—showing a rising trend to 1903; a sharp fall between 1903–7; a further rise to 1913; a setback during the war and lasting until 1921; a noted increase during the early 1920s;

[50] The comparative figures have been derived from various *Memoirs* of the Geological Survey of India.

[51] More sophisticated measurements of labour productivity—taking in output per man hour, per shift and per type of work—are being developed and will appear in a future paper. It has proved much more difficult to look at total factor productivity because we lack a proper measure of capital.

then, until 1941, a sharp drop for ounces per person—but a constancy for tonnage crushed. There was then some wild fluctuation during the Second World War—an instability which continued until nationalization. The trend for value per person is, of course, somewhat different, namely a steady improvement to the middle of the First World War; a plateau until the abandonment of the Gold Standard; a new plateau extending over 1932–41; a spectacular jump during the latter stage of the Second War; then a downward plunge in 1946—with no sustained improvement through to nationalization. In the circumstances of even greater depths and the depletion of quartz reserves, the physical achievement of the miners (and the management, of course) looks highly impressive: the tonnage of ore extracted (and crushed) remained remarkably constant throughout the inter-war period and, to a certain extent, this compensated for the long-run drop in ore quality as revealed below.

PENNYWEIGHT YIELDS OF FINE GOLD PER SHORT TON BY COMPANY IN SELECTED YEARS

	Mysore	*Champion Reef*	*Nundydroog*	*Ooregum*
1892	26.4	17.3	30.5	39.6
1899	31.0	29.5	22	16.8
1913	14.3	10.9	15.9	13.9
1924	10.1	8.3	8.8	13.2
1933	10.3	10.2	10.8	5.3
1940	7.4	9.8	6.9	6.9
1946	5.9	9.9	5.4	5.0
1951	6.7	8.3	5.1	5.1

SOURCE: Various *Annual Directors' reports* supplemented by *Memoirs* of the Geological Survey of India.

THE COMPOSITION OF THE WORK-FORCE: RACE, SEX AND AGE

The respective proportions of underground and surface workers on the K.G.F. have been derived and are presented in table 6 for each year between 1899 and 1946. For the period as a whole there was a 60:40 split and only on one single occasion, 1926, was the relative position reversed (49.8:50.2).[52] Throughout, shifts between the two were of a marginal order of magnitude, and by and large it seems that in years of high and rising profitability (e.g.

[52] When a higher-than-average rate of tailing recycling and ore re-treatment were being practised.

1902–12 and 1934–41) more workers would be directed towards the shafts underground, and vice versa. This average ratio is very much in line with contemporary mining experience both elsewhere in India as well as outside.

The sources also make it possible to derive a racial breakdown of workers as between Europeans, Anglo-Indians and 'Natives'. In terms of pay, status, managerial responsibility, formal training, skill, conditions of service and non-pecuniary benefits, the Europeans, of course, were at the top of the pile. Taken as a group they comprised just under 1 per cent of the total working community, and were slightly more in evidence on the surface (0.90 per cent) than underground (0.82 per cent)—although the line separating these two categories for many of the Europeans was often blurred. In both absolute as well as in relative terms the trend of European employment declined; however the fall was greater in the underground departments than on the surface.

NUMBER OF EUROPEAN EMPLOYEES

	1900	*1945*
Below ground	271	85
Above ground	237	115

The vast majority of the Europeans hailed from the UK, and Cornwall provided the greatest bulk. It was quite common for sons to follow fathers and nephews to follow uncles: and even the wives who accompanied them and lived 'on camp' (actually in quite luxurious bungalows with a generous complement of servants thrown in) tended to have some Kolar connections.[53] The influence of the local tin-mining, and the presence of the Camborne School of Mines near Redruth (which the original John Taylor had campaigned for in the early years of the nineteenth century),[54] were probably responsible for this and, of course, they did not simply restrict themselves to Kolar but went all over the world. As Hobsbawm has remarked, 'wherever there was hard-rock mining on the globe in the nineteenth century, groups of Cornishmen were to be found.'[55] All the British personnel enjoyed 'covenanted' status and in return for pledging themselves for a fixed term of service (three-year contracts, invariably renewed upon request) which

[53] This has been borne out with all of the interviews I have conducted with former Kolar employees. For a list of interviewees and correspondents see 'The economic growth of the K.G.F. . . .', p. 31.

[54] L.P.S. Piper, *A short history of the Camborne School of Mines* (Penzance, 1979), ch. 1, pp. 2f.

[55] E.J. Hobsbawm, 'What is the workers' country?', reprinted in his *Worlds of labour: Further studies in the history of labour* (London, 1984), p. 52.

included an expenses-paid furlough in Europe, they were entitled to a whole range of benefits including free housing, a furniture allowance, free fuel, lighting, a pension, medical service and the use of exclusive recreational facilities. They formed a close-knit community (partly captured in the only published—and best forgotten—novel of the K.G.F., written by one Mrs Penny[56]) and it is interesting to learn that all the formal social proprieties—such as the ceremony surrounding the exchange of cards upon their arrival—were scrupulously maintained right up until the Second World War. In addition to the British, a number of Italians were recruited in the early years of the twentieth century. The Mysore Census gives us an indication of their strength.

PERSONS RESIDENT ON THE K.G.F. BUT BORN IN ITALY

Persons	*Males*	*Females*	
1901	56	56	0
1911	121	116	5
1921	52	41	11
1931	—	—	—

SOURCE: *Census of Mysore* 1931, III, Table XI; 1921, II, Table XI; 1911, II, Table XI; 1901, II, Table XI.

All the Italians were employed as face workers, allegedly because of their experience in excavating marble. Forming a small and quite separate community, most of them seem to have dispersed after the Great War. Unlike the British, they never intended to setle permanently, and so did not bring over their wives: Australia (especially Victoria) was clearly a more attractive proposition.[57] Nevertheless, their presence was sufficiently visible so as to cause the Italian Consulate to make a few—admittedly desultory—enquiries about their terms of employment;[58] and even though the 1951 Census of K.G.F. records only thirteen persons (ten male) whose mother tongue was Italian, quite a few of them are even today remembered by old Kolar hands.[59]

The Eurasian—or, as later and more politely designated, 'Anglo-Indian'—

[56] F.E. Penny, *Living dangerously* (London: Hodder and Stoughton, *c.* 1925).

[57] An interesting account of Italian migrants to the Australian mines may be found in F.R. Pascoe's 'Italian immigrants in the Australian mining industry', paper presented to the International Mining History Conference, Melbourne, *op. cit.*

[58] Refer to the small file on 'Italian workers' in *Proceedings of the Foreign and General Department* of the Government of India, B39–41, (July 1911), National Archives of India, New Delhi.

[59] *Census of Mysore 1951*, part II, table D1 (I). Several of the Europeans I have interviewed recall their presence.

employees constituted 0.57 per cent of the underground workforce and 1.2 per cent of the surface workforce over 1907–40. In absolute numbers their strength below ground rose slightly (replacing, in some instances, the British), and on the surface they seem to have maintained their proportion of the total.

NUMBERS OF ANGLO-INDIAN PERSONNEL

	1900	*1941*
Below ground	96	1
Above ground	306	237 (including 24 females)

The pattern of their employment was quite job specific. Underground they either became gang foremen or skip and tram drivers; on the surface they gravitated towards driving the train engines, controlling the signalling of railway movements, working in the boiler and hoisting rooms (jobs long considered 'too responsible' to be left to Natives) and performing clerical duties—hence the two dozen women as recorded in 1945. Like their wider position within India, on Kolar they were caught between two worlds and seem to have suffered the same ignominious social fate.[60]

If the Europeans and Anglo-Indians constituted the thin silver of key positions, the indigenous male workers formed the base. As is evident from table 6, from the early 1890s—earlier figures are unavailable—they were the core of both the surface as well as the underground labour force. Thus Inspector James Grundy's special investigation of Kolar in October 1894[61] reveals that no women, girls or male children under the age of ten were to be found working below ground; and that only four boys aged below 16 were so employed.

Once established this pattern persisted and held for the remainder of the period. Males accounted for some 97 per cent of the total numbers employed below ground and just over 87 per cent of those on the surface.

Thus it is clear that adult males made up the overwhelming number of underground workers and dominated among those involved in surface operations. Over 1900–46 there was a more or less constant proportion of this division between sex and age, save for one brief spell in the 1920s which witnessed a slight trend upset with respect to the surface workers; then there was a marginal upward kink in the percentage of female and children (those under 12 years) which peaked in 1926 when, in combina-

[60] Their Christianity, of course, helped to bridge the gap with the 'blue-bloods'.

[61] J. Grundy, 'Report on the Inspectors of the Kolar Gold Field' in his *Report of the Inspector of Mines in India for the year ending 30 June 1895* (Calcutta, 1896), pp. 6–40.

JAMES GRUNDY'S ESTIMATES OF NUMBERS EMPLOYED IN OCTOBER 1894

A. Below ground (total) 7 006, of which:		
	Men	7 002
	Boys under 16	4
B. Above ground (total) 5 267, of which:		
	Men	4 383
	Boys under 10	11
	Boys 10–16	308
	Women over 16	469 (358 between 40–50)
	Girls 12–16	68
	Girls under 12	28

SOURCE: J. Grundy, *op. cit.*, pp. 38f.

NUMBERS OF INDIGENOUS EMPLOYEES

	1900		*1945*	
	Numbers	*% of grand total*	*Numbers*	*% of grand total*
Below ground	12 811	97.25	9 316	97.5
Above ground total	11 409		6 862	
of which: males	9 184	80.5	5 685	82.3
females	11 682		858	

tion, they accounted for 11.7 per cent of all workers and 25.8 per cent of those on the surface. This, however, was not at the expense of the indigenous menfolk at work above ground, but was caused by the greater demand for surface-wise ore treatment relative to mining itself (as noted above the proportion of those employed below ground fell off somewhat during that time for reasons already alluded to). Women and children then appear to have played only a minor supporting role in the K.G.F.[62] This, of

[62] I use the word 'appear' advisedly because there is some evidence that that part of the recorded workforce above ground which was under the aegis of the contractors may not be very accurate in terms of total numbers at work and sexual composition. Thus Grundy made the point that (in 1894) some of the contractors failed to keep a regular register of boys, girls and women (*ibid.*, pp. 38f). However, since there were far fewer contractors involved with surface operations than underground (and employing far fewer workers—as inferred from the Sreenivasan Report, *op. cit.*, pp. 7–11), and because of a general tightening of monitoring procedures over time, I do not think that the qualification seriously vitiates the figures presented in table 6.

course, is in keeping with the migratory labour force of the Transvaal gold mining industry, but contrasts with coal mining in the subcontinent and elsewhere (particularly the position before 1842 in the UK) where women, and to a lesser extent children, were of considerably greater importance, especially during the earlier phases of activity.[63] If we were interested in following up this comparative question and seeking an explanation why neither company managers nor labour contractors seemed to have much need to turn to women and children, then it must surely be that there were very few specific tasks that they were specially suited to perform on the K.G.F. Unlike the situation in the Indian collieries prior to the legislation of 1923 and 1929 (which prohibited women and children, respectively, from underground work) where a 'family' mode of mining was in vogue,[64] on Kolar only men working within the discipline of a formal shift system were employed from the very outset. Because of the geological conditions and a different system of ventilation and underground haulage than that which held in the coalfields, no premium was placed on small physique. Similarly, on the surface there was not much call for the sort of labour that was then considered to be best performed by women and children; and although their wage rates were well below those of virtually all the categories of surface male employees,[65] there were not so many functional overlays that they could be easily substitutable for the majority of the men. It is certainly not my impression that there was a problem of some sort of taboo in recruiting or holding on to women and children: quite simply it was a demand and not a supply-side question, and they were not wanted in substantial numbers. The pattern of their employment was accordingly quite narrow—they performed very general duties including surface excavation and clearing waste, maintaining ore dumps and tailings, carrying stores, working in the crushing mills and separation plants (where for some jobs nimble and dexterous finger-power was called for), storage work, loading and unloading materials, cleaning equipment, some sweeping and a miscellany of other unskilled labour.

Origins and Social Characteristics

In spite of their many imperfections and idiosyncracies, the state-wise Census reports enable us to derive some crude estimates of the birthplace origin of the K.G.F. population, and they also furnish us with certain data

[63] See N. Levy, *op. cit.*, for South Africa and for a discussion of the coal mining perspective see my 'Recruiting and organising and industrial labour force in colonial India', *op. cit.*, section II, 'The role of women and children'.

[64] For details see 'Recruiting and organising . . .', esp. p. 461f.

[65] This has been inferred from the data on wage rates by job rather than directly by sex.

about their social characteristics.[66] There are, however, two principal difficulties which stand in our way. First the K.G.F. was not singled out for separate Census treatment until 1901 the year that the so-called 'new town' was laid out; and this, of course, is some two decades after the pioneering miners had arrived on the site.[67] Secondly, the precise meaning of the unit designated as 'K.G.F. City' is elusive (see table 7) and therefore there is ambiguity within, and more seriously between, the succeeding Census volumes.[68] Skirting over the technical difficulties involved in arriving at a common spatial unit from this source over time, we can distinguish between two formally separable—but nonetheless interconnected—entities. The thirty square miles of territory lying between longitudes 12° 50′ to 13°, and latitudes 78° 18′ to 78° 21′ consisted of (1) the mining settlement proper and usually referred to as the Mining or Company Area; and (2) the surrounding eighty villages (approximately sixty in 1895) comprising an effective cordon between the mines and the rest of Kolar District.[69] After the end-of-century plague these villages, all centring on Bowringpet—now Bargarpet—Taluk (Col. Bowring being one of the noted Political Residents to the Mysore raj) came under a separate Sanitary Board (established in 1899), and then (in 1900) a separate Police Circle—both administered by the state government. Since the Census and a variety of other official sources seldom clearly differentiate these two categories, it is hard to demarcate exactly the actual mining population from that of the wider K.G.F. City population. Furthermore, although we know that at any one time a certain proportion of the mining labour force lived within the second category—either in a number of coolie lines off camp or in the villages themselves—we do not have any consistent measure of its changing magnitude. However, although we cannot obtain exact numbers, it is possible—by doing some elementary arithmetic on the few snippets of information at our disposal—to derive an indication of the broad picture.

[66] For a discussion of the value of the Census material as applied to another Mysore sector see J.D. Moore, 'Migration to Mysore plantations, 1871–1941' in M. Gaborieau and A. Thorner (eds.), *Asie du sud*, *op. cit.*, pp. 483–90.

[67] The only detail we have of the Census for 1891 is the enumeration of a mining population (including miners, workers, managers and agents) of 2 073 (1 371 as workers and 702 as dependents), vol. III, Table XVII. This is a long way short of the figure presented in table 3. The Census of 1881, more realistically perhaps, mentions that 59 miners, all men, were working in 'Uriya' (p. 85).

[68] Thus for 1901, 1911 and 1921 it is possible to derive two completely different estimates for the 'K.G.F. City' population.

[69] Towards the end of the period a third component of K.G.F. City was identified, i.e. the urban area under the aegis of the Sanitary Board. See the *Census* of 1941, part 1, p. 12.

Categories of Employment: Actual and Implied

	1921	*December 1929*
A. Total number of mining employees	23 648 (23 344)*	18 514 (18 454)*
(i) numbers living inside the mining area	16 717	13 462
(ii) numbers living outside	6 931	5 032
B. Total number of workers and dependents inside the mining area	51 031	
(i) less Mysore raj employees and dependents (approx.)	1 200	
(ii) less shop-keepers, hoteliers, traders and their dependents (approx.)	1 000	
Sub-total	48 831	48 166
(iii) Implied ratio of dependents to employees in mining area	2.06	2.60
C. Off-camp employees (6931) plus their dependents (11 000)...	17 931	12 982 (5 032 + 7 950)†
D. Employees and dependents on and off camp (48 831 + 17 931)...	66 762	61 148
E. Total K.G.F. City population (1921 Census)	87 682	85 103 (1931 Census**)
∴ F. The agricultural population of K.G.F. is 87 682–66 762...	20 920 (23%)	23 955 (28.1%)

Notes: *See table 3.

† The figure of 7 950 is based on the 1921 rate of 1.58 dependents off camp to each worker off camp.

** Since there is an 18–24 month gap between the Census and the Medical Department's data, I have adjusted the backward population extrapolation accordingly.

Sources: M.A. Sreenivasan's *Report*, *op. cit.*, pp. 4f and footnote 1 and the Mysore Census, 1921 and 1931.

Let us begin at 1941 and work backwards. The Census of that year, though its scope was adversely affected by the War, gives some valuable clues. For the first time it tells us that the villages within the rural remit of the K.G.F. Sanitary Board had a combined population of 26 900 (i.e. some 19.7 per cent of the total K.G.F. City population of 133 859 persons). If we extrapolate this back to 1921 using the rate of growth of population of Kolar District as a whole (18 per cent) then we arrive at a figure of 21 645. We would expect that this would be a slight over-estimate for the actual agricultural population in the K.G.F., since it includes the faster than average growing mining area within the calculation. In fact this is very close to the number we can derive from our second bit of information, which emanates from the raw statistics supplied to the Special Officer M.A. Sreenivasan in 1930 by the K.G.F. Medical Department (a central service run by John Taylor and Sons). This data when put together in the following format is revealing.

We can see immediately that there was a three-way division of population within the K.G.F. City designation. First, a majority—some 50 000 workers and dependents—lived on camp; second, some 18 000 lived off camp, either in the urban area or intermingled with the villagers; and finally, the remainder or 20 920 (i.e. only 725 less than our predicted—and upward biased—number) could be considered as the agricultural population who had little role in the mining industry. What is also noteworthy is that if we look at the other more uncertain figures for 1929, the agricultural population standing at 23 955 is once again close to our predicted number

	1891	*1901*	*1911*
1. Average daily numbers of employees at work (table 3)	9 038	25 060	25 942
2. Row 1 × the number of dependents assuming a ratio of 1:2	18 086	50 120	51 884
3. Row 1 + Row 2	27 124	75 180	77 826
4. K.G.F. City population according to Census: alternative B	24 111†	70 874	83 743
5. K.G.F. City population according to Census: alternative A	7 085*	38 204	48 635
6. Row 4–Row 5		32 670	35 108
7. Alternative (A) implied dependency ratio: Row 5: Row 1		1.52	1.87

Notes: † Since this is the only (and retrospective) Census estimate for 1891 it is not clear whether it should be placed in Alternative B or Alternative A.

*This rather ludicrous estimate appears in B.L. Rice's Gazetteer for *Mysore and Coorg* (Calcutta, 1908) p. 153.

of 23 770. The slightly enhanced proportion of agriculturists to the total for 1931 (28.1 per cent) over 1921 (23 per cent) is fully in keeping with the relative decline of the mining industry prior to the withdrawal from the Gold Standard. The final piece of information that we can draw upon relates to the perceived anomalies in the early Census Reports, especially those for 1901 and 1911. To appreciate the significance of these let us consider the following tabular statement.

Quite evidently the 2:1 ratio of dependents to workers (or rather to the average daily number of workers) which held in 1921 must be off-beam for 1901 and 1911, and of course for 1891. This is because row 3 is actually higher than the corresponding numbers in row 4 for the first two Census years and only slightly lower for 1911. Yet, if we were to focus on the figures given in K.G.F. City population alternative A, then again we would send up with an unlikely estimate for the residual agricultural population. Admittedly we would derive a more realistic dependency ratio (row 7) in the sense that the first two generations of workers might well have left a greater number of their dependents back home than later ones (and certainly the 'trend' estimate looks right for that judgment, i.e. 1:1.52 rises to 1:1.87) but this would seem to allow for a far too large or implied number living in the eighty villages and engaged in agriculture—row 6. It appears inconceivable that there could have been 14 000 more villagers in 1911 than in 1921 (35 108 as opposed to 20 920—row F of preceding table). Moreover, this residual shows a rising trend over 1901–1911 and yet, as we have already established earlier, this was a decade of considerable advance and prosperity for gold mining. Also the significant implied reduction of agriculturists between 1911–21 is not consistent with the population movement in Kolar District as a whole. Thus, assuming that the K.G.F. Census is accurate for both alternatives A and B, there seems only one possible explanation for the discrepancies: that employees and their dependents living off camp in the rural and urban areas were separately enumerated and that these numbers were proportionately greater in 1901 and 1911 than in 1921 and December 1929. From what we know about the administration of the K.G.F. City and the finances of the K.G.F. Sanitary Board, this is plausible,[70] but the direct evidence is far too flimsy to offer convincing proof one way or the other. So at the end of the day we are not much nearer to being able to separately identify the actual miners and their dependents from the overall K.G.F. City population for the period as a whole. In turn this means that for all the Census years we have discussed—

[70] The details are given in the *Annual reports of the Chief Inspector of Mines for Mysore*, and the *Annual reports and accounts of the K.G.F. Sanitary Board*, 1899–1915, *passim*.

with the partial exception of 1941—the birthplace and other social details do not enable us to differentiate between the mining and non-mining population in the optimum manner. Nevertheless despite this caveat we ought not to over-exaggerate the problem since in the first half of the twentieth century it is obvious that it was the fortunes of the mining industry which determined the shape of K.G.F. City and the nature of changes that took place there; and, for all their drawbacks, we can make some progress with the Census returns.

The first point we can establish is that throughout the period 1890–1946 the vast majority of the workforce (and, of course, their dependents) were born outside Kolar District itself, and indeed outside Mysore State. The fragments of information we have for the early years, when supplemented with rather firmer data for the later, indicate that around three quarters of the miners were non-Mysorean. Thus the 1941 Census reveals that of the 27 820 workers employed in that year, only 7 059 (or 77 per cent) came from Mysore: and this percentage seems to have held from almost the beginning of modern mining activity.[72] The bulk of the labour undoubtedly originated from the Madras Presidency and this can be partly seen from table 7. The respective Census volumes permit us to be a bit more exact. Contiguous North Arcot supplied the largest single district-wise contribution followed by Salem, Chittoor, Madras and far-away Malabar (inclusive of Cochin). This birthplace distribution is fully in line with the details of mother-tongues as given below.

Tamil was the Kolar Gold Field's lingua franca; and, as Special Officer M.A. Sreenivasan tells us, it was in that tongue that the grim epigram then current (1930) amongst the labour force was expressed: 'Keelay pona ponam, mele vanda panam' (If you go down, corpse—if you come up, coin).[73] Only 1.8 per cent or just over 500 persons of those engaged in mining in 1941 spoke the language of the state, i.e. Kannada, compared with approximately 70 per cent who spoke Tamil, 14 per cent Telugu, 6.5 per cent Malayalam, and 4.4 per cent Urdu.[74] In the wider K.G.F. City population tamil also dominated but, predictably, only to a much lesser extent (61.4 per cent): and it maintained this level even until 1951 (61.2 per cent). the K.G.F. also attracted a

[71] *Census of Mysore*, 1941, table 78, p. 100.

[72] As revealed in the succeeding reports of the *Chief Inspector of Mines for Mysore*, *passim*; the *Annual reports* of the Directors and of the Superintendents of the various gold mining companies; James Grundy's Report, *op. cit.*; G.F. Hatch's *Memoir* of the Geological Survey of India in the K.G.F., 33, (1902), pp. 61ff; M.A. Sreenivasan's *Report*, *op. cit.*, ch. 2; and, going beyond 1941, S.R. Deshpande's *Report on labour conditions in the gold mining industry* (Delhi, 1946), pp. 4f.

[73] M.A. Sreenivasan, *Report*, *op. cit.*, p. 97.

[74] *Census of Mysore*, 1941, part 1, p. 16.

ENUMERATION OF POPULATION BY MOTHER TONGUE
1941

Language	*Total KGF City population*	*Persons engaged in mining only*		*1951 Total KGF City population*
		Numbers	*%*	
Tamil	82 263	19 480	702	97 304
Telugu	26 214	3 861	13.8	31 514
Hindustani (Urdu)	9 777	1 233	4.4	12 812
Kannada	7 954	519	1.8	8 538
Malayalam	n.a.	1 756	6.5	
English	2 623			2 873
Hindi	n.a.			1 846
Marathi	1 101			1 846
Gujarati	n.a.			35
Marwari	n.a.			17
Punjabi	n.a.			5
Sudi	n.a.			3
Bengali	n.a.			4
Total of group identified		26 849	96.7	
Total number in Census	133 859	278 220		159 084

sprinkling of people from all over the subcontinent, but it would be wrong to think of the Settlement as being quite as cosmopolitan as many of the other modern industrial areas. But, needless to say, in 1941, sixty-six of the 87 registered moneylenders came from outside, and twenty years earlier the Census shows that there were as many as 420 Marwaris on the Field and virtually all of the menfolk (260) would have been *sowcars*.[75] The fall in the number of these moneylenders as evidenced in the 1951 Census (only 13 males and 4 females) is one sort of index of the decline of the industry!

In order properly to explain this pattern of birthplace origin, we would need to substantially extend our horizon and consider, inter alia, conditions on the land, relative population dynamics, and the means and cost of transport and communications. Given the relatively small number of persons involved this is not a very feasible or a rewarding task and I propose instead to suggest two lines of explanation. First, during our period, the indigenous Kannada-speaking Mysoreans do not seem to have been keen on entering the quite rapidly expanding modern labour market:[76] it was

[75] *Census of Mysore*, 1941, part II, table XVII.

[76] As is reasonably well known, the 'model' princely state of Mysore developed a strong

not simply a specific antipathy to mining work, but a generalized reluctance to leave the land and traditional pursuits. Thus the plantations of the Malnad were heavily reliant upon immigrant labour (especially from Madras Presidency and particularly from the adjacent South Canara District),[77] and so too were the industries which sprang up on the plains and in the cities of Bangalore and Bhadravati. Thus Balakrishna concludes his chapter on industrial development (1940) with the observation: 'It is obvious therefore that the composition of the industrial labour corps of Mysore consists of foreign elements to a great extent.'[78] As far as the population of Kolar District itself was concerned, it seems that two factors were at work. First, throughout our period and with the obvious exception of the years of acute famine, this overwhelmingly agricultural part of the state does not appear to have experienced any long-run decline in its agrarian economy; indeed the evidence suggests that it was a remarkably prosperous era. The Gazetteer goes as far as to say that 'being one of the healthiest districts in the South and with its good soil and a good system of irrigation with a large number of tanks, Kolar has been described as one of "nature's favourites"';[79] and in 1881—the very year that serious mining work began—the first Census Commissioner, B.L. Rice, contended that the life of the agriculturist in the area was 'rather an easy one. No such continuous toil is known to him as that which consumes the days and nights of his brother in north India'[80] He even went on to say that not only was 'the condition of the ryot extremely advantageous' but also that they were 'better off than any class of cultivator in any province of India that I am acquainted with'. The evidence of prosperity which he cited included many well-built roomy tiled houses; many cattle sheds; numerous grain pits; and a situation where there was a greater supply of food than demand, and hence its price was cheap.

The second factor is that the growth of the mining industry itself gave a stimulus to the local economy. Unfortunately a lack of suitable statistical data makes it impossible to derive any meaningful regional multiplier stemming from the influence of K.G.F. City;[81] however there is sufficient

industrial base in the first half of the present century and included textile plants, an iron and steel works and some light engineering.

[77] For details see J.D. More, 'Migration to the Mysore plantations', *op. cit.*, esp. table 2, p. 489. In fact between 1901–41 South Canara furnished well over half the plantation workers of Hassan and Kadure. North Arcot—on the other side of the state—also sent a contingent.

[78] R. Balakrishna, *Industrial development of Mysore* (Bangalore, 1940), p. 264.

[79] B.N. Sathyan (ed.), *op. cit.*, p. 90.

[80] B.L. Rice, *Report on the Mysore Census* (Bangalore, 1884), p. 33.

[81] The absence of any state-wise income accounts prior to Independence has been a major handicap to research in a variety of different ways.

qualitative information to suggest that there was a definite and positive fillip effect. The District benefited from a number of infrastructural improvements occasioned by the development of the mines, including a railway connection to the main Bangalore-Madras link (built between 1891 and 1898); an assured supply of filtered drinking water (from Bethamangala reservoir completed in 1905); plenty of irrigation water from two great public works projects—built primarily to service the mines—namely the dams across the Cauvery at Sivasamudrum (completed in August 1902) and, later on, at Krishnarajasagar; access to the electric transmission line carrying power from the h.e.p. stations and their relays to the K.G.F.[82] and many miles of metalled all-weather roads. With the continuing growth of K.G.F. City, 'Bangarpet assumed importance as a wholesale centre' for a wide range of crops including rice, chilies, onions and potatoes.[83] The wage rates for casual labour—especially agricultural—seem to have risen quite fast during the early decades, and the Gazetteer claimed that they were 'higher than elsewhere in the State'.[84] Further, in the Bangarpet (Bowringpet) Taluk there had been a 'noticeable increase in the agricultural resources of the people': indeed between the original land settlement of March 1890 and the assessment of 1924, the area under cultivation had grown from 45 543 to 58 482 acres; the value of the area under dry, wet and garden lands had increased by 72 per cent , 250 per cent and 600 per cent respectively; the number of houses had doubled; the number of cattle had risen by almost a third; and that of ploughs by 36 per cent.[85] Now whilst the normal population growth would account for some of this improvement, James Grundy was in no doubt about the specific advantages arising from the mines: thus in June 1895 he writes that 'it is plainly the case that such a great industry must be of great benefit to the surrounding country', and that

It may be seen in the everyday life of the people: at the railway stations, especially at or near the pay-days; at the daily and weekly bazars; at the monthly *hat* on

[82] Incidentally, the Cauvery power works not only proved to be a great boon for the K.G.F. Undertaking and its hinterland, but also helped to modernize the two principal cities of the State, Bangalore and Mysore (plenty of water, public lighting), and to provide a source of cheap energy to the cotton, wool, silk, oil and rice mills that began to spring up during the inter-war period. For some contemporary views of this externality-yielding process see the Dewan's *Address to the Mysore Representative Assembly*, 9 July 1924, Karnataka State Archives, and P.G. D'Souza's Speech to the Mysore Engineers Association, published under the title 'Industrial Progress in Mysore' (Bangalore, 1923), esp. p. 11.

[83] B.N. Sathyan (ed.), *Gazetteer, op. cit.*, p. 254.

[84] *Ibid.*, p. 295. Apparently, the wage push effect was felt as early as 1881: See the *Report on the administration of Mysore for 1880–81* (Bangalore, 1883), p. 31.

[85] *Ibid.*, ch. XI, pp. 338ff.

pay-days; and the springing up, with almost mushroom growth, of very large numbers of village huts; places for buying food and drink; and really fine and large buildings for a hospital, church, chapels, recreation halls and reading rooms, fire officials' bungalows, *musafir* bungalows, and a frequently used *kachahri*.[86]

Obviously, as Grundy suggests, the K.G.F. City itself—with the usual complement of residential housing, shops, godowns, restaurants and bazars—exerted a market pull on at least some local resources that might otherwise have gone untapped. Boom towns all over the world have this sort of character. But what all this amounts to is that the Kolar population appear to have decided that they could better live off—rather than on—the mines. Whether this was a 'rational' choice or not cannot be easily answered. This is because we would need to know very much more than we do about both subjective valuations as well as the pecuniary and non-pecuniary cost-benefit calculus (one that takes in the opportunity cost of the wage and the weighing-up of working conditions in the mines vis-à-vis alternatives on the land). In any event the Mysorean choice does not appear to have been understood or appreciated by certain sections of opinion in the State. Thus during the spurt of growth and high prosperity just before the onset of the First World War, the Indian Patriot ran a series of leading articles under the rallying cry of 'Mysore for the Mysoreans',[87] which bemoaned the fact that 'capital, skill and labour are all in the hands of the outsider' and that 'Mysoreans figure much less prominently than the Madras Tamilian.'[88]

Looking at this from the other side of the coin, for the immigrant Tamils the balance of advantage clearly lay the other way. Since both the eastern part of Mysore and the north-western sending districts of the modern Presidency shared similar geophysical and geomorphological characteristics,[89] it was not so much a question of the quality of the soil or monsoon as it was of agrarian structure. Towards the end of the nineteenth century agrarian conditions in North Arcot were rapidly approaching crisis. As John Harriss has shown, something like 85 per cent of all rural households in this dry zone were marginal, in that they either owned no land at all or had insufficient amounts to be able to produce enough for their own subsistence.[90] As a

[86] J. Grundy, *Report*, *op. cit.*, pp. 8f.

[87] *Indian Patriot* 28.11.1910, 3.12.1910 and 5.12.1910. The articles were written by someone who styled/himself or herself 'A Native of Mysore'.

[88] *Ibid.*, 28.11.1910.

[89] As mentioned previously the mines set up a demand for water which led to the development of a rather unique public works system which benefited the surrounding area; and B.L. Rice shows that the District as a whole, and K.G.F. City in particular, was relatively well endowed with tanks. See his *Mysore and Coorg Gazetteer*, *op. cit.*, pp. 144–62.

[90] J. Harriss, *Capitalism and peasant farming: Agrarian structure and ideology in northern Tamil Nadu* (Bombay, 1982), ch. 2.

result of various types of pressure stemming from British land policy and commercialization, a relatively small class of rich peasant farmers and small-to-medium-sized landlords became dominant and indeed, according to Harriss, have retained their hegemony to this day.[91] For this class the old-style patron-client relationships (which continued to exist in princely Mysore)[92] with low-caste landless labourers and under-tenants had little meaning—especially at times of famine (1876–8, 1896–7)—and so, when the opportunity presented itself, there was every incentive for these 'marginals' to migrate. Since the distances involved were not that great, and given the improved accessibility because of the railway, information and transport costs were being cut precisely when the mines were coming on stream. Moreover there was a precedent for cross-border population movement in the regular seasonal flow of agricultural workers from Madras into neighbouring Mysore, stretching back over many decades':[93] so the immigrants were not going into the unknown. We should also mention the existence of another enabling factor—the offices of the colonial state. In a literal sense this meant the co-ordination of the postal services between British India and the Mysore raj so that the Tamils could—if they chose—cheaply remit part of their cash earnings to their home villages. But, much more importantly, the Extradition Agreement between Madras and Mysore (Act XXI of 1879),[94] the co-operation between police forces and judiciaries over the theft, handling and transmission of items from the K.G.F. such as gold dust and explosives;[95] and the repeal of the already quite toothless legislation regarding the engagement and contract terms of labour recruited in the Presidency for work outside (Act V of 1866) in 1901,[96] all provided a useful 'externality' to the British owners and managers of the gold mines with respect to the availability of, and control over, their most vital input to the production process. Thus, as far as labour is concerned, in the most fundamental of senses—protection of British capital—it mattered not a whit that there were two formally separate administrations on either side of the Kolar border.[97]

[91] J. Harriss, 'What happened to the green revolution in South India? Economic trends, household mobility and the politics of an "Awkward Class."' Discussion paper 175, School of Development Studies, University of East Anglia, May 1985, pp. 14ff.

[92] Cf. B. Hettne, *op. cit.*, K. Puttaswamaiah, *op. cit.*, vol. 2. M. Shama Row, *Modern Mysore* (Bangalore, 1936), vol. 1 and B.N. Sathyan, *op. cit.*, ch. 8.

[93] C.H. Rao, *Mysore gazetteer*, *op. cit.*, vol. II, ch. IV.

[94] *Judicial proceedings* of the Government of Madras, G.O. 4–4–1894, No. 821, Tamil Nadu State Archives, Madras.

[95] *Judicial proceedings*, G.O. 22–11–1894, No. 2824, Tamil Nadu State Archives.

[96] *Public proceedings*, G.O. 22–4–1893, No. 322, Tamil Nadu State Archives.

[97] For a discussion of the general significance of the co-existence of direct and indirect

The caste and religious breakdown of the K.G.F. City population in the Census volumes for 1901–31 share the same problem as the birthplace, in that they do not differentiate the mining population from the remainder of the inhabitants. Nevertheless, they do show that a significant minority of this total were from the 'depressed classes'. Thus in 1921, of the five major divisions represented, the Adi-Dravida comprised 40.4 per cent followed by 'other Hindus' at 35.7 per cent, Indian Christians 11.3 per cent, Muslims 8.2 per cent, and Buddhists only 1.3 per cent.[98] Fortunately, once again the 1941 Census comes to our rescue and gives us details for the actual mining workforce.

THE COMMUNITY AND RELIGION OF THE WORKFORCE IN 1941

	Numbers	*% of total*
1. Brahmans of whom 62 were born in Mysore, and 93 outside	155	0.55
2. Other Hindu castes of whom 1 250 were from Mysore and 5 187 from outside	6 437	23.1
3. Depressed Classes (Adi-Dravida) of whom 3 329 were from Mysore and 10 646 from outside	13 975	50.2
4. Christians of whom 1 985 were from Mysore and 3 072 from outside	5 057	18.1
5. Muslims of whom 370 were from Mysore and 1 612 from outside	1 982	7.1
Total of above groups	27 606	99.05
Total numbers employed given in Census	27 820	

SOURCE: *Census of Mysore*, 1941, table 78, p. 106.

The adjustment clearly brings to the fore the very high proportion of Adi-Dravidas and Christians in the actual workforce, and taken together they formed just under 70 per cent of the total in that year.[99] The presence of the

ruled area, see C. Simmons and B.R. Satyanarayana, 'The economic consequences of indirect rule in India: A re-appraisal', *Indian Economic and Social History Review*, XVI, 2, (1978), pp. 185ff.

[98] *Census of Mysore*, 1921, part, II, tables XVI and XVII.

[99] Since the Adi-Dravidas also comprised some 43.1 per cent of the total K.G.F. City population in 1941—only marginally higher (2.8 per cent) than twenty years before, it seems safe to surmise that the proportion of the deprived classes in the workforce was around the same level for the earlier decades as it was then.

depressed classes in such large numbers is not all that surprising in view of the non-traditional and dangerous nature of the work itself—the Indian coal miners were similarly drawn from the Untouchables, other low castes and tribals;[100] and given the prominence and prestige of the Christian churches servicing the religious and social needs of the British and Anglo-Indian staff and their families, the high Christian allegiance proferred to the Census officers is also predictable. None of these Census volumes—not even the 1941 compilation—relate literacy to caste and religion, but it seems fair to assume that the bulk of the illiterates were from the depressed classes and the bulk of the literates in English were Christians. As late as 1941, two thirds of the male K.G.F. City population could not read or write in any language (for the female population it was just under 90 per cent), but as many as 5320 males were literate in English.

LITERACY IN K.G.F. CITY AND MYSORE STATE AS A WHOLE IN 1941

		K.G.F. City only		*Mysore State average*	
	Numbers	*%*	*(1951)*	*% only*	*(1951)*
1. Males literate	23 487	33.3	(44.7)	20.4	(30.3)
literate in English	5 320	7.5		3.8	
∴ illiterates	46 941	66.6	(69.7)	79.6	(69.7)
2. Females literate	6 505	10.3	(17.2)	5.3	(9.8)
literate in English	1 625	2.5		0.83	
∴ illiterates	56 926	89.74	(82.8)	94.7	(91.2)

SOURCE: *Census of Mysore*, 1941, II, table XIV, and 1951, II, table CIV.

Of course proportionately more people—especially males—were literate, more were literate in English in K.G.F. City than the wider Mysore State as a whole, and the trend was rising. However, despite any 'melting-pot' and perhaps even 'Sanskritization' effect that might have occurred through time, the fact remains that at the end of our period the greatest single chunk of the Kolar workforce was still regarded as coming from the lowest rungs of society and virtually all of these were illiterate.

RECRUITMENT AND ORGANIZATION

Setting aside the very special and temporary difficulties of holding on to

[100] See my 'Recruiting and organising an industrial labour force . . .', *op. cit.*, p. 458ff. For a comparison with cotton see (for Bombay) B.D. Morris, *The emergence of an industrial labour force*, *op. cit.*, pp. 71–83, and (for Cawnpore) Chitra Joshi, 'Kanpur textile labour: Some structural features of formulative years 1919–39', *Economic and Political Weekly*, special no. (1981); and with Tisco, see S.B. Datta, *Capital accumulation and workers' struggle*, *op. cit.*, pp. 29–39.

labour during the latter stages of the Second World War,[101] there was only one period—again of quite a limited duration—when the Undertaking seems to have encountered some difficulty in recruiting labour at the going wage. This was from the late 1880s down to the late 1890s—a matter of no more than a decade. The reasons for this comparatively short-lived 'problem' are not hard to identify. During exploration and extending to the first five years or so of operations, none of the mining companies complained about recruiting and maintaining sufficient labour for their purposes. Quite the contrary, both the *Prospectuses* and the early Directors' and Superintendents' *Reports* delivered to the shareholders spoke of an abundant supply of low cost labour—the wage rate being set at only 4–6 annas per day for men and 3–4 annas for women.[102] There was convincing unanimity about this, and the euphoric view stated by the 'Nundydroog Co. (in 1880) that 'any amount of good native labour could be procured for as little as 4 pence a day' was representative of the time.[103] However, once the workings got significantly deeper than the 300–400 feet level penetrated by the 'Ancients', we can begin to detect a change in attitude. From 1886 concern about supply adequacy began to be expressed, and in May 1887 the Superintendent of the Mysore G.M. Co. went as far as to write to the Mysore Residency in Bangalore requesting information to import Chinese labour—at 'fifty a time'—from the Hong Kong Colony in order to overcome the shortfall.[104] The Resident himself did not raise any objections, nor did the Government of India (though it opined that the proposed immigration 'should be kept within limits'). More surprisingly, the Mysore Durbar was not against the proposal. In fact this scheme never materialized—unlike, of course, the gold mines on the Rand, which imported over sixty thousand Chinese between 1904 and 1906[105]—but the fact that it was seriously considered at all is revealing. We should also note that it was around this time that the companies began to put pressure on the Political Resident in order to win support and public funds for greater control of this labour—and, needless to say, that official badgered the Durbar into providing a greater police presence and

[101] The best account of this period is to be found in the Directors' *Reports* of the four companies over 1941–45.

[102] Particularly the *Prospectuses* for Nundydroog, Mysore and Ooregum in 1880, and Nine Reefs for 1881. The Directors' and Superintendents' *Reports* for the four main-line companies were consulted for this period and all tell the same story.

[103] *Prospectus* of the Nundydroog G.M. Co., 6 Nov. 1880.

[104] Mysore Residency File No. 369, 1–9, 1887, in the Mysore Residency Papers, 12/2/27, India Office Records.

[105] See P. Richardson, *Chinese mine labour in the Transvaal* (London, 1982).

an improved administrative set-up to deal with labour troubles.[106]

In addition to the question of greater depths, several factors combined to explain this decade of uncertainty. First of all the demand for manpower was growing extraordinarily rapidly, and seems to have exceeded the limited supply of willing workmen from the immediate neighbourhood. Secondly, the high bankruptcy rate amongst the early companies must have had a disheartening effect: people laid off were not automatically given jobs elsewhere. Thirdly, and as we have seen, it took a few years before the improvements in communications and transport filtered through, and so knowledge of employment opportunities in the mines was sparse. Fourthly, on 11 September 1897, the most serious accident—until then, that is—in Indian mining history occurred at Champion Reef. Fifty-two men died and several hundred were badly injured in a particularly horrifying accident—one that is very vividly described by the hard-pressed Inspectorate.[107] In brief, what happened was that one of the surface staff made an elementary blunder, which ultimately led to over one hundred men falling on top of one another down the succession of steeply inclined ladders that were in place from the shaft bottom. Apart from having a profound long-run effect on the mode of conveying men to and from the underground workings—within five years of the disaster cages for ascent and descent had replaced the primitive system of ladders[108]—this fearful tragedy naturally frightened off some existing workers and must have put off many potential new entrants. Finally, and most seminally, in 1898–9 there was a major outbreak of bubonic plague in the lines: it quickly spread to the surrounding villages and caused great panic.[109] Within the Mining Area itself, 615 cases were diagnosed between October 1898 and December 1899, resulting in 453 deaths; the corresponding figures for the villages were 335 cases and 261 deaths. The Chief Inspector of Mines for Mysore, W.F. Smeeth, informs us that on a single day in February 1899, when the plague was at its most virulent phase and quite out of control, 'about 5000 coolies left in a body'.[110] It was that disease and the consequent disruption

[106] *Proceedings of the Foreign Department*, Internal Branch, File 99–108 'A', October 1900, and File 164 'B', Feb. 1902. National Archives of India.

[107] A.R.C.I.M.M. 1897, pp. 97ff. Even the Resident felt moved to inform his masters in Calcutta that 'there has been a fearful accident in the Champion Reef mines owing to mismanagement in regulating ascent of coolies crowding up; the shaft became blocked, panic ensued and many coolies lost their hold and fell to their death'. Letter dated 15 September 1897 and printed in J. Grundy's *Report of the Chief Inspector of Mines in India*, 1897, p. 126.

[108] A.R.C.I.M.M. 1902, pp. 4f.

[109] Details are to be found in the A.R.C.I.M.M. 1899, pp. 26–31.

[110] *Ibid.*, p. 30.

it caused to mining which led to the establishment of the Sanitary Board, and finally prompted the Managing Agents to raze the old infected lines and build a new town.

Literally from the turn of the century, the problem of labour supply disappears. The scope and tenor of the entries in the surviving handwritten 'Weekly minutes of meetings', covering April 1899–March 1902, change dramatically: from an almost exclusive preoccupation with labour matters (especially the health of the community) in the months up to February 1900, the Minutes reveal an attention to simple routine and, for the modern reader, they become quite anodyne. Once the plague crisis had been overcome, the management no longer seem to have discussed labour supply in problematic terms. This change of mood is also reflected in the other sources, and the Annual Directors' Reports of the various companies, the Reports of the Inspectorate, and the Reports of the Administration of the State begin to take a very casual and laid-back attitude towards labour: quite simply the issue had ceased to provoke concern or much detailed comment. This can be partly explained by the steps taken to improve living and working conditions (as far as the latter is concerned there was an element of compulsion introduced through the Mysore Mines Regulation Act of 1897 and the ensuing derivation of Mining Rules)[111] and partly because after 1907 there was no need to further expand the number of jobs (table 3). Certainly, after that peak year for employment the Undertaking could easily cope with their raw labour needs.

As far as the supply of 'skilled' and 'semi-skilled' labour is concerned,[112] there is no evidence that the companies experienced any general difficulties of recruitment—although they did of course frequently bemoan the loss of certain 'irreplaceable' individuals (invariably British), especially during the latter stages of the Second World War. Since the wages and perks of most of the European covenanted staff were attractive relative to what could be earned in the UK, there does not seem to have been any problem in recruiting the necessary quantity or quality; and as for the Anglo-Indians, this avenue of employment was considered most suitable. The semi-skilled posts were apparently easily filled with indigenous labour. The largest category was that of the mestries or foremen attached to the various underground departments—drilling, blasting, tramming and

[111] For details of the Act and the first round of Rules see the A.R.C.I.M.M. 1897–1906, and the *Committee reports* of the Govt. of Mysore, 'G' 2 & 3, and 'M' 11 & 12, in the Karnataka State Archives.

[112] To sidestep the many conceptual difficulties associated with the definition and meaning of 'skill'—for which see S. Wood (ed.), *The degradation of work? Skill, de-skilling and the labour process* (London, 1982)—I propose simply to accept the conventions of the K.G.F. Undertaking.

so on. After the passage of the Mines Regulation Act, many of the mestries were required to hold a valid certificate of competence issued by the Mines Inspectorate. In order to meet this need the Undertaking stepped up its provision of elementary schools and organized evening and day-release classes which prepared the men for their examinations. Annually after 1898 there would be between 400 and 500 men who had to go through the examina-tions, and since the certificates had to be periodically renewed, this became an ongoing process.[113] Most of the other semi-skilled posts both underground and on the surface were learned 'on the job'; and since the pace of the technological change in mining, conveying, crushing, milling, ore-treatment and assaying was rather slow-paced after 1903–05 (when electricity replaced coal) there was little call for a new cadre of highly trained manpower. Needless to say, there were always enough clerks to fill the various offices.

To complete this picture of labour recruitment and relate it to the way in which it was organized, disciplined and controlled, we need to consider the role of the contractors. The surviving documents do not suggest the presence of many 'pure' labour recruitors, i.e. intermediaries who simply contracted to obtain a stated number of hands and deliver them to the manager at the pit-head for a given per capita commission. In this respect the K.G.F. experience contrasts with that of the great plantation industry in the north-east and also with the gold mines of the Witwatersrand. The species of contractor active in Kolar was the working or raising contractor, who bore a strong functional resemblance to the Indian colliery *ticcardars*, the middle-men of the pre-revolutionary Chinese (Manchurian) coal mines, and the butties of the early British coal industry.[114] These men—to my knowledge, no women are ever reported to have done this—contracted with the company management to perform a specified task for a given rate of remuneration and usually within a stipulated time. Typically the jobs were the toughest, unpleasantest, most physically demanding and most dangerous of all. Having successfully tendered for a job the contractor would then have the responsibility of hiring sufficient labour and then supervising the work—usually doing most of this personally: in the words of the Mines Inspector in 1896, 'he usually acts as his own mestri or head of the party'.[115] He would supply the tools and materials himself (which, for the most part, were purchased from the company) and then pay the wages. In theory he was under the

[113] Details in the A.R.C.I.M.M. 1899–1946, *passim*.

[114] For the three cases see my 'Recruiting and organising an industrial labour force...', *op. cit.*, pp. 471–82; T. Wright, 'A method of evading management...', *op. cit.*; and A.J. Taylor, 'The sub-contract system in the British coal industry' in L.S. Preswell (ed.), *Studies in the industrial revolution* (London, 1960), pp. 224–30.

[115] A.R.C.I.M.M. 1896, p. 56.

general direction of the mining manager, and of course had to comply with the normal mining laws and obey the non-statutory regulations laid down by individual companies.

The importance of the contractors is not easy to accurately estimate for two main reasons. First, the contractors themselves rarely kept regular muster rolls, wage books or invoice and payment slips—as M.A. Sreenivasan found to his dismay in 1930.[116] Secondly, the company check that was kept on them—particularly during 'rush jobs'—was perfunctory in the early decades, and only marginally better from 1930 onwards. The first hard piece of quantitative evidence we possess is that contained in Sreenivasan's *Report* and the following figures have been extracted from it.

RELATIVE STRENGTHS OF CONTRACTOR AND COMPANY-WISE EMPLOYMENT, 1929

	Contractors		*Company*		*Totals*
	Numbers	*% of Total*	*Numbers*	*% of Total*	*Number*
1. Underground	6 271	56.1	4 845	34.6	11 116
2. Surface	1 993	25.7	5 757	74.3	7 750
3. Underground and surface	8 264	43.8	10 602	56.1	18 866

SOURCE: M.A. Sreenivasan's *Report, op. cit.*, p. 9.

It will be observed that even at this comparatively late stage in the career of the gold fields the contractors were represented in strength. In 1929 they controlled over half of the underground workforce and a quarter of the surface: in all just under 44 per cent of all employees were contractors' men. Qualitative evidence suggests that the further back in time we go the greater the reliance upon contractors for underground labour—but it is unlikely that they ever formed more than two thirds of the complement below surface.[117] Again, after 1929 there is nothing in the data which would lead us to suppose that their position was substantially eroded: indeed the good fortune that the industry enjoyed between 1931 and 1940 probably enhanced their hold. During the Second World War, however, they came under attack from several different quarters—organized labour (such as it was) was very opposed to their presence, and the companies themselves came round

[116] M.A. Sreenivasan, *Report, op. cit.*, p. 9.

[117] An impression gained from a detailed examination of the Inspectorate records and the Directors' and Superintendents' *Reports*.

to the view that they were an anachronism.[118] Certainly the 1946 Labour Investigation Committee found that their numbers and importance had recently dwindled and were definitely on the wane.[119] Out of 19 936 workers only 6358 (or 32 per cent) were employed by the contractors—virtually all of them underground. The pattern of their deployment had also remained the same, i.e. they were concentrated on the arduous task of machine mining (716 mestries, 1371 coolies), hand-jumping (328 mestries, 1876 coolies), tramming (363 mestries, 1320 coolies) and packwalling (25 mestries, 134 coolies). By 1949, although a few were still in existence, Sundara Rajan informs us that not only had many been eliminated, but also that the remaining rump were no longer permitted to collect labour nor even to pay their wages.[120]

If we compare the terms and conditions of contract with company labour there seems little doubt that over the long term, and increasingly after 1930, contract labourers were much the worse off. Although wage rates (most of them on a piece rate basis) tended to be higher for contract work simply by virtue of the harder physical demands it usually involved, there was a far greater incidence of absenteeism, and hence monthly earnings tended to be significantly higher for those on the company ticket. On the basis of Sreenivasan's data[121] it seems that in 1929 the average monthly absentee rate for contract men was 22 per cent (percentage of absentees to total expected), whereas it was only 7.7 per cent for company employees. Indeed for contract work underground, the figure was as high as 36.3 per cent (10.3 per cent for company staff). Given that many of the tasks were piece-rated, this meant that the average monthly income for contract labour was some Rs 7 less than for company workers (Rs 15 as against Rs 22).[122] Writing some fourteen years later on the relative rates of absenteeism and earnings as between these two categories, the Deshpande Committee came to much the same findings.[123] There is also some evidence that the contractor pushed his labour more intensively and for longer hours at a single stretch.[124]

[118] Cf. the Directors' *Reports* for the four companies, the Inspectorate *Reports* over 1940–46, and the evidence submitted to R.D.B.K. Matthan in the *Proceedings of the General and Revenue Department*, G.O. No. D6583–6–1 and C85–40–34-, 17/4/1942, Karnataka State Archives.

[119] Labour Investigation Committee, *Report on labour conditions in the gold mining industry* (Delhi, 1946), *passim*.

[120] V.M. Sundara Rajan, 'Production bonus on Nundydroog Mine', *Bulletin* of the K.G.F. Mining and Metallurgical Society, xiv, 72 (Feb. 1949).

[121] M.A. Sreenivasan, *Report*, *op. cit.*, ch. 3.

[122] *Ibid.*, p. 14.

[123] *Report* of the Labour Investigation Committee, *op. cit.*, section 5.

[124] Thus Sreenivasan writes: 'A contractor, finding in the morning that a number of his

Thus there were more accidents associated with contract labour, witness the warning given as early as 1896 by John Evans, Inspector of Mines, that

> it is, I am afraid, hopeless to expect that a contractor or his subordinates will ever take sufficient precautions against accidents unless under very careful supervision. Every moment spent in any other work than for what he is paid is a direct loss to the contractor. It sometimes happens that under adverse circumstances he may receive scarcely any remuneration for a month's work and in such a case it is only natural that he should sacrifice everything to increase the results.[125]

But of course Evans, with his official's hat on, was missing the commercial point: it was precisely the lack of managerial supervision which made the system profitable for the companies—at least in the short run. They really could not have it both ways: 'economical' mining, *and* elbow distance direction and monitoring. We should also mention that contract staff were not normally entitled to any of the benefits (such as the attendance bonus, rice advances and fuel allowance) enjoyed by some of the company employees—benefits which increased in scope and generosity after the strike troubles of 1930.[126] Further, it was widely recognised that the system lent itself to a great deal of abuse and corrupt practice. Much of this has obviously been swept down abandoned shafts and there is little in the way of surviving evidence, but in the 1940s when the system was on its way out and the fear of coming forward to speak against it had diminished, some idea of its deleterious nature was brought out into the open.[127]

Despite this division into contract and company employees, and notwithstanding the difference this made to the working life of the miners—including their respective earning capacities—on the whole it was a remarkably permanent and stable labour force. In marked contrast to the migrant labour system in vogue in the South African gold mining industry, and the fluctuating and seasonally oscillatory system *in situ* in the Indian coalfields, the Managing Agents and the senior company staff of the Undertaking must have consciously and purposefully decided to create a settled community of miners and their families. Now although the surviving documents do not

workmen have not turned up to work, is not unwilling to find men among those present that will work a "double shift", i.e. two shifts on end.' Apparently this (illegal) arrangement was not always disliked by atleast some of the men since, as Sreenivasan found, 'I have been told that some men rather like to work a "double" and get the whole of the next day off. I have heard of one particular man who stays underground for two whole days and nights, and emerges on the third day, to spend the next three days according to his own conception of an orgy'. M.A. Sreenivasan, *Report*, *op. cit.*, p. 8.

[125] A.R.C.I.M.M. 1896, p. 56.

[126] A.R.C.I.M.M. 1931–46, *passim*.

[127] Evidence submitted to and Report of R.D.B.K. Matthan, *op. cit.*, and *Report* of the Labour Investigation Committee, *op. cit.*, *passim*.

permit us to be absolutely precise about when such a decision was taken, the evidence contained in the handwritten 'Weekly minutes of meetings' kept in the Record Room at Ooregum, unmistakably points to the very last few months of the nineteenth century and the first year and a half of the twentieth as the crucial period. Immediately before then—in 1898—we have, on the good authority of the Chief Inspector of Mines, the statement that

> The mining population is not a regular and settled one, but is partly made up of men who come to earn and save money for a time, and then return home to their families.... The workmen's proper names and addresses are not known to the officials.[128]

As we have already seen, after the 'ladders' accident at Champion Reef in 1897 and directly following on from the devastating plague of 1898–9, it began to dawn on the management that it might actually pay them to spend money and time in improving both the working conditions and the living environment. The time was opportune: this was the period of great prosperity so that the necessary financial means were available; the ore reserve position seemed sound, so that they could afford to take a long view, and, icing on the cake, the Companies had just completed a successful round of negotiations with the Mysore raj on the renewal of their property rights (secured for the next thirty years) and their royalty payment obligations (a modest 5 per cent on sales plus 2.5 per cent on dividends).[129] From 1900, then, and starting with the construction of the new town—which, conveniently, the Undertaking's own engineering and construction workers built—we can chart the improvements to the quality of life. Recognising the range and scope of these does not mean that conditions were idyllic or even good relative either to need or to what they might otherwise have been under a differnt economic system; nor should it imply that there was a continuous and steady enhancement of conditions and amenities over time. References to Kolar as being some sort of 'model mining camp' seem to me very wide of the mark;[130] and although there is not much (objective)

[128] A.R.C.I.M.M. 1899, p. 21.

[129] Though their original leases ran on until 22 March 1910, as early as June 1901, the Undertaking engaged the services of the famous English barrister, the Hon. M.F. Napier, to negotiate their renewal. Napier's hefty fee (paid for by the five individual companies) was obviously a good investment since even the Chief Inspector of Mines, commenting on the terms, wrote that, 'Considering the past prosperity of the mines and the magnitude of the concession which has now been acquired, the companies ought to, and I believe do, consider themselves to have been favourably treated', A.R.C.I.M.M. 1901, p. 11. In my view this was one of the classic understatements of that year!

[130] This phrase-redolent of the kind of comments made (to my mind much more fairly) about Jamshedpur comes from the 'Special number' of the London *Times* on 'Gold', 20 June 1933, p. 109.

doubt that K.G.F. City was a better place in which to work and live than many other mining towns in India, and certainly a much better place than the infamous compounds in central and southern Africa,[131] it would be a grave error of judgment to suggest that work and life for the vast majority was anything other than a grim struggle. Since within the confines of this paper we cannot properly discuss the subject of working and living conditions in any depth, let me present and then briefly comment upon two telling sets of statistics. First, using the annual returns submitted to the Mysore Mines Inspectorate over 1899–1946, I have compiled a time series of nominal and real monthly wages for European and indigenous employees (table 8). Putting aside the niceties of percentage point accuracy, the meaning of an 'average' worker, the methodology of the index derivation, the exchange rate adjustment, and the choice of the price deflator, I would just make the following general observations. First, there was a substantial and sustained wage disparity between indigenous and European labour which, at its apex in 1917, stood at the ratio of 22.1:1 (column 4). In fact the wage gap on Kolar was always greater than that of the allegedly extreme case of racial discrimination—South Africa. Secondly, between 1899 and 1916, the 'golden years' for Kolar, the nominal wage index remained remarkably constant—and indeed partly because of the inflation during World War I, real wages were cut by 40 per cent (between 1913 and 1918). Again, over the prosperous years of 1931–35, money wages actually fell and (at a time of falling commodity prices) real wages only rose very marginally. Finally, it is difficult to detect any secular improvements in real wages for the Indian staff: and even if 1945 is regarded as a special and unrepresentative year, the average Indian employee's real pay packet bought 31.2 per cent less than it did in 1900.[132] Furthermore, we know from the two budget studies done in 1930 and 1944 that there was a very high degree of indebtedness amongst the indigenous workers.[133] Of Sreenivasan's representative sample of fifty families, no less than forty-nine were in the miserable situation where monthly expenditure exceeded combined monthly income; and when broken down further, the average outlay on food per adult male per day was a mere 2 annas 7 pice, that is, rather less than the cost of feeding the convicts in Bangalore Central Jail.[134] Things do not seem to have greatly

[131] Cf. C Van Onselen, *Chibaro; African mine labour in Southern Rhodesia 1900–1933* (London, 1976), and C. Perrings, *Black mineworkers in Central Africa: industrial strategies and the evolution of an African proletariat in the Copperbelt 1911–41* (London, 1977).

[132] The average European real wage was also 11.6% less in 1945 than in 1900, but the considerable difference in absolute levels must have eased the strain.

[133] Cf. M. A. Sreenivasan, *Report*, op.cit., ch. 5, and the *Report* of the Labour Investigation Committee, *op.cit.*, ch. 10.

[134] M. A. Sreenivasan, ibid., pp. 18f, 21.

improved over the following decade and a half, and the Labour Investigation Committee found that 'more than fifty per cent of the total number of workers employed in the mines were in serious debt'.[135] Finally, on admittedly very shaky and uncertain ground, we should also note that the comparative history of Kolar workers was not wildly out of line with wages in the modern sector elsewhere in India.[136] If, in an absolute sense, they were higher than those in the coal mines of Bengal and Bihar and, during the latter part of the inter-war period, the Calcutta jute mills, they were below that for other groups of workers, including the Bombay and Ahmedabad cotton operatives.[137] We can therefore conclude that the K.G.F. Undertaking paid as much—but no more—as they needed in order to recruit and permanently hold on to their Indian labour. And this wage was not so much a function of the real selling price of gold as it was of conditions on the land. As good capitalist employers they were quick to seize on the fact that because alternatives open to labour were so limited the wage could be set close to—if not below—subsistence. They encountered little organized resistance from the rank and file of the miners; in fact no real trade union emerged before the Second World War, and the few strikes that occurred before 1942 were easily quashed.[138]

The second set of statistics concerns the accident rates—a reasonably sensitive indicator of working conditions, especially those underground.

[135] *Report* of the Labour Investigationl Committee, p. 19.

[136] The problems of deriving a satisfactory index of money and real wages for the modern sector legion: thus Professor Morris writes that 'more heroic assumption have been introduced than the frail data can bear', and that some of the estimates 'cannot be taken too seriously', in his 'The growth of large scale industry', *Cambridge economic history of India*, vol. 2 op.cit., p. 646. I suspect that virtually leveryone who has worked in this area would concur with this pessimistic view; cf. A Heston's chapter 'National income' in the same *Cambridge economic history*, vol. 2, esp. pp. 401–9; K. Mukerji, 'Levels of living of industrial workers' in V. B. Singh (ed.), *Economic history of India 1857–1956* (Bombay, 1975), pp. 638–59; D. Kumar & J. Krishnamurthy, 'The evolution of labour markets in India', op.cit., ch. VIII; and S. Sivasubramonian, 'Income from the secondary sector in India, 1900–47', *Ind. Econ. & Social History Rev.* xiv, 4 (1977).

[137] Needles to say, the detailed movement and long-run trends of real and money wages in the different industries exhibited some characteristics unique to those industries. Por comoarative purposes I have used A. K. Bagchi's *Private investment in India 1900–39* (Cambridegd, 1972), ch. 5; and the four articles by K. Mukerji, all in *Artha Vijnana* and covering real wages 1900–1951 in the Bombay cotton industry (no. 1, 1 (1959)), jute (2, 1 (1960)), the Ahmedabad cotton industries (3, 2 (1961)) and the textile mills in western India (4, 2 (1962)).

[138] Despite the one-sidedness of industrial relations over the period 1881–1946 it would be wrong to assume that labour was totally supine. For a short discussion of this see the *Report* R. D. B. Matthan, op.cit., esp. parts 13 and 14 and the *Report* of the Labour Investigation Committee, op.cit., ch. 8.

Table 9 shows the annual number of fatalities and of serious accidents over the period 1891–1946. Without going into details, we can see that the total human cost of gold mining operations on Kolar amounted to no less than 3398 lives—an average of 61.8 deaths each year. Entirely excluded from these casualties were the miners who died as a result of contracting silicosis—which the Undertaking adamantly refused to recognise as constituting an industrial disease until they were forced into it by government—but not until as late as July 1936.[139] Even after that date, however, the sums the company distributed annually for working men's compensation were derisory. Gold mining was undoubtedly a highly dangerous activity, and despite a great deal of effort to reduce the risk of disaster, the great depths, the extraordinary high underground temperatures, and the constant danger of rock bursts, were always threatening. Further, if we assume away geophysical differences and seek to draw a parallel with the Witwatersrand experience, the death rate per £100 000 of gold output was consistently far higher in Kolar throughout this period—implying a lower rate of labour productivity; and after 1916, the death rate per 1000 persons employed was also generally in excess of that in South Africa.

It is therefore clear that the management did not secure its settled labour force by paying generous wages and/or providing a reasonably safe working environment. How then did they do it? The management certainly took advantage of the plight of the Tamil immigrants, but that is by no means the complete story. They also acted positively and sought to buy the commitment of their labour by investing in a wide range of social infrastructure—including low-rental housing, day and night schools, canteens, hospitals, parks, pit-head baths, shops, clubs, *pucca* roads, perennial pure water supply, home electricity, regular refuse collection, the employment of teams of sweepers to keep the city clean, child welfare programmes, maternity provision, rehabilitation units, a dairy, the occasional issue of subsidized rice rations, and the organization and active encouragement given to cultural and sporting events. They were also keen on inculcating a spirit of loyalty to a mine, to a company and to the Undertaking as a whole, and this was largely done through the medium of particularly favoured, team-leading individuals. In addition to the carrot, the management also kept a useful stick in reserve. Not only did they enjoy the support of the Mysore raj in terms of police and judiciary services, but they financed a not-so-small 'protection force' of their own. In 1901 this private army consisted of 232 constables, 16 *daffedars*, 20 *jamadars*, 4 chief constables, 5 inspectors and 22 detectives—all under the command of a British Superintendent of

[139] Government Order, No. p. 846—Legis 7–36–1, 31 July 1936, in the *Proceedings* of the Government of Mysore, Committee Reports 'G'. Karnataka State Archives.

Police; they were also armed with 74 sniper carbine rifles.[140] Needless to say, the Managing Agents were quite opposed to any labour association and took steps to infiltrate any society which they felt had the potential for turning into an organized body of workers. Of course, later on in the period they had to bow to the inevitable, but they successfully prevented the emergence of anything remotely resembling a real trade union until the 1940s. On the only pre-war occasion when serious trouble did blow up—i.e. between 1 and 28 April 1930—the management dealt with the problem in a ruthless way: the police and army were called out to dispel a crowd, 44 persons were shot and 2 died.[141] But once it was all over and the resistance had crumbled, the management were far-sighted enough to speed up and extend their welfare activities considerably.

The net result of this mixed strategy was well summed up by the independent journal *The Mining World*. In a special feature on Indian gold mining in 1937, the editorial ran as follows: 'Labour in the Kolar goldfield, which is practically all native, is more than adequate, and as satisfactory as one could wish. It is cheap, reliable, adaptable, and pleasant to work with . . . and the relationship between employers and employees is excellent'.[142] This is borne out by the Deshpande Committee's finding (in 1944) that a large proportion of the workers had a long record of service:

LENGTH OF SERVICE IN 1944

Years of work	*% of the labour force*
0–1	12
1–5	17
5–10	30.5
10 or longer	40.5

SOURCE: *Report of the Labour Investigation Committee, op. cit.*, p. 7.

The motive for wanting a stable and settled workforce was clear: the demand for gold was highly regular; to be cost effective the capital equipment, plant and machinery installed in the mines needed to be worked consistently; the shafts, stopes and winzes needed constant daily attention and proper routine maintenance to remain open; and water had to be regularly pumped out, just

[140] Abstracts of the K.G.F. Administration Reports were usually appended to the A.R.C.I.M.M.

[141] The best surviving account of the troubles of April 1930 appears in the A.R.C.I.M.M. 1929–30, pp. 19–21.

[142] *The Mining World and Engineering Record*, 26 June 1937.

as air had to be regularly pumped in and filtered. Before the age of new technology those mining industries, or sub-branches of the industries, which needed a smooth and continuous flow of input provision and output despatch, necessarily had to ensure that they possessed a reliable corps of labour on hand; and the Kolar Gold Field Undertaking was one such example.[143] Far from being an act of benevolence or even paternalism, the social investments in K.G.F. City and environs had a compelling economic logic.

The Labour Process

The most noteworthy feature of the 'labour process' on the Kolar Gold Field before nationalization was its highly planned nature. As we have seen, there was a definite role assigned to the 'disorganized' contractors so that they too slotted into the general scheme of things. Within the guiding principle of up-to-date hard-rock mining technology, a logical structure of work organization and personnel management quickly evolved. Let us proceed to sketch out its major characteristics.

To begin with, from the early 1890s—if not earlier—the managers decided that for underground operations they would work round the clock. In order to make this tolerable they formally divided the labour time into three shifts of eight hours each. As can be seen from the table below, up until 1898 it was possible for the men to work seven days a week, and in fact a majority of miners, including those under the contractors, put in an average of 56 hours a week. After 1899 and lasting right until 1946, the average number of hours worked ranged from the high to the mid-40s, so that most of the underground company staff had at least one day off in seven. The trend was also down, and by the end of the period the average company employee underground was working 42–43 hours. In fact the 'effective' number of hours worked was always rather less than these figures would suggest: even in the 1890s the Inspectorate claimed that it was not feasible for a man to perform continuous hard labour for more than 4–6 hours a day—the balance of the time was necessarily taken up by recuperation, rest, and the journey to and from the working stopes.[144] With regard to the distribution of men between the three shifts, it seems that the managers tried to equalize the work, but the first shift was always the one to carry out blasting.

[143] Another, in the Indian context, was the captive collieries of integrated firms such as the mines owned by TISCO and the various railway companies. For a discussion of the former case and a brief consideration of the latter, see my 'Vertical integration and the Indian steel industry: the colliery establishment of the Tata Ironand Steel Company,1907–56' *Modern Asian Studies*, 1 (1977).

[144] A.R.C.I.M.M. 1899.

Average Hours of Labour per Week per Company Employee 1894–1946

	Underground	*Surface*	*Mills cyanide dept, and engineering dept*
1894–98	56 (7×8)	63 (7×9)	n.a
1899–1922/3	48 (6×8)	54 (6×9)	54
1926	48	54	
1927	48	54	
1928	48	54	
1929	48	54	
1930	47	54	
1931	46	55	
1932	46	54	
1933	47	56	
1934	46	56	
1935	46	55	
1936	47	56	
1937	47	56	
1938	47	55	
1939	47	56	
1940	46	56	
1941	47	56	
1942	45	55	
1943	44	54	
1944	43	53	
1945	42	53	
1946	43	52	52
	Shifts		
	7 am to 3 pm: 1st	7 am to 5 pm	7 am to 3 pm
	3 pm to 11 pm: 2nd		3 pm to 11 pm
	11 pm to 7 am: 3rd		11 pm to 7 am

Source: *Reports of the Chief Inspector of Mines for Mysore*, 1896–1946, *passim*.

The surface workers were always required to labour longer than their counterparts underground. They only worked one daylight shift of nine hours duration—with one hour, at noon, formally given over to tiffin. After 1899 they too worked for six rather than the full seven days. Those workers employed in the crushing mills, the reprocessing plant (under the Cyanide Department after 1902) and the Engineering Department worked six days at nine hours per day. However, they—especially the last-named department had to synchronize their work with that of those labouring underground, so they adhered to the three shifts per day system.

We next turn to the content of this labour time, and how it was divided up between the various departments. Let us begin with mining itself. In the

1880s and early 1890s and closely following the tracks of the 'Ancients', shafts were sunk through the quartz so as to minimize the excavation of barren rock—and this almost certainly accounts for the high d.w.t. returns given above. But with the continued development of the industry, the technique had to be phased out simply because it became increasingly difficult to hoist ever-larger tonnages through the twisted and often tortuous passages which directly followed the line of the reefs. So from the mid-1890s it became standard practice to sink straight shafts which were either vertical or followed particular inclines. As mining penetrated to even lower depths it eventually became necessary to sink secondary, and ultimately tertiary, shafts to link up with the primary ones. Once the shafts were ready, work proceeded on gaining access to the actual lodes and this was done through a whole network of winzes leading on to the working areas or stopes. By 1946 well over 500 miles of such tunnels had been dug out—a veritable honeycomb of intricate passageways. The hard rock was drilled (by machinemen and hand-jumper men) and then explosives were set to blast away the stratas of rock and quartz. Timber-men and packwallers then moved in to support the roof and sides. The broken ore was loaded into trucks and carried along the tramways (by stuff-coolies and trammers) to the shaft bottom and thence it was winched up to the surface. The Engineering Department was responsible for the installation and working of all the plant and machinery, and they also handled the water pumping and air ventilation tasks.

Once the ore reached the surface it was conveyed to the crushing and roller mill, and then was pulverized into manageable lumps. It was then removed to the strip mills and the reprocessing plants where, ultimately, the residual gold was obtained. Also on the surface was the General Office of the Company, which received and then despatched the bullion (by train to Madras and later Bombay), paid the salaries of the company staff, and kept all the stores. The Assay Office, the Survey Office, and the Safety First Office were all located nearby and, of course, the other Departments already mentioned maintained their own office premises above ground.

The resulting internal division of labour within the undertaking can be seen from the categories of workers presented in table 10. In 1945 there were no less than thirty-eight separately listed categories of workers, including the contractors' labour, and for each of them there was an appropriate grade of pay. This is a sophisticated hierarchy—notwithstanding the unmistakable racial overtones—and it went back to the earliest days of operation. There was little horizontal or vertical mobility between the jobs, despite the fact that the management never developed a formal apprenticeship system. The distinction between piece- and time-rated terms was clear, and the management formally differentiated between 'skilled' and 'unskilled' labour. In fact, after 1930 they sent on to the Mines Inspectorate a breakdown between these two groups, and as the following table shows, the ratio between the two stayed more or less the same over this limited time period.

AVERAGE WEEKLY EARNINGS OF SKILLED AND UNSKILLED LABOUR, 1930–46

	'Skilled' labour Rs-As-P	*'Unskilled' labour Rs-As-P*
1930	7–15–6	3–12–2
1931	8–0–6	3–9–4
1932	7–14–0	3–9–7
1933	8–4–8	3–13–0
1934	7–13–10	8–11–3
1935	8–1–1	3–11–3
1936	7–15–9	3–12–11
1937	8–2–2	3–12–0
1938	8–1–3	3–13–8
1939	7–15–9	3–14–3
1940	8–2–6	4–0–9
1941	8–6–9	4–6–7
1942	9–10–6	5–6–4
1943	10–4–9	6–0–7
1944	10–7–9	5–13–5
1945	11–6–0	6–3–3
1946	13–8–4	7–14–7

SOURCE: Derived from the Inspector of Mines for Mysore, 1930–46, *passim*.

At a rather less formal level, the managers seem to have evolved a definite idea about the relative merits and work biases of each different community that made up their indigenous workforce. Thus the Superintendent of the Ooregum Mine (one R. Bullen) supplied a detailed note on the 'mental and physical' attributes of his workers to F.W. Hatch in 1901, which today makes rather amusing reading. For Bullen, the Moplahs were 'far better than any of the other coolies in sinking shafts and stopes'; the Canarese were 'excellent underground men'; the Tamils were 'superior machinemen'; the Wudders were 'only good for shallow earth excavation'; and the Telegus could 'turn their hand to any unskilled work underground'.[145] Throughout the period this feeling of a community division of labour was echoed many

[145] F. W. Hatch, *Memoir*, op.cit., p. 61.

times over.[146] Even M.A. Sreenivasan caught the habit—though his branding was rather more precise than most. [147] Whatever be the causes of this 'specialization', it does seem to have had a real meaning for the contemporaries.

3. CONCLUDING COMMENTS

This paper may be seen as a first step towards a modern reconstruction of the history of the Kolar gold mining labour force in the period from the opening up of the area down to the first nationalization. In view of what was said in section 1 about the undevelopment of Third World labour studies, it will have come as no surprise that this working community has received no critical secondary attention: quite simply, and like many of the other mining and industrial settlements in the subcontinent, it has been ignored. Moreover, because the industry itself has been in sharp and terminal decline since the 1950s, the thousands of men and women who were involved in this most strenuous and dangerous of work situations are now virtually forgotten; today they seem little more than ghosts haunting the hundreds of miles of underground shafts, galleries and worked-out stopes. Yet, as I have tried to show, not only do they have a fascinating past, but they have played an important role in both the growth of India's mining sector, and also in the wider economic development of the 'model' princely State of Mysore. Though rather small beer in world terms, in southern India the mines were of considerable significance and they generated many indirect—as well as obviously direct—influences upon the regional economy and society. Further, since the mines were owned and operated by private British capital, their hugely successful exploitation yielded a handsome and regular dividend for the fortunate shareholders—who included magnates like Lord Ribblesdale, as well as the more modest investors numbering, at any one time, several hundred individual investors.[148]

Aside from the existence of the auriferous lodes themselves, the key factor in the opening up and subsequent working of the mines was undoubtedly the availability of a cheap and pliant labour force. It has been the burden of this paper to show the manner in which labour was recruited, from where it originated, its major features and characteristics, and the ways in which it was organized, appeased and controlled—in short, how it was appropriated by foreign capital within the broad context of colonial rule in

[146] For example, it is frequently to be found in the Reports of the Directors and Superintendents and, of course, in the various A.R.C.I.M.M.

[147] M. A. Sreenivasan, *Report*, op.cit., pp. 4ff.

[148] The details of sahreholding in the companies are to be found in the BT31, Company Files Series in Companies House, City Road, London (for Champion Reef), and in the Public Record Office, Kew (for the others).

general, and that of princely—or indirect—rule in particular. The major conclusion we have reached is that immediately after the turn of the century the indigenous part of the labour force—the overwhelming majority—took on many of the characteristics of a permanently settled industrial proletariat. This is not to suggest that it resembled in every detail the 'classical' European (especially British), North American or even Japanese mining proletariats. As we have seen, although the Kolar miners shared certain common features with them, they also displayed a number of distinctive differences. We have also tried to point out some of the more important ways in which the Kolar proletariat compares and contrasts with the gold miners of the Transvaal and the coal miners of eastern India. In fact the greatest difference with the later two cases was the question of stability: whereas they were both essentially migrant systems (although it must be said that the nature of the migrancy differed), on the K.G.F. the workers were settled. The chief explanation for this concerns the strategy of the management rather than anything attributable to the action of the labourers. That is, since the companies required an uninterrupted and smooth production run in order to function with maximum profitability, the managing agents quite deliberately decided over 1899–1901 to stabilize its workforce. By a curious but effective mixture of non-wage incentives and, on the one hand, a tough measure of labour control allied with a system of contracting out on the other, they succeeded in creating a reliable and, for the most part, committed, body of workers.

As far as the actual labour process itself is concerned, we are handicapped by an absence of data stemming from within the rank and file of the workers themselves. We lack the bottom-up sort of perspective which is necessary properly to grasp the process through the eyes of the great majority who experienced it at first hand. Instead we have had to rely upon a variety of sources written by managers, inspectors and other official and semi-official observers. Thus we too have encountered the problem of trying to make sense of a phenomenon at second remove; and indeed the vantage point itself is somewhat suspect on account of its high elevation and tinted telescopic lens. But given the lack of any real alternative, we have had little choice. In any event, since a good many of the objective conditions governing the form and quality of the working and living environment inhabited by the Kolar miners were determined by the companies—and not the workers—the procedure we have adopted has some logical as well as practical justification. After all, we should not lose sight of the fact that the core of the K.G.F. labour force came from the depressed, downtrodden, illiterate and poverty-stricken castes of what is now Tamil Nadu—a collection of people who were hardly in a position strongly to influence the fundamental material and social shape of the world of Kolar Gold Field City.

TABLE 1

SELECTED INDICES OF OUTPUT (VOLUMES AND VALUES), PROFITABILITY AND DECLARED DIVIDENDS, 1891–1945 (1900 = 100)

5 year average	*Output volume (ounces)*	*Output value (£)*	*Dividend*	*Profitability (Mysore G.M. Co. only)*
1891–95	37.98	39.18	36.84	31.84
1896–1900	82.01	83.55	85.25	91.5
1901–05	113.33	115.68	110.86	102.12
1906–10	107.17	111.45	82.58	114.6
1911–15	110.31	114.71	88.32	120.54
1916–20	100.28	108.39	52.00	65.35
1921–25	79.30	96.53	36.17	50.84
1926–30	72.00	83.09	32.36	42.1
1931–35	64.52	107.20	50.13	46.74
1936–40	62.34	126.48	56.70	62.66
1941–45	45.34	153.11	23.04	36.96

NOTE: Profitability refers to the gross profit in the revenue account minus the royalty payment. A profit rate estimate (net profits expressed as a percentage of market valuation) has also been derived and can be consulted in 'Golden imperialism . . .', *op. cit.*,

SOURCES: Annual Directors' Reports of the various companies, and *Annual reports of the Chief Inspector of Mines for Mysore*, 1899–1946, *passim.*

TABLE 2

COST BREAKDOWN FOR TWO SAMPLE YEARS

	1925		1938	
	£	%	£	%
A. *Input Costs*				
Coal	41 721	4.05	9 893	0.82
Firewood	1 478	0.14	978	0.08
Cauvery and mines power	181 565	17.64	211 720	17.49
Timber	50 790	4.93	14 762	3.70
Granite	—	—	16 676	1.38
Cement	14 660	1.42	30 638	2.53
Gelatine	25 245	2.45	26 360	2.18
Dynamite	15 184	1.47	29 826	2.46
Detonators	3 112	0.30	4 115	0.34
Fuses (ord)	0	—	25 620	2.12
Electrical fuses	49 311	4.79	69 921	5.78
Steel castings	3 758	0.36	3 692	0.31
Candles	11 700	1.14	314	0.03
Calcium carbide	—	—	14 358	1.19
Mercury	1 008	0.10	156	0.01
Granite	35 485	3.45	18 294	1.51
Zinc	2 799	0.27	1 930	0.16
Steel	4 507	0.44	4 385	0.36
Steel bars	4 921	0.48	18 795	1.55
Iron castings	9 877	0.96	6 215	0.51
Shoes & dies	3 919	0.38	3 081	0.25
Wages	568 459	55.22	668 517	55.24
B. *Total Costs*				
Total mining costs	644 685		987 222	
Total milling costs	150 401		148 806	
Total re-treatment costs	133 152		18 994	
Total	928 238		1 155 022	
C. *Wages as a per cent of total cost*		56.4		57.9

SOURCES: *Annual report of the Chief Inspector of Mines for Mysore*, 1925 and 1936, *passim*.

TABLE 3

TOTAL EMPLOYMENT ON THE KOLAR GOLD FIELDS, 1891–1951

1 *Year*	2 *Average daily numbers at work*	3 *Index of (2)*	1 *Year*	2 *Average daily numbers at work*	3 *Index of (2)*	4 *Numbers in service*
1884–90	N.A.	N.A.	1922	23 297	94.75	
1891	9 038	36.76	1923	20 604	83.80	
1892	11 773	47.88	1924	19 836	80.68	
1893	13 930	56.66	1925	19 347	78.69	
1894	12 237	50.17	1926	18 742	76.23	
1895	12 100	49.21	1927	18 918	76.94	
1896	16 709	67.95	1928	18 829	76.58	
1897	22 395	91.08	1929	18 454	75.06	
1898	21 597	89.30	1930	17 312	70.41	
1899	21 093	85.79	1931	18 388	74.79	
1900	24 587	100.00	1932	18 816	76.53	
1901	25 060	101.92	1933	20 263	82.41	
1902	26 268	106.84	1934	21 514	87.50	
1903	27 458	111.68	1935	22 271	90.58	
1904	29 494	119.96	1936	22 973	93.44	
1905	30 328	123.35	1937	24 239	98.58	
1906	32 261	131.21	1938	24 031	97.74	
1907	34 641	140.89	1939	24 380	99.16	28 315
1908	28 801	117.14	1940	25 467	103.58	29 035
1909	28 702	116.74	1941	24 836	101.01	28 635
1910	26 888	109.36	1942	21 436	87.18	27 187
1911	25 942	105.51	1943	20 717	84.26	24 815
1912	26 086	106.10	1944	17 498	71.17	22 478
1913	25 237	102.64	1945	16 412	66.75	21 194
1914	25 904	105.36	1946	17 948	72.99	22 075
1915	27 008	109.85	1947			19 488
1916	25 270	102.78	1948			20 430
1917	24 531	99.77	1949			23 841
1918	24 517	99.72	1950			23 663
1919	24 409	99.28	1951	19 031		22 849
1920	23 925	97.31	1959			17 501
1921	23 344	94.94	1977			11 658

SOURCES: Directors' *Reports* of the various companies, the *Annual reports of the Chief Inspector of Mines for Mysore*, 1895–1946, *passim*, various numbers of the *Statistical abstracts of Mysore State* and selected *Records* of the Geological Survey of India.

TABLE 4

EMPLOYMENT BY MINING COMPANY 1895–1946

	Mysore		*Champion Reef*		*Nundydroog*		*Ooregum*		*Others**		*Total of columns 1–4*	
	1		*2*		*3*		*4*		*5*		*6*	
Year	*No.*	*(%)*	*No.*	*(%)*	*No.*	*(%)*	*No.*	*(%)*	*No.*	*(%)*	*No.*	*(%)*
1895	2 877	30.1	2 271	23.7	1 958	20.5	2 466	25.8	0	0.0	9 572	100.0
1896	3 656	27.6	4 650	35.1	2 205	16.6	2 739	20.7	0	0.0	13 250	100.0
1898	4 397	27.1	6 299	38.8	2 407	14.8	3 113	19.2	0	0.0	16 216	100.0
1899	4 299	20.4	6 197	29.4	2 208	10.5	3 433	16.3	4 956	23.5	21 093	76.5
1900	5 683	23.1	6 764	27.5	2 796	11.4	3 449	14.0	5 895	24.0	24 587	76.0
1901	5 682	22.7	7 288	29.1	2 873	11.5	3 882	15.5	5 335	21.3	25 060	78.7
1902	7 295	27.8	6 507	24.8	2 954	11.2	4 202	16.0	5 310	20.2	26 268	79.8
1903	7 701	28.0	6 913	25.2	3 483	12.7	4 672	17.0	4 689	17.1	27 458	82.9
1904	8 220	27.9	7 590	25.7	4 306	14.6	4 360	14.8	5 018	17.0	29 494	83.0
1905	8 156	26.9	8 382	27.6	4 213	13.9	4 671	15.4	4 906	16.2	30 328	83.8
1906	8 194	25.4	8 716	27.0	4 122	12.8	4 491	13.9	6 738	20.9	32 261	79.1
1907	8 334	24.1	8 696	25.1	3 918	11.3	4 589	13.2	9 104	26.3	34 641	73.7
1908	9 047	31.4	7 442	25.8	4 426	15.4	4 624	16.1	3 262	11.3	28 801	88.7
1909	9 707	33.8	7 023	24.5	4 304	15.0	4 840	16.9	2 828	9.9	28 702	90.1
1910	8 707	32.4	6 913	25.7	4 334	16.1	4 930	18.3	2 004	7.5	26 888	92.5
1911	8 548	33.0	6 492	25.0	4 294	16.6	4 884	18.8	1 724	6.6	25 942	93.4
1912	8 258	31.7	6 922	26.5	4 453	17.1	4 881	18.7	1 572	6.0	26 086	94.0
1913	8 591	33.9	6 696	26.4	3 908	15.4	4 504	17.8	1 628	6.4	25 327	93.6
1914	9 270	35.8	6 551	25.3	4 220	16.3	4 324	16.7	1 539	5.9	25 904	94.1
1915	9 790	36.2	6 487	24.0	4 256	15.8	4 531	16.8	1 944	7.2	27 008	92.8
1916	8 596	34.0	5 871	23.2	4 239	16.8	4 690	18.6	1 874	7.4	25 270	92.6
1917	9 063	37.0	5 117	20.9	4 207	17.1	4 303	17.5	1 841	7.5	24 531	92.5
1918	9 160	37.4	4 813	19.6	4 284	17.5	4 292	17.5	1 968	8.0	24 517	92.0
1919	9 238	37.9	4 746	19.4	4 176	17.1	4 374	17.9	1 875	7.7	24 409	92.3
1920	8 405	35.1	5 190	21.7	3 963	16.6	4 514	18.9	1 853	7.7	23 925	92.3
1921	7 948	34.1	4 925	21.1	3 561	15.3	4 807	20.6	2 103	9.0	23 344	91.0
1922	7 382	31.7	4 919	21.1	3 930	16.9	4 928	21.2	2 138	9.2	23 297	90.8
1923	6 451	31.3	4 217	20.5	3 521	17.1	4 325	21.0	2 090	10.1	20 604	89.9
1924	5 948	30.0	3 927	19.8	3 538	17.8	4 406	22.2	2 017	10.2	19 836	89.81
1925	6 143	31.8	3 835	19.8	3 299	17.1	4 161	21.5	1 909	9.9	19 347	90.1
1926	6 033	32.2	3 874	20.7	3 381	18.0	3 740	20.0	1 714	9.1	18 742	90.9
1927	6 025	31.9	3 729	19.7	3 381	17.9	4 106	21.7	1 677	8.9	18 918	91.1
1928	6 119	32.5	3 622	19.2	3 300	17.5	4 127	21.9	1 661	8.8	18 829	91.2
1929	5 759	31.2	3 610	19.6	3 258	17.7	4 209	22.8	1 618	8.8	18 454	91.2
1930	5 285	30.5	3 557	20.5	3 248	18.8	3 743	21.6	1 479	8.5	17 312	91.5
1931	5 729	31.2	3 564	19.4	3 710	20.2	3 783	20.6	1 602	8.7	18 388	91.3
1932	6 566	34.9	3 810	20.2	4 488	23.9	3 852	20.5	100	0.5	18 816	99.5
1933	6 599	32.6	4 206	20.8	5 357	26.4	4 101	20.2	0	0.0	20 263	100.0

TABLE 4 (*Contd.*)

	Mysore		*Champion Reef*		*Nundydroog*		*Ooregum*		*Others**		*Total of columns 1–4*	
	1		*2*		*3*		*4*		*5*		*6*	
Year	*No.*	*(%)*	*No.*	*(%)*	*No.*	*(%)*	*No.*	*(%)*	*No.*	*(%)*	*No.*	*(%)*
1934	6 970	32.4	4 471	20.8	5 806	27.0	4 267	19.8	0	0.0	21 514	100.0
1935	7 010	31.5	4 624	20.8	6 176	27.7	4 461	20.0	0	0.0	22 271	100.0
1936	7 163	31.2	4 555	19.8	6 628	28.9	4 627	20.1	0	0.0	22 973	100.0
1937	7 199	29.7	5 162	21.3	6 838	28.2	4 682	19.3	358	1.5	24 239	98.5
1938	6 983	29.1	5 139	21.4	7 032	29.3	4 877	20.3	0	0.0	24 031	100.0
1939	7 178	29.4	5 345	21.9	7 108	29.2	4 740	19.4	9	0.0	24 380	100.0
1940	7 385	29.0	5 678	22.3	7 557	29.7	4 847	19.0	0	0.0	25 467	100.0
1941	7 140	28.7	5 040	20.3	7 142	28.8	4 704	18.9	810	3.3	24 836	96.7
1942	6 760	31.5	4 519	21.1	6 527	30.4	2 822	13.2	808	3.8	21 436	96.2
1943	6 517	31.5	4 250	20.5	5 865	28.3	3 289	15.9	796	3.8	20 717	96.2
1944	5 407	30.9	3 622	20.7	4 567	26.1	3 095	17.7	807	4.6	17 498	95.4
1945	5 249	32.0	3 685	22.5	4 416	26.9	3 101	18.9	0	0.0	16 412	100.0
1946	6 382	35.6	3 548	19.8	5 105	28.4	2 913	16.2	0	0.0	17 948	100.0
Average	7 063	30.9	5 333	23.3	4 338	19.0	4 166	18.2	1 990	8.7	20 900	91.3

NOTE: *Mainly consists of Balagat G.M. Co.

SOURCES: Directors, *Reports*, and the *Annual reports of the Chief Inspector of Mines for Mysore*, 1895–1946, *passim*.

TABLE 5

LABOUR PRODUCTIVITY, 1891–1946

Date	*Ounces per person*	*Pound per person*	*Tonnage of ore crushed per person*
1891	14.43	55.80	N.A.
1892	11.08	52.85	N.A
1893	14.87	56.34	N.A.
1894	17.16	65.03	N.A.
1895	21.19	80.46	N.A.
1896	19.24	73.54	N.A.
1897	17.78	66.40	N.A.
1898	19.12	72.97	15.63
1899	21.16	79.57	16.10
1900	20.71	76.43	16.34
1901	21.15	76.74	17.97
1902	20.31	74.79	21.35
1903	21.77	83.18	24.98
1904	20.60	78.77	24.78
1905	20.34	78.26	25.76
1906	17.52	67.19	23.07
1907	15.45	59.15	21.18
1908	18.60	71.38	25.03
1909	19.00	72.89	25.76
1910	20.37	78.33	29.12
1911	21.39	82.10	30.65
1912	21.51	82.74	30.99
1913	22.16	85.20	32.07
1914	21.71	83.62	31.15
1915	21.15	80.46	29.55
1916	21.94	84.02	30.41
1917	21.87	84.22	30.01
1918	20.57	78.94	29.12
1919	19.88	76.46	28.78
1920	19.76	91.67	28.13
1921	18.10	86.20	27.48
1922	18.44	76.74	28.89
1923	18.49	85.05	31.55
1924	19.79	92.45	34.60
1925	20.34	87.01	35.82
1926	20.43	87.05	34.20
1927	20.18	86.04	33.75
1928	19.96	85.20	34.68
1929	19.71	83.91	35.75
1930	19.01	80.55	34.21
1931	17.97	84.81	31.65

TABLE 5 (*Contd.*)

Date	*Ounces per person*	*Pound per person*	*Tonnage of ore crushed per person*
1932	17.52	102.23	33.00
1933	16.57	102.88	32.56
1934	14.93	102.71	31.56
1935	14.64	103.04	31.84
1936	14.45	100.73	31.96
1937	13.63	95.12	31.66
1938	13.04	96.87	32.72
1939	12.90	99.88	32.89
1940	11.36	95.92	29.90
1941	11.51	100.30	32.38
1942	12.14	132.27	29.83
1943	12.17	184.57	31.46
1944	10.73	152.64	26.85
1945	10.26	156.22	27.45
1946	5.97	106.92	18.67

TABLE 6

CATEGORIES OF UNDERGROUND AND SURFACE LABOUR, 1899–1946 (% OF TOTAL)

	Below ground				Surface						
1899	1.56	0.42	54.93	56.91	0.77	1.29	34.11	6.93		43.09	100.00
1900	1.27	0.40	50.17	51.94	0.98	1.22	37.55	8.41		49.16	100.00
1901	1.18	0.55	54.57	56.30	0.92	1.09	33.38	8.31		43.30	100.00
1902	1.15	0.35	59.17	60.66	0.99	1.17	39.95	7.32		39.34	100.00
1903	1.13	0.36	64.63	59.93	0.85	1.06	31.81	6.34		40.07	100.00
1904	0.95	0.34	59.63	59.93	0.85	1.06	31.81	6.34		40.07	100.00
1905	0.94	0.37	66.91	68.22	0.79	1.00	22.96	7.04		31.79	100.00
1906	0.96	0.34	65.17	66.47	0.76	0.97	26.89	4.91		33.53	100.00
1907	0.96	0.32	66.62	67.91	0.78	0.89	24.58	5.09	0.74	32.09	100.00
1908	1.07	0.27	61.96	63.30	0.75	0.94	29.34	5.28	0.39	76.70	100.00
1909	1.07	0.36	60.13	61.56	0.88	0.90	31.41	4.35	0.90	38.44	100.00
1910	1.21	0.37	60.85	62.43	0.82	0.91	31.41	4.35	0.90	38.44	100.00
1911	1.11	0.43	60.78	62.32	0.86	1.00	29.84	5.19	0.79	17.38	100.00
1912	1.07	0.37	61.01	62.45	0.91	0.95	29.58	5.54	0.55	37.54	100.00
1913	1.10	0.36	57.55	59.02	0.92	0.95	32.56	5.89	0.59	40.98	100.00
1914	1.01	0.34	58.33	59.69	1.04	0.93	30.89	5.89	0.59	40.98	100.00
1915	0.84	0.40	59.32	60.56	1.02	0.95	30.21	5.23	1.83	39.44	100.00
1916	0.80	0.45	58.07	59.32	1.11	1.06	30.21	5.72	2.58	40.59	100.00
1917	0.75	0.48	56.33	57.55	0.99	1.17	31.28	6.20	2.81	42.45	100.00
1918	0.68	0.44	55.79	56.91	0.91	1.15	30.84	6.77	3.41	43.93	100.00
1919	0.60	0.46	55.00	56.07	0.85	1.13	30.70	7.05	4.20	43.93	100.00
1920	0.54	0.60	56.65	57.99	0.92	0.93	30.87	5.77	3.62	42.11	100.00
1921	0.60	0.48	55.12	56.19	0.97	1.08	31.65	6.48	3.63	43.81	100.00
1922	0.58	0.49	52.75	53.83	1.12	1.29	33.88	6.63	3.26	46.17	100.00
1923	0.59	0.51	50.57	51.68	1.16	1.35	35.48	7.00	3.33	48.32	100.00
1924	0.60	0.45	51.86	52.92	1.14	1.40	34.96	6.34	3.24	47.08	100.00
1925	0.61	0.48	50.69	51.79	1.13	1.44	35.39	6.89	3.35	48.31	100.00
1926	0.65	0.52	48.62	49.79	1.11	1.44	35.93	7.68	4.05	50.21	100.00
1927	0.70	0.53	49.78	51.00	1.08	1.45	35.80	7.22	3.45	49.00	100.00
1928	0.71	0.53	49.80	51.04	1.07	1.57	35.72	7.22	3.38	49.95	100.00
1929	0.75	0.55	51.56	52.97	1.05	1.55	34.48	7.22	2.84	47.13	100.00
1930	0.83	0.66	51.75	52.85	1.09	1.62	35.82	6.75	1.88	47.15	100.00
1931	0.83	0.55	51.35	52.85	1.09	1.62	35.82	6.75	1.88	47.15	100.00
1932	0.82	0.66	56.12	57.60	0.89	1.49	31.75	5.82	2.47	42.40	100.00
1933	0.82	0.70	57.58	59.10	0.93	1.39	30.72	5.55	2.41	40.90	100.00

TABLE 6 (*Contd.*)

	Below ground						*Surface*				
1934	0.81	0.81	59.56	61.17	0.76	1.36	39.40	4.97	2.33	39.83	100.00
1935	0.80	0.90	61.70	63.40	0.72	1.31	27.77	4.48	2.33	36.60	100.00
1936	0.80	0.94	61.98	63.72	0.71	1.30	29.10	4.34	0.84	36.28	100.00
1937	0.75	1.00	62.32	64.08	0.67	1.26	29.06	4.12	0.80	35.82	100.00
1938	0.75	0.95	62.91	64.62	0.65	1.35	29.01	3.77	0.61	35.39	100.00
1939	0.73	1.00	62.85	64.58	0.63	1.31	29.67	3.81	0.00	35.42	100.00
1940	0.62	0.93	63.27	64.91	0.60	1.23	29.35	4.01	0.00	35.19	100.00
1941	0.50	0.73	65.36	66.59	0.47	0.90	32.04	NA	NA	33.41	100.00
1942	0.51	0.73	62.78	64.03	0.50	0.93	34.55	NA	NA	35.97	100.00
1943	0.47	0.66	62.97	64.09	0.52	0.87	34.52	NA	NA	35.91	100.00
1944	0.52	0.74	58.62	59.98	0.51	0.99	39.52	NA	NA	40.12	100.00
1945	0.52	0.91	56.76	58.19	0.70	1.44	34.44	5.23	0.00	41.81	100.00
1946	0.53	1.04	57.59	59.15	0.65	1.49	34.38	4.32	0.00	40.85	100.00
Averages:											
1899/1906	1.11	0.39	59.92	61.42	0.86	1.10	30.01	6.62		38.58	100.00
1907/1940	0.82	0.57	57.70	59.08	0.90	1.20	31.20	5.63	1.98	40.92	100.00

NB: For 1941 to 1944 figures for adult male Indian surface workers include adult females and children.

SOURCES: See table 3

Table 7

Population and Birthplace, 1891–1961

	Total KGF population	*Males only*	*Born in Mysore State: numbers*	%	*Born in Kolar District: numbers*	%	*Born in Madras Presidency numbers*	%	*Born in North Arcot numbers*	%	*Born in Salem District: numbers*	%	*Born in Malabar District: numbers*	%
1891	24 111	NA	NA	NA	NA	NA	NA	NA	NA	NA	NA	NA	NA	NA
1901(a)	38 204	22 492	6 312	16.5	2 440	...	30 923	80.9	16 678	43.6	2 686	7.0	1 510	3.
(b)	70 874													
1911(a)	48 635	27 960	10 846	22.3	7 248	...	36 215	74.4	19 825	40.7	3 451	7.0	2 013	4.
(b)	83 743	47 487												
1921	87 682	47 487	38 097	43.4	32 661	...	47 561	54.2	24 017	27.3	4 926	5.6	2 016	2.
1931	85 103	45 051	47 309	55.6	43 424	...	36 176	42.5	20 697	24.3	2 972	3.5	1 763	2.
1941	133 859	70 428	76 041	56.8	71 211	...	55 485	41.4						
1951	159 084	79 384												
1961	146 811	74 015												

Note: The horizontal rows (a) probably exclude the population lying outside both the mining area proper and the urban area under the jurisdiction of the KGF Sanitary Board; rows (b) therefore cover the total KGF City designation.

Sources: Census of Mysore 1901–61, *passim*, supplemented with information from the Gazetteers.

Table 8

Annual Wages (earnings) for European and Indian Employees in the K.G.F., 1899–1946

1	2	3	4	5	6	7	8	9
Date	*Average monthly money wage per European employee*	*Average monthly money wage per Indian employee*	*Wage gap. Ratio of European: Indian*	*South African gold mines*	*Nominal wage index for Europeans*	*Real wage index for Europeans*	*Nominal wage index for Indians*	*Real wage index for Indians*
1899	16.9	1.43	11.8:1		95.6	112.6	99.3	116.9
1900	17.68	1.44	12.2:1		100.0	100.0	100.0	100.0
1901	19.72	1.45	13.6:1		111.5	117.6	100.7	106.2
1902	20.04	1.41	14.2:1		113.3	124.5	97.9	107.5
1903	19.26	1.54	12.7:1		108.9	128.3	106.9	125.9
1904	21.55	1.41	15.2:1		121.9	139.7	97.9	112.2
1905	21.45	1.52	14.1:1		104.1	109.8	105.5	111.3
1906	21.66	1.5	14.4:1		122.5	110.0	104.2	93.5
1907	22.01	1.47	14.9:1		124.5	106.0	102.1	86.9
1908	22.60	1.51	14.9:1		127.8	104.3	104.9	85.5
1909	21.27	1.44	14.8:1		120.3	95.2	100.0	79.1
1910	24.19	1.52	16:1		120.3	114.3	100.0	95.0
1911	25.05	1.51	16.6:1	11.7:1	141.6	127.3	104.8	94.2
1912	25.74	1.57	16.4:1		145.6	127.6	109.0	92.8
1913	28.35	1.51	18.7:1		160.3	130.7	104.8	85.5
1914	27.63	1.61	17.1:1		156.2	123.6	111.8	88.4
1915	28.19	1.52	18.5:1		159.4	112.7	105.5	74.6
1916	32.46	1.49	21.8:1	12.0:1	183.6	113.5	103.4	63.9
1917	35.05	1.58	22.2:1		198.3	103.0	109.7	59.8
1918	36.12	1.87	19.3:1		204.3	91.8	130.1	58.4
1919	36.96	2.16	17.1:1		209.0	84.6	150.5	60.9
1920	37.7	1.89	13.1:1		213.6	83.6	201.8	78.7
1921	39.6	1.86	21.3:1	15.0:1	224.3	99.1	129.6	57.2
1922	40.58	1.86	21.8:1		229.5	104.0	129.5	58.1
1923	44.09	2.24	10.7:1		249.4	114.7	155.6	71.6
1924	44.82	2.14	20.0:1		253.5	115.8	155.3	70.9
1925	45.64	2.24	20.3:1		258.1	128.5	156.2	77.7
1926	47.30	2.23	21.2:1		267.5	142.9	156.1	83.3

TABLE 8 (*Continued*)

1	*2*	*3*	*4*	*5*	*6*	*7*	*8*	*9*
Date	*Average monthly money wage per European employee*	*Average monthly money wage per Indian employee*	*Wage gap. Ratio of European: Indian*	*South African gold mines*	*Nominal wage index for Europeans*	*Real wage index for Europeans*	*Nominal wage index for Indians*	*Real wage index for Indians*
1927	43.52	2.23	19.5:1		246.1	131.4	156.1	83.4
1928	43.80	2.20	19.9:1		247.7	135.0	153.9	83.9
1929	45.71	2.26	20.2:1		258.5	145.0	157.0	88.1
1930	44.88	2.42	18.5:1		253.8	173.0	168.5	114.8
1931	47.28	2.45	19.3:1	11.3:1	267.4	220.6	170.4	140.6
1932	48.14	2.48	19.4:1		272.3	236.6	172.6	150.0
1933	43.76	2.43	18:1		247.5	225.2	169.2	153.9
1934	42.03	2.37	17.7:1		237.7	210.9	165.2	146.5
1935	42.12	2.4	17.5:1		238.3	206.9	166.7	144.9
1936	42.67	2.59	16.5:1	11.5:1	241.3	209.7	180.1	156.5
1937	45.2	2.68	16.8:1		255.6	198.5	186.2	144.6
1938	45.86	2.6	17.6:1		259.4	215.6	180.9	150.4
1939	45.58	2.69	16.9:1		257.8	188.5	186.9	136.6
1940	46.39	2.72	17.1:1		262.4	172.7	189.5	124.7
1941	n.a.	n.a.		12.1:1				
1942	n.a	n.a.						
1943	n.a.	n.a.	17.1:1					
1944	49.99	2.92	15.8:1					
1945	49.03	3.11			277.3	88.4	216.1	68.8
1946	56.81	4.23	13.4:1	12.7:1				

NOTES: Column 2 is a composite average which includes all European employees enjoying 'covenanted' status. Anglo-Indian ('Eurasian') employees—or 'non-covenanted' staff—have been excluded: between 1934–38 their average wage was £13.26 p.m. (5.26:1); before 1934 information is not available for this category.

Column 3 has been expressed in £ sterling at the existing exchange rates. For the years of exchange instability, 1917–22, the following rates were used: 1917 Rs 15 = £1; 1918 Rs 13.7; 1919 Rs 12; 1920 Rs 10.2; and 1921 and 1922 Rs 16.

Column 5 has been extracted from F. Wilson's *Labour in South African gold mines 1911–69* (Cambridge, 1972), table 5, p. 46.

Columns 6–9: the base year is 1900.

Columns 7 & 9: The price deflator used for this exercise has been derived from M. Mukherjee, *National income of India: trends and structure* (Calcutta, 1969), table A2.11, p. 94.

SOURCE: *Annual reports of the Chief Inspector of Mines for Mysore*, 1899–1946, *passim*.

TABLE 9

ACCIDENTS ON THE K.G.F., 1891–1946

	1	2	3		4	
Date	*No. of deaths in Mysore*	*No. of serious accidents in Mysore*	*Death rate per 1000 employed*		*Death rate per £100 000 of output*	
			a) Mysore	*b) Transvaal*	*a) Mysore*	*b) Transvaal*
1891	25		2.70			
1892	34		2.80			
1893	38		2.70			
1894	39		3.17			
1895	50		4.05	4.64	5.14	3.34
1896	33		1.97	4.95	2.60	4.22
1897	47		4.88	4.31	6.52	2.91
1898	53	81	2.45	4.64	3.26	2.68
1899	38	91	1.80	n.a.	2.26	n.a.
1900	64	178	2.61	n.a.	3.35	n.a.
1901	57	147	2.29	n.a.	3.90	n.a.
1902	58	157	2.21	3.83	2.90	1.94
1903	69	155	2.52	n.a.	3.02	n.a.
1904	45	204	1.53	n.a.	1.94	n.a.
1905	76	205	2.51	n.a.	3.23	n.a.
1906	70	342	2.30	5.83	3.23	3.97
1907	60	336	1.92	4.98	2.89	3.01
1908	90	357	3.09	4.4	4.37	2.65
1909	114	347	3.64	5.53	5.0	3.26
1910	74	350	2.72	4.46	3.5	2.75
1911	89	326	3.35	4.33	4.12	2.6
1912	90	219	3.36	4.02	4.11	2.23
1913	112	231	4.38	3.96	5.10	2.17
1914	61	177	2.28	3.35	2.76	1.74
1915	70	219	2.59	3.27	3.22	1.83
1916	93	138	3.52	3.22	4.19	1.84
1917	69	118	2.81	2.59	3.34	1.46
1918	71	97	2.90	2.47	3.67	1.46
1919	68	147	2.79	2.41	3.64	1.38
1920	85	101	3.55	2.38	4.68	1.43
1921	68	125	2.91	2.19	4.22	1.29

TABLE 9 (*Continued*)

	1	*2*	*3*		*4*	
Date	*No. of deaths in Mysore*	*No. of serious accidents in Mysore*	*Death rate per 1000 employed*		*Death rate per £100 000 of output*	
			a) Mysore	*b) Transvaal*	*a) Mysore*	*b) Transvaal*
1922	72	131	3.09	1.85	4.03	1.16
1923	78	149	3.79	2.50	4.45	1.34
1924	69	157	3.48	2.56	3.65	1.33
1925	71	160	3.62	2.32	4.16	1.19
1926	47	155	2.45	2.20	2.82	1.12
1927	56	176	2.64	2.75	3.07	1.41
1928	43	149	2.28	2.24	2.68	1.18
1929	73	181	3.74	2.58	4.46	1.33
1930	40	154	2.31	2.47	2.86	1.28
1931	131	160	7.12	2.31	9.32	1.22
1932	74	168	3.39	2.28	5.28	1.17
1933	54	239	2.67	2.29	3.78	1.32
1934	56	280	2.18	2.04	4.10	1.37
1935	53	230	1.98	2.12	3.82	1.54
1936	59	193	2.14	2.10	4.18	1.58
1937	46	176	1.93	2.09	3.27	1.55
1938	49	135	2.60	1.89	2.10	1.41
1939	51	118	1.80	1.74	3.81	1.26
1940	40	225	1.38	1.66	3.25	1.19
1941	28	242	0.98	1.57	2.30	1.13
1942	56	209	2.10	1.42	5.15	1.01
1943	42	223	1.69	1.45	8.92	0.99
1944	17	157	0.76	1.41	2.13	0.97
1945	24	184	1.13	1.42	3.35	1.01
1946	9	160	0.41	1.51	1.60	1.10
Total no. of deaths 1891–1946	3 398					

SOURCES: *Annual reports of the Chief Inspector of Mines for Mysore*, 1895–1946, *passim*.

TABLE 10

JOB SPECIFICATIONS IN 1945–46*

	Europeans		Anglo-Indians	Indians	
Work designation	*Numbers*	*Earnings (£/month)*	*Numbers*	*Numbers*	*Earnings (Rs/month)*
Superintendents	4				
Chief underground agents	4	91.67			
Assistant underground agents	36	54.65		5	
Chief cashiers	4				
Accountants	17				
Doctors	6			3	
Storekeepers	10				
Watch establishment	6				
Foremen	80	33.00	200	100	
Assistant foremen				200	
Miners		27.73		13 000	109.41
Machinemen				1 000	30.27
Hardjumper mestries				200	42.13
Hardjumper men				2 000	35.46
Blasters				200	43.09
Timber mestries				100	30.06
Timber men	12	27.61		400	24.59
Staff mestries				100	35.48
Staff men				300	24.55
Shiproad mestries				100	43.64
Shiproad men	4			200	25.8
Landers and bellmen				500	29.67
Chief engineers	6	85.94			
Assistant engineers	24	50.45		25	
Engineering foremen		32.13	16	50	
Carpenters	3			250	42.35
Smiths				100	49.33
Engine drivers	24	27.86	60	240	34.25
Boiler smiths				50	49.4
Surfacemen (coolies)				500	22.16
Chief surveyors	4	84.38			
Assistant surveyors	10	40.03		2	

TABLE 10 (*Continued*)

Work designation	*Europeans*		*Anglo-Indians*	*Indians*	
	Numbers	*Earnings (£/month)*	*Numbers*	*Numbers*	*Earnings (Rs/month)*
Chief metallurgists	4	78.18			
Assistant metallurgist	23	46.69		2	
Millmen	24	23.29		420	
Fitters		31.82		1 000	55.5
Loco Drivers			80	120	56.09
Trammers				1 000	23

NOTES: *Unavoidably the numbers are for 1946 but the pay is for 1945. The numbers, especially for European and Anglo-Indian staff, do not precisely tally with the Inspectorate records—probably because they are taken from a slightly different original muster roll source. Indian numbers have been rounded off.

SOURCES: *Report of the Chief Inspector of Mines for Mysore*, 1946, supplemented by information (on numbers) received from Mr. Hugh Stapleton.

Effects of International Labour Migration on the Economic Growth of Bangladesh

BÉATRICE KNERR

1. INTRODUCTION

During the last decade hundreds of thousands of workers from Bangladesh have migrated to the oil-exporting countries of the Middle East on temporary labour contracts. The enormous flow of remittances became the country's most important source of foreign exchange. Obvious repercussions on the domestic economy, and the country's urgent need for foreign exchange, led to increasing government intervention. Bangladesh is one of the poorest countries—with a per capita income of US $130 p.a. It is ranked as the second poorest country of the world and by far the poorest in Asia (World Bank 1985b:174–5) and the first goal of its Five-Year Plan is 'to ensure an equitable growth in order to bring about visible improvement in the standard of living of the people through adequate supplies of basic needs' (Bangladesh Bureau of Statistics 1985:901). Therefore a conscious migration policy has to be shaped in such a way that it serves this goal as far as possible. It is the aim of this paper to consider the economic costs and benefits of international labour migration for Bangladesh under the government's present policy.

The next section gives a brief overview of the general relationship between growth and international labour migration. This will establish the analytical base for the subsequent investigation of the special situation of Bangladesh. Section 3 considers the consequences of the loss of labour for Bangladesh against the background of the domestic labour market; section 4 analyzes the effects of the use of remittances and the effectiveness of government intervention, and considers distributional aspects. Section 5 present some thoughts on the future prospects of the demand for labour from Bangladesh.

2. THE FRAMEWORK OF EVALUATION

Economic growth, defined in terms of domestic product, could be achieved either by technical progress, by capital accumulation—including human, social and physical capital—or by taking into production idle resources if there is enough demand for the additional products. To assess the growth impact of international labour migration on the sending country, we must consider how these variables are affected by the three major streams crossing the borders: emigrating workers, the backflow of their foreign savings, and returning migrants. This is the analytical base for answering the question: what are the costs and benefits of these movements, in terms of losses and gains of real per capita income?

2.1 The Loss of Labour

If labour force mobility is allowed, people will tend to move to places where the reward of their work is greatest and where their economic situation will improve. The loss of social product for the sending country depends on the kind and quantity of labour emigrating. Depending on the opportunity costs, i.e. the output lost because of their departure, there are five categories (see fig. 1):

1. Migrants who were unemployed at home and whose departure does not cause any loss of production in their home region. The people staying behind will have a higher per capita income because they no longer have to share with the migrants. The money eventually spent for or by the migrant will now be spent by others; so there is no significant decline in aggregate demand.
2. Migrants who were employed but can be replaced easily and with no cost by previously unemployed or underemployed persons, so that there are no or negligible opportunity costs.
3. Migrants who can be replaced by others taken out of the pool of unemployed and underemployed, but whose replacement is not costless because new entrants must be trained and the work requires experience. In this case production losses and additional costs of training will occur for some time.
4. Migrants who cannot be replaced in the foreseeable future. The higher their qualifications and the scarcer their skills in the home region, the higher the costs for the economy. In these cases several negative effects are often cumulative: first, the migrant's direct production is lost; and secondly, there may be a loss of other jobs, for example because certain machines can no longer be repaired.

Fig. 1 : Categories of emigrating labour force according to opportunity Costs

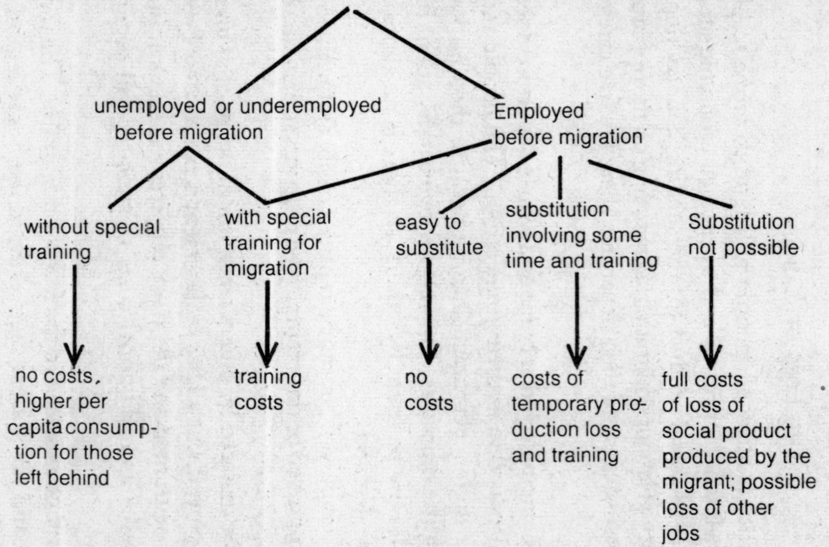

This also has a dynamic aspect. With increasing labour emigration certain categories of workers, who were in surplus before the migration started, may become increasingly scarce and their replacement more and more difficult and expensive.

5. Migrant workers who, in order to get a job abroad, received special education or training paid for by themselves or by the government. In this case migration causes an input of resources in advance. Such costs might occur in addition to the opportunity costs already mentioned.

2.2 The Remittances of Foreign Savings

Generally migrants save an important share of the money earned abroad. It is either sent regularly to the family at home or brought back when the migrant returns. The impact of remittances on the economic growth of the sending country depends on (see fig. 2):

1. The use of remitted foreign exchange. Migrants either spend it themselves or sell it to banks or private importers, including people who travel abroad.
2. The use of the remittances by migrants and their families after they have changed it into domestic currency.

2.2.1 THE USE OF FOREIGN CURRENCY

The migrant can use his foreign exchange to import goods, sell it to enterprises or private persons, or exchange it for domestic currency at the central state bank.

If the central state bank buys the foreign exchange, it becomes available to the public sector and subject to the plans of political decision-makers. At the same time more domestic currency becomes available to the private sector. These transactions are reversed when foreign exchange is sold to the private sector.

If the migrants sell their foreign exchange to traders, or import goods themselves, the domestic money supply will not increase. As the supply of foreign exchange increases, its price will tend to fall if it is not effectively fixed by the government, and the additional foreign exchange will be used for goods and services that otherwise would not be imported. If these goods and services replace domestic products—and this depends not only on the prices and the preferences of the consumers but also on existing import regulations—their producers will be faced with declining prices and incomes. At the same time domestic purchasing power shifts to other goods.

Long-term growth effects could be achieved by the import of productive capital goods, provided there is enough domestic or foreign demand for the

Fig. 2: Use of remittances

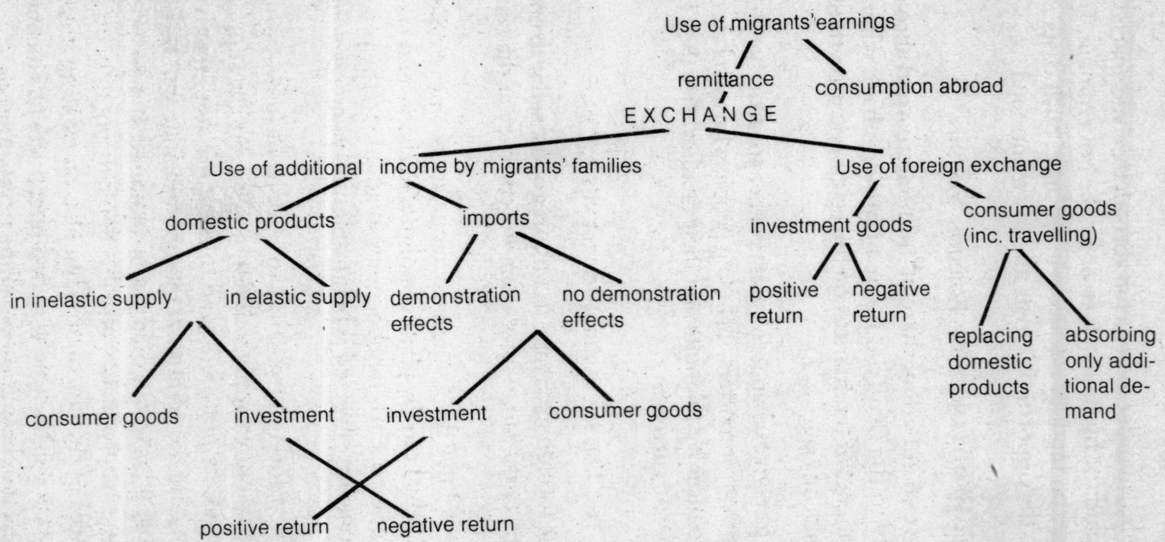

products. In a labour-surplus economy this could create new jobs, depending on the technology.

2.2.2 THE USE OF ADDITIONAL INCOME BY MIGRANTS' FAMILIES

Let us assume that the foreign currency has been exchanged for domestic currency. Migrants can use the additional income they earned abroad either for saving and investment or for consumption.

As income elasticities differ among goods, sometimes even being negative, not all sectors of the economy will be equally affected by the increasing purchasing power of migrants' families. The higher the share spent on domestic goods and services, the more the additional income that will be created for other producers and suppliers through keynesian multiplier effects. Demand can be directed to domestic products if the government succeeds in imposing effective import restrictions. But demand for domestic goods will only result in real growth of the social product if there are idle resources which can be mobilized. If the goods demanded and/or productive resources are in inelastic supply, then increasing demand will result in higher prices, which could lead to inflation in the whole economy.

Obviously there might be a conflict between short-term and long-term consumption. If a large share of income is consumed immediately, the boom will be over as soon as remittances decline, because a recession in the host country will quickly affect the sending country. But if a larger share of the additional income is used for investment, then immediate consumption will be smaller but it may lead to higher and more stable income later on, provided that it is used to produce goods and services for which there will be domestic or foreign demand in the future.

2.3 The Remigrants

People coming back from abroad may contribute to the economic growth of their home country if the output per unit of their labour input is higher than the potential output before their departure. The criterion for this is not the individual output of the worker but the total output of the economy. For example, if someone who was unemployed before his departure finds a job when he comes back, this does not result in any increase in output if he is just replacing someone who is now unemployed or if the work is only divided between more people. Remigration results in a positive growth effect if the migrant was able to learn something abroad that will be useful at home and increase his productivity. This effect is multiplied if he can pass on this know-how to others.

3. THE COSTS AND BENEFITS OF LABOUR EMIGRATION FROM BANGLADESH

3.1 Labour Scarcities and Surpluses in Bangladesh

The Bangladesh labour market is characterized by high rates of unemployment and underemployment which are caused by high population growth, insufficient education and vocational training, and a stagnation in the number of jobs offered.

For years the Bangladesh labour force has grown by nearly 3 per cent yearly (see table 1) and every year about 800 000 more people enter the labour market. The labour force of 27 397 000 in 1985 will grow to 43 931 000 in the year 2000 (Bangladesh Bureau of Statistics 1985:206). Since rates of population growth during the last years exceeded 2 per cent (see various issues of the World Banks' *World Development Report*) this trend will continue for some decades.

About 75 per cent of the population—67 per cent of the men and 87 per cent of the women—are illiterate. There is no compulsory school attendance. Only 7 per cent of.girls and 23 per cent of boys aged 12–16 go to school. Vocational schools are few and have low standards. Not more than 3 per cent of the young people between 17 and 22 years old have the chance to go to university or to receive vocational training; yet 87 per cent of these study general subjects like philosophy, literature or law, and only 13 per cent receive a technical or specialist education (World Bank 1985a, vol. III: 43).

Table 1

Annual Growth Rates of The Labour Force per Year, 1976–83

Year	*Growth rate*	*Population of working age as percentage of total population*
1976	1.6	49
1977	2.3	51
1978	2.4	54
1979	3.3	54
1980	2.4	55
1981	2.9	55
1982	2.9	55
1983	2.8	54

Source: World Bank (ed.), *World development reports*, 1978–85, and own calculations.

On the demand side, there is a vicious circle of low incomes, low demand

and low investment. Over recent years the demand for labour has stagnated, partly because of a lack of investment which in turn is due to the small domestic and foreign demand for goods produced in Bangladesh. Gross capital formation in the fiscal year 1984–85 amounted to US $349m, or 11 per cent of GDP; but only $81m, or 2.6 per cent of GDP, were gross domestic savings (Bangladesh Bureau of Statistics 1985:692). There is hardly any direct investment from abroad. The country's external debt, at over $400m, is nearly 40 per cent of GNP, causing a high outflow of capital to service the debt.

In 1980, for example, gross investment amounted to only $1000 for each new entrant to the labour market (World Bank 1984:87). Bangladesh is at the bottom of the international scale, below even Ethiopia which is the world's poorest country in terms of income per capita. Since the industrial sector is small and technically backward, it employs only a small part of the growing labour force. The agricultural sector, which employs nearly 80 per cent of all workers, cannot absorb the additional labour supply (Vereinigung für Internationale Zusammenarbeit 1986:19). As Q. M. Khan (1985:1055–6) points out, moderate demand keeps prices, production and employment low. Moreover, the lack of social capital, especially roads, energy and water supply, contributes to the low productivity of the farm labour force. As landlessness is very common—about 3.9m or 32.8 per cent of rural households are landless (Sinha 1984:36)—self-employment is a solution for only part of the rual population. The service sector is a pool of hidden unemployment; and given the level of skills, there is no significant employment-creating effect from the export sector. Part of the cheap unskilled labour force cannot be mobilized for industrial exports because there are not sufficient complementary inputs of equipment and management, nor is there an adequate infrastructure to support industrial expansion (World Bank 1985a, vol. II: 72–3).

Population pressure is leading to significant internal migration. This is shown by the fact that population growth rates—except in the largest urban centres, Dhaka and Chittagong—are highest in the regions with the lowest population densities: Chittagong Hill Tracts with 6.5 per cent, Dinajpur, Rajshahi and Patuakhali with nearly 3 per cent each (see fig. 3). Between 1974 and 1981 Chittagong Hill Tracts gained more than one-third of its population by immigration from other regions; Bandarban, the region with the lowest population density, gained more than 16 per cent (see table 2).

The gap between domestic demand for and supply of labour widens steadily, resulting in widespread and rising unemployment and underemployment. In rural areas people work only 185 days a year on average,

Figure 3: Population density in the regions of Bangladesh

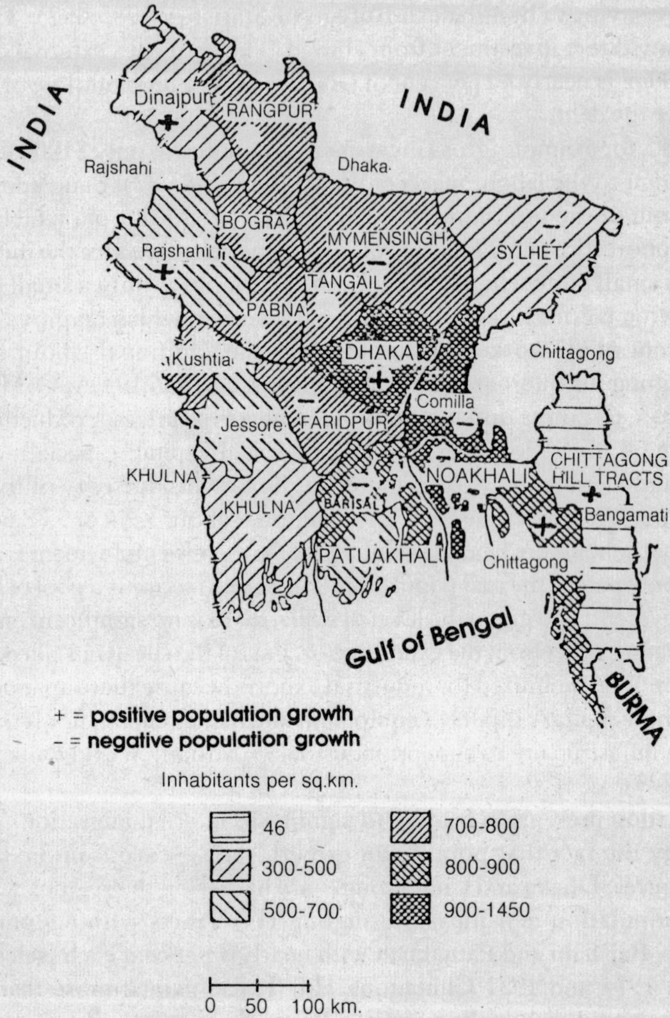

Statistisches Bundesamt 830642

and they do not earn enough to support a family (World Bank 1985a, vol. III: 18). In the towns, more and more people join the informal sector. Hidden unemployment is common in the smallholder sector and in the urban service sector (*ibid.*: 29, 31). Estimates of urban unemployment range from 20 per cent to 50 per cent of the potential labour force, and the number of unemployed rises by 900 000 each year (Ali 1981:1). There is also widespread disguised unemployment in the public sector. Government ownership of a significant part of industry results in a rigid employment structure, because labour in the nationalized state-run enterprises is rather inflexible. Worker mobility is low and staff are rarely dismissed. If, for example, a worker leaves one of the older state-run jute factories, the government saves money because these enterprises do not fire older workers and are heavily overstaffed (Kibria and Tisdell 1985).

TABLE 2

INTERNAL MIGRATION IN BANGLADESH: REGIONS WITH LARGEST POPULATION GAIN AND LOSS BETWEEN 1974 AND 1981

Region	*Population gain*	*Population 1981 (in thousands)*	*Population density 1981*	*(1) as percentage of (2)*
	(1)	(2)	(3)	(4)
Chittagong Hill Tracts	+231 568	602	180	35.4
Bandarban	+ 29 576	180	104	16.4
Dacca	+736 321	10 340	3 585	7.1
Dinajpur	− 66 907	3 300	1 302	2.0
Chittagong	+102 714	5 664	1967	1.8
Rajshahi	+ 67 718	5 440	1 490	1.2
Patuakhali	+ 15 855	1 897	1 200	0.8
Bogra	+ 8 786	2 814	1 875	0.3
Sylhet	−145 153	1 189	1 189	−12.2
Faridpur	−183 953	1 851	1 851	− 9.9
Mymensingh	−144 254	1 816	1 316	− 7.9
Barisal	−121 290	1 710	1 610	− 7.0
Comilla	−211 515	2 787	2 787	− 7.0
Noakhali	−125 711	1 868	1 868	− 6.7

SOURCES: Bangladesh Bureau of Statistics, 1985; World Bank 1985a, vol. III; and own calculations.

A high level of education is no guarantee of employment. Especially for graduates in more general subjects, there is not sufficient demand. A study carreid out by the BMET revealed that 63.8 per cent of 'administrative, managerial and related' workers are underutilized in Bangladesh. At the beginning of the 1980s, 61 per cent of qualified trainees who had passed the Technical Training Centre of the BMET were unemployed for one year, 20 per cent for two years and 17 per cent for more than three years.

On the other hand insufficient technical and specialist education, resulting in a lack of skilled craftsmen and professionals, creates a serious bottleneck for the country's development, a fact which givers of foreign aid have already recognized. In 1979, for example, the International Development Agency provided a credit of $25m, which was earmarked for vocational training. Insufficient education and vocational training is also a decisive bottleneck for the export sector. Categories with an overall deficit are, above all, medical specialists, graduate doctors, engineering graduates, engineering technicians and craftsmen, medical technicians and agricultural professionals (Ali 1981:163–4; World Bank 1985a, vol. III: 57–8). In spite of high unemployment and underemployment, the government had 50 000 posts vacant in 1981 because of failures in administration and shortages of suitable manpower (Ali 1981:2). The lack of human capital includes the unskilled labour force. A 1985 study by the World Bank (1985a, vol. I:4) concludes:

> The base of skilled craftsmen and professionals is small. Even the excess pool of unskilled labour should not be simply regarded as an attribute which leads to a 'comparative advantage' for labour-intensive industrialization. The poor health and nutritional status of the members of industrial labour force, together with the lack of even basic education, can lower their productivity per dollar earned to below that of employees earning substantially higher real wages in other potentially competing countries.

This is in line with the efficiency wage hypothesis developed by Leibenstein (1951) and Stiglitz (1976, 1982), which states that a worker's productivity increases with the wage rate, and that below a certain level of consumption his productivity will be very low.

The coexistence of a large surplus labour force and a scarcity of certain skills in the country is mainly the result of the educational bias described above, which gives low priority to technical skills and vocational training and high priority to 'white-collar' university education.

One can easily predict that within the next few decades it will not be possible to create the number of jobs needed within Bangladesh, and there is no possibility of settlement migration in neighbouring countries. They have problems with their own labour markets and are neither willing nor able to accept migrants from Bangladesh on a larger scale. As a dramatic example of this, one could cite the Assam conflict of 1982.

As a result of this labour surplus, the money income of the majority of the population, especially in rural areas, is very low. It is estimated that in 1981, 23 per cent of the population had an income of less than $3 a year, and about 55 per cent had less than $6 (Statistisches Bundesamt 1984:66).

In 1984 the wage rate for skilled workers was around $1 a day, for unskilled workers around $0.80 (see table 3), construction being the leading sector since 1973. In most sectors real wages decreased markedly over the last decade, especially in agriculture and jute textiles (see table 4). The wage differential has changed more and more in favour of skilled workers (see table 5). In state enterprises the minimum wage rate for industrial workers was fixed at $25 a month in 1984. Wages are comparatively high for technicians. Laboratory assistants in Chittagong, for example, earned about $35 a month in 1984, and car mechanics $0.20 an hour (based on Statistisches Bundesamt 1985:78–9).

3.2 Foreign Demand

The export of manpower from present-day Bangladesh started in 1922 with the passing of the British Emigration Act. Migrants from the territories

Table 3

Wage Levels of Skilled and Unskilled Workers in Bangladesh 1973–1984 (US $ per day)

	1973	*1978*	*1981*	*1983*	*1984*
Agriculture					
skilled	0.79	—	0.94	0.82	0.84
unskilled	0.66	—	0.80	0.61	0.59
Fishery					
skilled	0.80	0.73	1.28	1.05	1.28
unskilled	0.64	0.58	1.02	0.84	0.76
Textile (large-scale manufacture)					
skilled	—	0.83	1.23	1.08	1.14
unskilled	—	0.55	0.94	0.81	0.83
Jute processing (large-scale manufacture)					
skilled		0.69	1.10	1.03	1.07
unskilled		0.55	0.92	0.79	0.78
Cottage industry		0.51	0.77	0.66	0.93
Construction					
skilled	1.51	1.53	2.13	1.95	1.94
unskilled	0.79	0.78	1.07	0.92	0.94

Source: Statistisches Bundesamt 1985.

TABLE 4
AVERAGE DAILY REAL WAGE OF UNSKILLED WORKERS, 1973–84
(TAKA PER DAY AT 1973–4 PRICES)

Sector wages	*1973–4*	*1978–9*	*1979–80*	*1980–1*	*1981–2*	*1982–3*	*1983–4*
Agriculture	6.69	6.48	6.20	6.53	5.90	6.13	6.15
Fishery	5.23	5.88	7.63	8.57	8.23	7.73	6.74
Small Scale Industry	5.03	5.73	5.94	6.49	5.95	5.89	7.89
Cotton textiles	5.53	6.25	6.37	6.65	5.95	5.62	5.73
Jute textiles	7.61	5.45	5.76	6.49	5.82	5.47	5.54
Matches	6.40	5.91	5.42	5.43	5.43	5.32	5.54
Engineering	6.23	6.30	5.75	6.06	6.03	5.74	5.98
Vegetable oils	5.53	5.75	5.34	5.40	5.20	4.53	4.93
Construction	7.10	7.70	7.42	7.59	7.20	6.58	7.71
INDEX (1973–4 = 100)							
Agriculture	100	97	93	98	88	92	92
Fishery	100	112	146	164	157	148	129
Small Scale Industry	100	114	118	129	118	117	157
Cotton textiles	100	113	115	120	108	102	104
Jute textiles	100	72	76	85	74	72	73
Matches	100	92	85	85	85	83	87
Engineering	100	101	92	97	97	92	96
Vegetable oils	100	104	97	98	92	82	89
Construction	100	108	105	107	101	93	109

SOURCES: World Bank 1985a, vol. II: 20, 28, and own calculations.

now comprising Bangladesh were, however, very few in number until the 1950s (Ali 1981:4). Then for a decade mostly unskilled workers emigrated, especially from Sylhet District. In the 1960s emigration to Great Britain fell sharply and was restricted to a few professionals and skilled workers. Today it has no significance for Bangladesh and it will not be dealt with in this paper. By far the greatest international market for Bangladeshi labour is in the oil-producing countries of the Middle East, where the major incentive of demand for foreign workers are:

1. earnings from oil exports;
2. a local population too small to put into effect government plans to develop infrastructure and industry;
3. low participation of the local population in the labour market, partly because of the tradition of confining women to home work and agriculture;
4. a strong preference for 'white-collar' jobs and avoidance of jobs that 'make the hands dirty'. This attitude is reinforced by a policy which gives

TABLE 5

RELATION BETWEEN WAGES OF SKILLED TO UNSKILLED LABOUR, 1974–1984

Fiscal Year	*1974–75*	*1975–76*	*1976–77*	*1977–78*	*1978–79*	*1979–80*	*1980–81*	*1981–82*	*1982–83*	*1983–84*
Agriculture	1.20	1.24	1.23	1.21	1.17	1.29	1.25	1.29	1.37	1.44
Average of all industries	1.29	1.34	1.42	1.44	1.40	1.33	1.43	1.40	1.37	1.42
Jute textiles (state-owned)	1.18	1.23	1.31	1.34	1.35	1.27	1.40	1.34	1.29	1.37

SOURCE: Own calculations from Bangladesh Bureau of Statistics 1985.

many privileges to state employees and assumes responsibility for giving public sector jobs to as many people as possible. As this is reflected in the education of the labour force, the result is a lack of human capital in technical professions and handicrafts (Birks & Sinclair 1980).

The most stable of these factors are the socio-cultural circumstances; the least stable are the earnings from the oil exports, as can be seen from recent events on the oil market. These factors lead to short-run fluctuations in the demand for labour, especially as labour contracts are limited to short periods.

During the first years of high and steadily rising earnings from oil exports, Middle Eastern countries followed a development strategy which emphasized building up a physical infrastructure, and this created a high demand for unskilled and semi-skilled workers. As this period is over, the demand for labour has changed in structure.

In 1972, 800 000 foreign workers lived in the oil-producing countries of the Middle East, the overwhelming majority of them from Arab countries. With the sudden rise of oil prices in 1973, the demand for foreign labour force increased sharply. In 1975 their number had already doubled. Now the supply of Arab workers became inelastic. At that time the south and east Asian supply was 'discovered' (see fig. 4). Between 1976 and 1981 the number of immigrants from Bangladesh increased from 6087 to 55 787, which means that on average it doubled every year (see table 6). Their number was estimated at about 191 000 in 1982, which corresponds to 0.4 per cent of Bangladesh's labour force. Over recent years the growth rates fell and even became negative. In 1984, 56 753 Bangladeshi workers emigrated, which amounts to 0.1 per cent of the total domestic labour force. Saudi Arabia, Kuwait, the UAE and Oman together absorb more than 70 per cent of the migrants (see table 6). Saudi Arabia is becoming increasingly important, in absolute and relative terms. Today it employs one third of all Bangladeshi migrants.

3.3 Migration Policy

Because of government intervention, and intervention from outside which goes beyond the mere pull effect of higher wage rates, the migration process in Bangladesh is subdivided into three stages:

1. Until 1972 emigration by Bangladeshi workers was practically not controlled or organized by any government or private agencies. The number of Bangladeshis working abroad was insignificant; nevertheless they paved the way for the following initiatives.
2. Between 1972 and 1975, the period of the oil boom, several unofficial delegations visited Bangladesh to recruit workers for the Middle East.

Fig. 4: Gross outflow of international contract migration from selected Asian countries 1976-82.

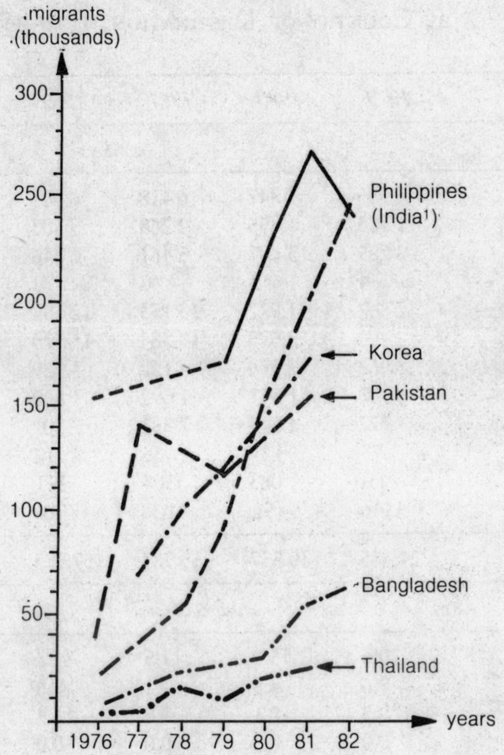

1) 1976 data for India were taken from 1975; 1977 and 1978 are estimated.

Source: Birks & Sinclair 1980.

As a result the number of migrants rose sharply. The recruitment process brought with it many malpractices and the government's first attempts to cope with this problem were not very successful.

TABLE 6
STRUCTURE OF MIGRANTS (NET)
BY COUNTRY OF DESTINATION, 1979–1984

	1979	*1980*	*1981*	*1982*	*1983*	*1984*
			Numbers			
UAE*	5 055	4 847	6 418	6 501	6 615	5 302
Qatar	1 383	1 455	2 268	5 505	7 541	2 643
Kuwait	2 289	3 687	5 461	6 846	10 283	5 697
Iran	4	2	0	0	0	534
Iraq	2 362	1 927	13 153	12 152	4 932	4 701
Saudi Arabia	6 490	8 695	13 384	14 770	11 462	20 587
Lybia	1 967	2 976	4 162	1 929	2 209	3 386
Bahrein	827	1 351	1 392	1 860	2 473	2 825
Oman	3 777	4 745	7 351	7 309	10 351	10 091
Jordan	73	127	66	140	42	1
Singapore	110	1 083	304	211	728	0
Others†	146	92	1 046	1 760	2 322	640
Total	24 485	30 537	55 787	57 575	58 441	56 635
			Percentages of total			
UAE	20.6	15.9	11.5	11.3	11.3	9.4
Qatar	5.6	4.8	4.1	9.6	12.9	4.7
Kuwait	9.3	12.1	9.8	11.9	17.6	10.1
Iran	0.0	0.0	0.0	0.0	0.0	0.9
Iraq	9.6	6.3	23.6	21.1	8.4	8.3
Saudi Arabia	26.5	28.5	24.0	25.7	19.6	36.4
Lybia	8.0	9.7	7.5	3.4	3.8	6.0
Bahrein	3.4	4.4	2.5	3.2	4.2	4.1
Oman	15.4	15.5	13.2	12.7	17.7	17.8
Jordan	0.3	0.4	0.1	0.2	0.1	0.0
Singapore	0.4	3.5	0.5	0.4	1.2	0.0
Others	0.8	0.3	1.8	0.4	4.0	1.1
Total	100	100	100	100	100	100

*Comprising Abu Dhabi, Dubai, Ajman, Fujairah, Ras al Khaimah, Sharja, Umm al Qaiwain.

†Algeria, Nigeria, Uganda, Malaysia, Ethiopia, Lebanon, Syria and others.

SOURCES: Bangladesh Bureau of Statistics, 1985:217, and own calculations.

3. From the mid-seventies the export of labour came to be of major economic and political concern in Bangladesh. In 1976 the government founded the Bureau of Manpower, Employment and Training (BMET) to solve the enormous and worsening problems of the labour market. Among other things, it is required to handle the export of manpower. At the same time the government introduced several laws to control and stimulate the flow of remittances and to encourage migration.

Today the government tries hard to export more labour. In 1982 it declared that it planned to send 70 000 more workers abroad in each of the following years. In recent years it pursued this goal by means of getting control of and information about potential labour markets, and by developing marketing strategies which include visits to the host countries by the Minister for Labour and Manpower (Arab News, 12 April 1985, p. 2). Since 1982 private agents have to seek government permission for each job they arrange. Migrant workers have to register at a government office, which they have also to inform about their terms of contract.

3.4 Forms of Migration

Whereas migration to the United Kingdom was nearly all settlement migration, and most migrants obtained British citizenship after four or five years, international migration from Bangladesh today is contract migration, i.e. movements of workers to another country where they will not settle but only offer their labour for the time specified in their job contract. Most contracts are for one or two years. In 1979, for example, more than 66 per cent of contracts of non-professional migrants were for only one year, 33 per cent for two years and only 0.13 per cent for more than three years (Ali 1981:31). The migrants go without their families and live together in shared accommodation. As highly qualified people have the opportunity to sign long-term labour contracts, professionals like engineers, doctors or managers tend to stay longer.

Migration is organized in six ways:

1. By the BMET. Besides collecting offers and requests, it keeps a list of people registered as 'surplus labour' by state public sector enterprises. Assistance by BMET has become less and less significant (see fig. 5). In the first year of its existence it handled nearly 87 per cent of all manpower exports, but its share fell rapidly to only 20 per cent manpower exports.
2. By licenced agents, the so-called 'passage brokers'. They are very numerous, but only a few arrange for jobs more than once.

3. By private parties seeking ad hoc permission from BMET.
4. By foreign embassies in Bangladesh. They handle only a very small volume.
5. By Bangladeshi enterprises with contracts for work in the Middle East.
6. By individual efforts, for example through friends and relatives already working in the Middle East.

Money passes from migrants to those who help them to find a job abroad. The number of Bangladeshis applying for a job abroad has always exceeded the number of jobs offered. For example in 1979 there were 165 000 persons registered at the BMET for jobs in the Middle East, but only one-fifth actually left during the following year (Ali 1981:26, Bangladesh Bureau of Statistics 1985:217). This shortage of job offers gives state employees and private agencies a chance to make money as intermediaries. Those who hand out jobs receive part or all of the difference between the actual salary in the Middle East and the salary the individual applicant would be willing to accept, in various ways. It is not surprising that private agents, who are paid by the employer and are not allowed to take money from the employee, often do just this even if they fail to deliver the job they have promised. It goes without saying that private agents are not the only ones to take commission from migrants. State employees, and people who use their informal contacts, may also expect a reward. Of course figures for these payments are hard to get. According to Ling (1984:34), recruiting agencies throughout South-East Asia routinely exact $500–1000 from every worker bound for the Middle East, without guaranteeing a job; payments in Bangladesh are unlikely to be lower, though this depends on wage levels in the Middle East.

3.5 The Occupational Structure of Migrant Labour

A sample survey of 10 per cent of migrants working in the Middle East in 1978 and 1979 showed that roughly half were skilled workers (see table 7). Over the last decade, however, the occupational structure changed according to the development priorities of the host countries. At the beginning of the migration movement, nearly 40 per cent of emigrants were construction workers, which reflected the strong emphasis on the building of infrastructure; their share declined very rapidly to only 6 per cent. A similar trend shows up in the number of emigrating engineers, the only group whose number declined in absolute terms (see table 8). Emigration of industrial workers, professionals, doctors and nurses, in contrast, displays the most significant growth rates. The increasing emigration of doctors and nurses is especially alarming, although Bangladesh has a relatively high proportion of medical staff.[1]

As a consequence of high unemployment and underemployment among unskilled workers, the cost of their departure in terms of production foregone is zero or very close to it. As studies of the relation between factoral income and caloric intake have shown that there is significant redistribution of personal incomes (Sinha 1984:38), consumption by those left behind will rise and the country's per capita income will increase.

TABLE 7

CLASSIFICATION OF MIGRANTS BY SKILL, 1978–79 (SAMPLE SURVEY)

Skills	*% of total* Main category	Sub-category
Professional workers	5.40	
engineers		2.16
doctors		1.18
Technical workers	2.58	
Skilled workers	48.88	
construction workers		30.17
transport equipment operators		9.15
service workers		4.98
production workers		3.77
Semi-skilled workers	10.53	
construction, transport and production workers		3.81
fisherman and agricultural workers		3.14
Unskilled workers	28.08	
construction workers		25.28
Skill not known	4.53	
Total	100.00	

SOURCE: Ali 1981.

[1] 7,812 people per doctor and 22 570 per nurse; cf. 17 990 and 3 148 for other low-income countries except PR China and India, or 5 995 and 1 945 for middle-income countries. (World Bank 1985b)

TABLE 8

MIGRANTS BY OCCUPATION (NET MIGRANTS ONLY)

Year	*1976*	*1977*	*1978*	*1979*	*1980*	*1981*	*1982*	*1983*	*1984*
					Numbers				
Construction workers	2 366	1 792	2 266	2 053	2 590	3 393	2 641	3 814	3 779
Vehicle drivers	824	567	1 308	1 950	1 070	2 575	3 587	1 881	1 448
Workers (all skill levels)	944	2 898	7 826	8 791	17 706	31 478	34 870	40 410	37 886
Technicians	359	1 466	5 744	4 657	4 247	10 357	7 597	6 113	4 992
Engineers	215	322	728	213	194	36	175	67	60
Doctors, nurses paramedicals	142	608	381	148	274	273	224	492	2 003
Professionals	211	836	470	74	385	1 905	2 805	3 371	3 836
Catering workers	543	490	1 007	1 124	1 836	2 653	2 604	2 225	1 229
Miscellaneous	483	6 746	3 079	5 475	2 271	2 917	3 072	827	1 450
Total	6 087	15 725	22 809	24 485	30 573	55 787	57 575	58 441	56 753
					Percentages of total				
Construction workers	38.9	11.4	9.9	8.4	8.5	6.1	6.6	6.5	6.7
Vehicle drivers	13.5	3.6	5.7	8.0	3.5	4.6	6.2	3.2	2.6
Workers (all skill levels)	15.5	18.4	34.3	35.9	57.9	56.4	60.6	69.1	66.8
Technicians	5.9	9.3	25.2	19.0	13.9	18.6	13.2	10.5	8.8
Engineers	3.5	2.0	3.2	0.9	0.6	0.1	0.3	0.1	0.1
Doctors, nurses, paramedicals	2.3	3.9	1.7	0.6	0.9	0.5	0.4	0.8	3.5
Professionals	3.5	5.3	2.1	0.3	1.3	3.4	4.9	5.8	6.8
Catering workers	8.9	3.1	4.4	4.6	6.0	4.8	4.5	3.8	2.3
Miscellaneous	7.9	42.9	13.5	22.4	7.4	5.2	5.3	1.4	2.6
Total	100.0	100.0	100.0	100.0	100.0	100.0	100.0	100.0	100.0

SOURCE: Bangladesh Bureau of Statistics 1985:218, and own calculations.

However, the loss of highly qualified labour may involve real costs to the country, even though there are many educated and highly skilled unemployed people in Bangladesh. Assuming that private sector wages reflect the real scarcity of each group, we can multiply the money income of these groups by the number going abroad, in order to estimate the costs caused by their departure. Thus in 1979 the cost to Bangladesh of emigration by professionals and technicians alone was about $5 911 458.[2]

As the structure of the demand for labour is changing in the Middle East, and as more and more highly qualified people—especially professionals, skilled workers, doctors, nurses and technicians—are induced to leave the country, the opportunity costs for Bangladesh are increasing over time. The groups with the highest growth rates of emigration, namely medical specialists, doctors and professionals, are also the deficit groups in Bangladesh. The only deficit group faced with declining foreign demand are engineers (there is also a shortage of construction workers; but this, as will be shown, depends on money remitted by migrants).

Some migrants receive special vocational training in private or public institutions for the sole purpose of getting a job in the Middle East. Therefore, the costs should be included in a calculation of migration costs if the resources employed, like teachers, rooms and materials, would otherwise be useful. It is reported that recently more and more small private institutions have appeared in Bangladesh, advertising with slogans like 'We are training for Saudi Arabia'. The government, too, is paying increasing attention to training for migration. As for a long time the demand for foreign labour in the Middle East was concentrated on construction, this has dominated the government's training courses. The Bangladesh economy may benefit later if the migrants acquire skills which are scarce in the country. However, the structure of the demand for labour in Bangladesh is very different from that in the Middle East; especially when the construction boom in Bangladesh, caused by migrants' remittances, comes to an end.

3.6 The Migrants' Regions of Origin

Half of the migrants come from Chittagong, Dhaka and Sylhet (see table 9). The first two are among the regions with the highest rates of population growth, which are partly caused by internal migration. The reason for this concentration is that the recruiters seldom travelled outside Dhaka and Chittagong, where the infrastructure is comparatively good and travelling

[2] 4 657 technicians and 385 professionals emigrated (see table 8). On average the technicians received 1 450 takas and the professionals 2 360 takas monthly (Ali 1981: 211), making 91 934 994 takas altogether.

is easier than in other regions. As soon as migration out of one region has started then it continues under its own momentum because of demonstration effects and contacts with friends and relatives working abroad, a phenomenon that can be observed in every labour-exporting country. The third important migration region, Sylhet, is the only region in Bangladesh which was heavily involved in migration to Britain. In all three regions the per capita income is significantly higher than the all-Bangladesh average (see table 9), showing that migration has a bias in favour of economically more developed regions; remote areas are mostly excluded. Therefore direct regional growth effects hardly occur in backward regions which lack infrastructure.

On average the proportion of migrnts coming from rural areas is higher than the share of rural population of their home regions (see table 9), thus displaying a bias of direct growth effects in favour of rural regions.

4. THE COSTS AND BENEFITS OF REMITTANCES

4.1 The Importance of Remittances in the Balance of Payments

Workers' remittances are today the most important source of foreign exchange for Bangladesh. Over the last few years they have nearly doubled, and now amount to more than 5 per cent of GNP. They reached their peak at $629m in 1984, when they paid for nearly half the imports and reached an amount of nearly 80 per cent of the country's export earnings (see table 10).

4.2 Remittance Policy

The Government of Bangladesh aims to maximize the inflow of remittances, and to direct as much of the remitted money as possible into productive investment.

4.2.1 THE INFLOW OF REMITTANCES

Legally each worker is obliged to remit 25 per cent of his pay from abroad, but this is hard to control and to enforce. Until 1975 workers avoided sending their money to Bangladesh through the banking system, because they had to change money at the official rates which overvalued the taka, and not on the black market. As an incentive to those working abroad, in 1975 the government set up the Wage Earners Scheme (WES), which is the main instrument of remittance policy. Under this scheme Bangladeshis employed abroad are allowed to hold foreign currency accounts in domes-

TABLE 9

ORIGIN OF MIGRANTS BY REGION, 1977 AND 1978

Region	*Percentage of total migrants*	*Percentage of population migrated*	*Percentage of migrants from rural areas*	*Gross regional product per capita (in current takas)* 1979–80	1983–4	*Percentage of rural population*
Chittagong	28.19	0.21	87.38	3234	5158	79.0
Dhaka	12.51	0.05	34.46	2397	3677	70.0
Sylhet	11.25	0.06	89.30	2229	3613	97.2
Noakhali	7.03	0.07	96.81	1959	3022	97.9
Comilla	2.83	0.07	93.06	1919	3178	95.8
All other regions*)	2.85	—				
Region not known	35.44					
Bangladesh	100.00			2139	3459	9.2

*Each with less than 1 per cent of migrants.

SOURCES: Ali, 1981:366ff; Bangladesh Bureau of Statistics 1985:84ff; and own calculations.

tic banks, so that no additional local currency enters the economy. They can use this foreign currency to import specific goods or to travel abroad,[3] or they can sell it together with their special import licences at a market rates called the 'import-permit' (IP) rate. The difference between the IP and official rates fell from 52 per cent in 1977 to 7.8 per cent in 1984, mainly because of the official devaluation of the taka against the dollar (Reza 1984:30–1). These special import regulations contrast with the strict official allocations of foreign exchange and the trade regulations that usually apply to imports into Bangladesh. The WES list comprises around 100 items. Though migrants have the right to import directly, this is done mostly by importers to whom they sell their foreign exchange/import licences at one of the daily auctions in the bank or through bilateral deals.[4] The foreign exchange is bought from migrants' accounts and sold to final users by dealers who pocket a margin of at least two paisa per dollar (Reza 1984:27). Another potential advantage from money earned abroad is lost by the migrants at the auctions, because the buyers often co-operate to hold down the price of foreign exchange. So the buyers make an extra profit at the expense of the migrant workers, who are not organized at all (Ali, 1981).

As migrants complain about the lack of banking facilities at their work place, delays in the transfer process and ignorance of the bank staff, some of them still send their money home through private agents or change it in their host country. Sometimes the money is remitted home through British banks. Thus part of the money which is statistically registered as transmitted from Great Britain has its origin in the Middle East (UN/ESCAP 11–12).

4.2.2 INVESTMENT POLICY

As explained above, lack of capital is seen as a major bottleneck to the economic development of Bangladesh. As an incentive for investment, the government of Bangladesh offers migrants to buy development bonds of various denominations with interest rates higher than those on bank deposits, and to invest directly in industries. The effective rate of interest for Wage Earners' Development Bonds is 23 per cent for bonds issued in 1981 and maturing in five years. This is one of the highest rates of all National Savings Schemes.

[3] The limit for those travelling by air is $100 for neighbouring countries and $300 for other countries.

[4] Until 1979 migrant workers had the right to use their foreign exchange while they stayed abroad and there to arrange the import of certain goods, namely transport vehicles, machinery and equipment into Bangladesh. In 1979, however, the government announced an embargo on dfirect shipment of most goods under the WES.

TABLE 10

FLOW OF Workers' REMITTANCES TO BANGLADESH

Year	Remittances (millions of US$)	Remittances as a percentage of Export earnings	Imports	GDP	Net National Product (factor costs)	Debt service
1976	23.4	5.8	3.1	—	—	36.1
1977	80.4	17.8	6.5	—	—	122.2
1978	110.3	19.1	8.5	—	—	72.2
1979	121.4	18.4	7.9	—	—	140.5
1980	249.4	32.0	10.2	1.7	1.8	314.0
1981	386.0	48.8	14.9	2.8	2.9	391.0
1982	329.0	42.8	14.3	3.1	3.2	291.7
1983	629.0	79.7	41.8	5.2	5.3	435.9
1984	550.0	68.3	27.1	4.2	4.3	332.0
1985	494.6	74.0	30.5	5.1	5.1	—

SOURCES: World Bank, *World development reports*: Bangladesh Bureau of Statistics 1985; OECD 1984.

In contrast, the lending rate of the Bangladesh Bank in 1985 was 10.5 per cent; for fixed deposits of three years and over it was 15 per cent (Bangladesh Bureau of Statistics 1985:S.87).

4.3 USE OF REMITTANCES

As a rule migrants sell their foreign currency to importers against takas. So the impact of remittances on the economic growth of Bangladesh depends on (see fig. 2).

—the way the takas are spent by he migrants' families.
—the goods and services imported with the foreign exchange.

4.3.1 USE OF REMITTED MONEY BY MIGRANTS' FAMILIIES

Average as well as marginal savings ratios within the same income groups are higher in households which receive remittances than in households who do not. Whereas remittance-receiving households in rural areas save on average half their income, other households with the same income save only 1.8 per cent. In urban areas the figures are 39.2 per cent and 4.2 per (Ali 1981:104).

A sample survey showed that more than half of migrants' investments are in land and buildings (see table 11). In rural areas nearly 37 per cent of

TABLE 11

INVESTMENTS IN BANGLADESH BY MIGRANTS, 1978–79

Sector	*Total investment (in US $1000)*	*Percentage of total investment*
Agriculture	6.4	1
Industry	48.2	5
Business	50.5	5
Land and buildings	543.5	54
Bank deposits (savings or fixed account)	358.7	35
Total	1 007.3	100

SOURCE: Ali 1981 and own calculations.

remitted money was spent on purchase of land and about 20 per cent on construction and improvement of houses. The figures for urban households were 23 per cent and 20 per cent. The result is rising land prices in areas with the highest migration rates (see table 12). Though the purchase of land is not productive investment for the economy as a whole, there could be a positive growth effect if this land mobility implied a transfer to a more productive use; but there is no hint of this. High and rising land prices will make it difficult or impossible for other buyers to compete with migrants' families. A positive growth effect could also occur if the seller of the land used the money received for productive investment. Normally, however, the reasons for selling land are different. The net result is that 'in the rural areas where there is a concentration of such migrants, land prices go up so high that small farmers and farmers with very little land are tempted to dispose of their holdings at a lucrative price instead of cultivating their uneconomic holdings; in the process they themselves swell the rank of landless peasants' (Ali 1981:74).

Since one fifth of migrants' investments is spent on building houses, it is not surprising that increasing remittances caused industries related to construction to grow significantly more than others (see fig. 6). From 1974 to 1978 the production index of cement rose by 600 per cent and that of processing of stone and earth by 500 per cent; the index of all other industries did not even double. Since the construction industry is labour-intensive, employment in this sector grew rapidly from the beginning of the migration process. Whereas between 1961 and 1974 it fell by 7 per cent, against an increase of 1.4 per cent in total employment, it grew by an annual rate of nearly 30 per cent in the decade 1974 to 1984, a period in which total employ-

TABLE 12

ANNUAL RURAL LAND PRICE INDICES BY REGION

Region	*1973–4*	*1974–5*	*1975–6*	*1976–7*	*1977–8*	*1978–9*	*1979–80*	*1980–1*	*1981–2*	*1982–3*	*1983–4*
Chittagong	179	221	304	380	546	737	871	1286	1637	2042	2437
Comilla	490	701	1000	1266	1477	1623	1741	1603	1876	2109	2354
Noakhali	242	366	479	678	733	892	1016	1352	1727	2136	2512
Sylhet	288	358	384	434	485	542	579	857	1156	982	1211
Dhaka	258	410	563	779	981	1216	1573	1679	1805	1884	2141
Bangladesh	259	352	432	577	690	832	959	1132	1245	1249	1367

SOURCE: Bangladesh Bureau of Statistics 1985:677.

ment increased by only 3.3 per cent (Based on Bangladesh Bureau of Statistics 1985:194). At the same time wage increases in the construction sector were above the average of other sectors (see table 4). The very high income elasticities for food (see table 14) will raise demand for agricultural products in the country through multiplier effects. They will last as long as there is new investment in construction but will be crowded out if no more income from abroad enters the economy.

Houses built by migrant families are regarded as unproductive durable consumer goods. However, the extremely bad housing situation in Bangladesh makes this expenditure a high priority. In the countryside people usually live in huts of bamboo which have to be rebuilt every two years and provide no water or hygienic facilities. In urban areas slums are very common. On an average there are two rooms for each family, and in each room there are three persons (Statistisches Bundesamt 1984:66). Therefore investment in housing is specially significant for welfare.

The government's attempt to stimulate productive investment with development bonds has not yet succeeded. In the 1983–4 fiscal year less than 0.5 per cent of remittances were absorbed by this programme. In earlier years its share amounted to not more than 0.2 per cent: deposits under the Wage Earners' Development Bond Scheme rose from $300 000 in 1980–1 to $2 500 000 in 1983–4.[4] In spite of generally low demand, there are oppor-

TABLE 13

CONSUMPTION PATTERNS OF URBAN AND RURAL HOUSEHOLDS OF MIGRANT FAMILIES

Consumption	*Household expenditure in %*	
	urban	*rural*
Food and drink	47.82	53.03
Clothing and footwear	7.07	7.55
Personal effects	1.82	2.48
Rent, house repair etc.	9.46	2.33
Fuel and light	2.95	3.73
Furniture	1.20	1.13
Domestic servants	4.72	5.21
Recreation	3.44	1.03
Festivals and ceremonies	4.93	5.76
Others	16.59	15.44
Average monthly income, US$	344.25	344.64
Average monthly expenditure, US$	209.02	172.25

SOURCE: Ali 1981.

Fig. 5: Organization of labour migration from Bangladesh, 1976-9

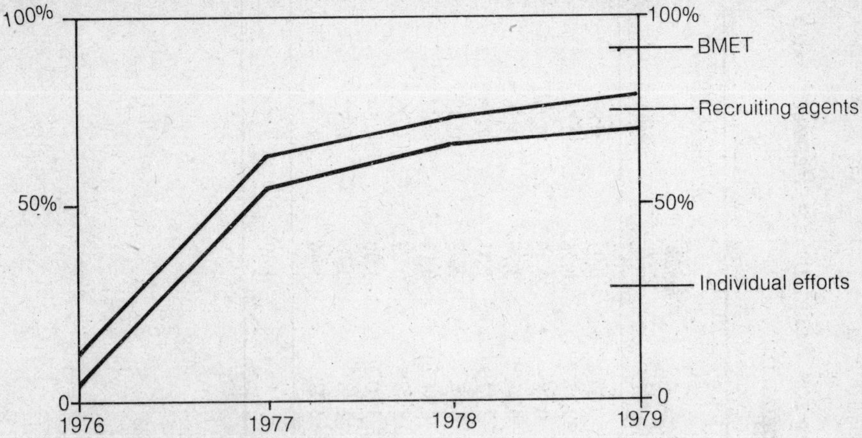

Source: Own calculation from figures of World Bank staff working paper 454.

tunities for productive investment, especially in the jute industry. The production of the jute mills in Bangladesh is not constrained by lack of demand for their product, and the shortage of yarn is one of the major causes of low productivity in the jute-weaving factories.Many mills with spinning capacity have recently extended their spinning operations to three shifts because of the present shortages of yarn (Kibria & Tisdell 1985:1159; Zingel 1983:90). New investment in this sector could have positive effects on export earnings and employment. However, as Bangladesh holds more than three quarters of world exports of jute (FAO, *Trade yearbooks*) it is not clear whether higher supply would increase export earnings or bring them down because of falling prices.[5]

With rising incomes, migrant families adapt to the consumption pattern of the income group they now belong to. Half the money is spent on food and drinks; the other main expenditure categories are clothing and footwear, domestic servants, and festivities and ceremonies (see table 13). The most important food item is rice, with nearly 40 per cent of food expenditure (see table 14).

Many studies suggest that the consumption level in Bangladesh is a problem of purchasing power and not one of insufficient domestic production capacities. Therefore supply and employment will increase with rising

[5] Based on Bangladesh Bureau of Statistics 1985: 588; exchange rates from IMF, *International financial statistics* (various issues).

Table 14
Main Categories of Food Expenditure, and Income Elasticities for Agricultural Products and Clothing of Urban and Rural Households

	Consumption patterns					Income elasticities		
	nation-wide	urban average	migrants	rural average	migrants	nation-wide	urban	rural
Total food expenditure	100	100	100	100	100	0.91	0.87	0.95
Rice	54.5	41.2	24.99	55.1	39.72	0.96	0.64	1.02
Wheat	7.8	8.9	4.21	7.7	0.98	−0.45	−0.21	−0.52
Milk	2.6	2.8	8.71	2.6	6.43	3.75	1.66	2.95
Edible oil	5.9	6.7	4.44	5.8	3.77	1.31	1.16	1.32
Meat	2.4	4.4	6.16	2.9	4.85	2.38	2.43	2.28
Vegetables	5.1	5.4	8.03	4.9	6.84	0.13[a]	0.67	0.34[a]
Fish	7.5	8.5	12.64	7.3	8.88	0.[illegible]4	0.95	0.83
Fruit	1.3	1.4	4.44	1.3	5.80	1.60	1.64	1.59
Spices	6.2	4.0	2.04	6.4	2.88	0.40[b]	0.92	0.34[b]
Sugar	0.7	3.0	2.57	0.5	3.02	3.36	1.64	3.82
Clothing				5.3		1.39	1.43	1.40

Sources: World Bank, Staff working paper no. 454; FAO 1983; and own calculations.

Notes: [a] The coefficient is not statistically significant at the one per cent level of probability.
[b] The coefficient is not statistically significant of the five per cent level of probability.

demand. For cereals, Khan estimated a Cobb-Douglas production function with a production elasticity for labour of 0.6 (Khan 1985); therefore a one per cent increase in production results in a 1.6 per cent increase in employment in rural areas. Though the price of cereals will climb, hitting people with a high propensity to consume the most, Khan concludes: 'An increase in income-earning opportunities would raise the level of effective demand.... Thus at low prices the situation of the poor will be even worse' (Khan 1985:1060). Significant production reserves of cereals could be mobilized by rising demand, creating employment in the agricultural sector. The effect will be strongest on rice, which has a high income elasticity and a high budget share. Income elasticities are highest for milk, followed by meat, sugar and edible oil, but these products have only small budget shares. They are significantly negative for wheat, which also has a small budget share.

Though a substantial part of the cereals and milk products consumed in the country are imported—about 28 per cent of all imports are food, with wheat being the most important item after petroleum—it need not follow that rising incomes will generally affect food imports because these are mostly food aid—especially from the EEC, Australia, Canada and the World Food Programme—all of which goes into the public distribution system for certain target groups which are unlikely to include migrants' families (Ahmad 1983:181–2). Increasing demand for edible oil, which has an income elasticity of 1.3 per cent and makes up 4.4 per cent of household food expenditure, could have a minor effect on the balance of payments because it is imported commercially. The same holds for sugar, which has an income elasticity of more than 3 per cent.

4.3.2 THE USE OF FOREIGN EXCHANGE

By far the largest part of imports from remittances is financed under the WES: its share of the country's total imports increased steadily from 3.4 per cent in 1974–75 to nearly 20 per cent in 1981–82 (Reza 1984:40–1). Most of these imports are finished consumer goods and raw materials, especially textiles. On average between 30 per cent and 40 per cent of the foreign exchange is spent on the import of finished consumer goods (see tables 15 and 16), especially second-hand clothing. Although its share fell from nearly 18 per cent in 1976 to 4 per cent in 1982, its total import value has stabilized at around $10m. Imported clothing can replace domestic production to a large extent. Since this sector cannot compete with the very cheap second-hand clothing, these imports will have negative growth effects and reduce the demand for domestic labour. Considering the high imports of cheap textiles, it is probably no coincidence that the domestic textile industry has the lowest growth rate of any group of manufactured

TABLE 15

COMPOSITION OF GOODS IMPORTED UNDER THE WAGE EARNERS SCHEME 1975–1979
(IN MILLIONS OF US$ FOR MAIN CATEGORIES AS PERCENTAGE OF TOTAL)

	1975		*1976*		*1977*		*1978*		*January–June 1979*	
	value	%	*value*	%	*value*	%	*value*	%	*value*	%
Consumer goods of which	13.950	34.2	22.405	46.8	25.678	37.3	29.669	30.1	20.398	32.7
second-hand clothing	5.173	12.7	8.532	17.8	11.064	16.1	10.235	10.4	4.935	7.2
betelnuts	0.314		2.066		1.668		1.794		1.069	
spices	1.193		1.731		1.847		1.781		0.817	
cars	—		1.196		2.483		5.847		1.844	
Capital goods of which	2.130	5.2	2.527	5.3	2.674	3.9	6.069	6.2	4.477	7.1
trucks and buses	0.242		0.532		0.541		3.072		2.414	
factory machines	0.628		1.111		1.069		1.311		1.181	
office machines and equipment	0.247		0.099		0.304		0.316		0.024	
tools and workshop equipment	0.253		0.248		0.159		0.311		0.321	
fruit	0.538		1.208		0.852		1.457		0.535	
filter cap cigarettes	0.673		0.454		0.360		0.843		1.049	
reconditioned engines and machinery	—		—		—		0.023		0.140	

Raw materials of which	24.651	60.5	22.919	47.9	40.465	58.8	62.764	63.7	37.406	60.1
cotton and synthetic textiles	11.808	29	11.243	23.5	11.502	16.7	22.078	22.4	12.357	19.6
dyes and chemicals	2.517	6.2	3.869	8.1	1.519	2.2	4.399	4.5	4.607	7.2
Totals	40.716	100	47.852	100	68.818	100	98.503	100	62.283	100

SOURCE: Own calculations from Ali, 1981:360ff.

[1] Transactions in US$ at the market exchange rate; period average as given by the International Monetary Fund.

TABLE 16

IMPORTS UNDER WES BY MAJOR COMMODITY GROUPS, 1981–82

Commodity	*US$*	*% of total*
I. Consumer goods[1]	90 702	31.7
of which		
dairy products and eggs	11 445	4.0
fruits and vegetables	4 578	1.6
coffee, tea, cocoa and spices	4 006	1.4
sugar, sugar preparations and honey	20 029	6.3
other food (including live animals)	3 720	1.3
beverages and tobacco	572	0.2
vegetable oils and fats	35 479	12.4
clothing	10 873	3.8
II. Raw materials[2]	127 325	44.6
of which		
crude fertilizer and crude minerals	2 289	0.8
chemical elements and compounds	11 159	
dying, tanning and colouring materials	4 864	1.7
medical and pharmaceutical products	2 861	1.1
textile yarns etc.	32 618	11.4
iron and steel	31 760	11.1
other raw materials	41 774	14.6
III. Capital goods	56 653	19.8
of which		
machinery other than electrical	13 448	4.7
electric machinery	9 442	3.3
transport equipment[3]	33 763	11.8
Other manufactured goods, not classifiable	7 440	2.6
Other items	6 295	2.2
Total	286 123	100

[1] Classification into categories I–III.
[2] Except coal, petroleum and precious stones.
[1] Classification into consumer and capital goods, as in table 15, was not possible.

SOURCE: Own calculations with data from Reza, 1984:45–6.

goods in Bangladesh (see fig. 6). Moreover imports of consumer goods might have demonstration and ratchet effects: people who get acquainted with them may change their preferences and as a result these imports may be hard to reduce when foreign exchange remittances fall.

Most of the imports financed by remitted foreign exchange are raw materials. Between 30 per cent and nearly 50 per cent are cotton and synthetic tex-

Figure 6: Index of industrial production in Bangladesh, 1974 to 1984.

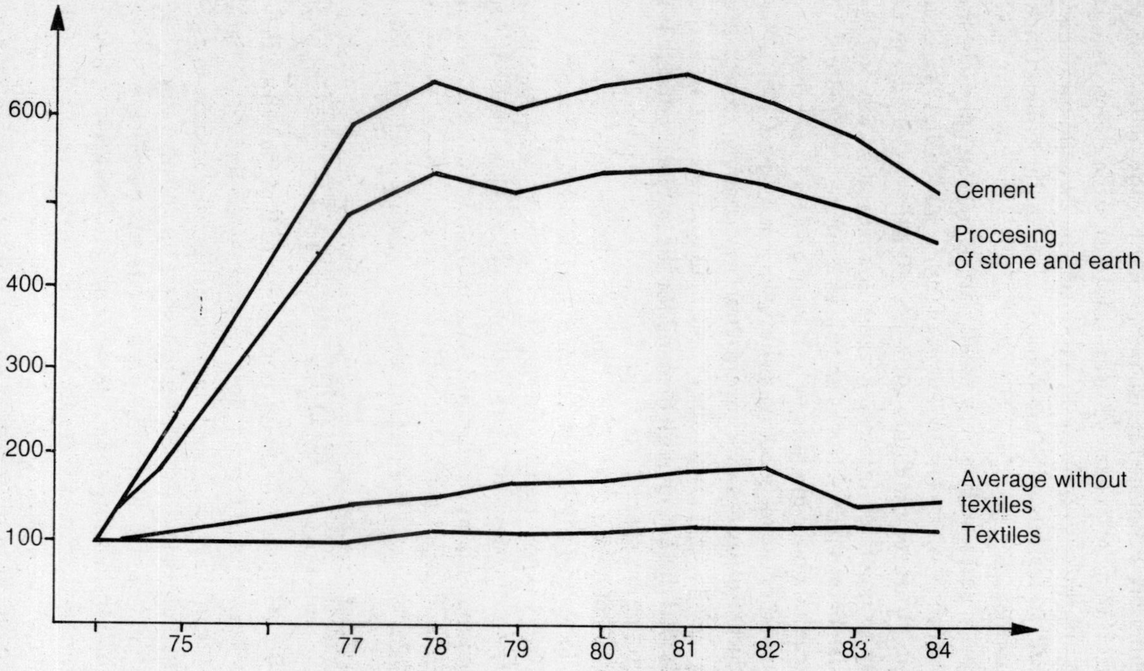

Source: Own calculations with data from Statistisches Bundesamt 1985.

tiles, which constitute the biggest single share of imports under WES. Obviously these will be used for producing consumer goods, namely clothing. Imports of raw materials might have better effect on labour demand than the import of finished consumer goods, because at least they will be processed within the country. However, as most of these imports are textiles, and thus substitutes for domestic products, the demand for domestic raw textiles will suffer. Since 1981 iron and steel are gaining importance among WES imports.

For many years, only a very small part of the foreign exchange—less than 8 per cent—was spent on import of capital goods. In 1981–82 its share increased. However the figure of nearly 20 per cent, shown in table 16, shows an exaggerated increase because it was statistically impossible to distinguish between cars, trucks and buses as in the years before. Allowing for this, capital goods might have a share of around 15 per cent.

The import of capital goods could bring into the country new technologies and productive capacities which are essential for economic growth. In contrast to imported consumer goods, they could help to create income in the longer run, provided there is enough demand for the goods produced. It is often difficult to import spare parts. Especially in the jute-spinning industry, the shortage of imported parts is one of the most important bottlenecks. According to Kibria and Tisdell replacement of parts is a long process, because all the machinery is imported but the import of parts is subject to a cumbersome administrative process and a shortfall of funds actually released: 'An inadequate maintenance system in this nationalized industry accentuates the frequency of mechanical breakdown in older machinery and thereby reduces the average number of spindles in older mills' (Kibria & Tisdell 1985:1159).

6. FUTURE PROSPECTS

The export of labour and foreign remittances to Bangladesh are determined by oil revenues of the main host countries (see fig. 7). These depend, among other things, on the oil-importing countries' success in developing new technologies and substitutes to reduce oil consumption. Research in this field and public campaigns to save energy, have been intensive and successful. Furthermore some suppliers of petroleum which have become very important in recent years are not willing to join the OPEC cartel, and even some of its members do not co-operate. In view of this situation and the development of oil revenues during the last years, another oil boom seems unlikely in the near future; stagnation or decline is more probable. This will have an adverse effect on the demand for foreign labour in the Middle East. As it will decline, the first workers to be released will most

Fig. 7: Growth rates of international contract migration from main Asian sending countries and revenues of oil exports of main receiving countries 1977-1984.

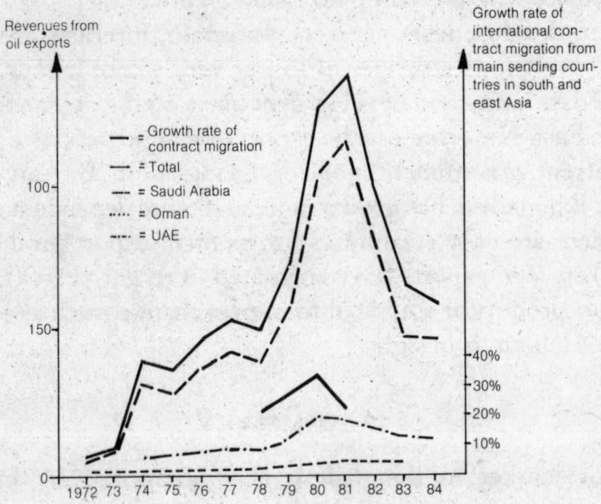

Sources: Own calculations with data from IMF, International financial statistics, and sources of fig. 5.

probably be from south and east Asia. Migrant workers from Arab countries have certain advantages: no language problems, lower travel costs, better understanding of the labour market situation and of employers in the host countries. For most of them, going to another Arab country does not even mean 'going abroad'. As the stage of intensive infrastructural development in the oil-exporting countries of the Middle East has approached its end and more emphasis is put on industrial development, the structure of demand for foreign workers changes. Now more and more skilled workers are needed for the new industries, while demand for workers with low skill levels is declining. However highly skilled workers are scarce in Bangladesh. The educational level in other supplying countries, like Egypt, the Philippines and Malaysia, is significantly higher, which leads to stronger competition. The development will probably result in loss of higher qualified labour and higher costs to the economy of Bangladesh. It is clear from the classification of people who registered their names with the Employment Exchange as seeking foreign employment that there is a large number of highly qualified people willing to emigrate. More than half of those registered at the end of the 1970s held masters' or bachelors' degrees, diplomas, or certificates of intermediary or secondary education (Ali 1981:26).

For Bangladesh, oil prices have a two-sided effect: when they are high, labour demand from the Middle East tends to increase. At the same time the country's foreign exchange expenditure on oil is rising (see fig. 8). So there is a possibility of compensating for rising oil prices.

As future developments are very uncertain, forecasts are not easy to make; and as there is a danger of losing very scarce labour, Bangladesh cannot build its long-term development plans on the demand for labour in the Middle East. Nevertheless the export of manpower has a high priority among current government policies (Bangladesh Bureau of Statistics 1985:931). Bangladesh has grown more and more dependent on exporting labour. There are easy substitutes for its main export product, jute, and earnings from jute exports have stagnated in recent years (table 17). No other export product or source of foreign exchange, such as a new market for exported labour, is in sight.

7. SUMMARY

The labour market in Bangladesh is characterized by high rates of unemployment and underemployment and falling wages, which are due to high population growth, stagnating demand for labour and insufficient education and vocational training. This caused hundreds of thousands of contract workers to migrate to the Middle East where wages and demand for labour are high. As these workers' skills are mostly in excess supply in Bangladesh, their migration has not caused significant losses of production. However their remittances are now the country's main source of foreign exchange. This is used mainly to import consumer goods and raw materials for their production, especially second-hand clothing and textiles which compete with domestic production. Only a small part is spent on the import of capital goods.

Migrants have high rates of saving, and they invest especially in land and buildings. This results in high growth rates of construction industries and rising land prices. Migrant families' consumption patterns differ only slightly from those of other families in the same income groups, and most of their additional consumption increases demand for domestic products. Some sectors, especially construction industries, are booming, but this will be over as soon as demand for foreign labour in the Middle East loses its importance. The end of the intensive building of infrastructure in the Middle East, and the development of new industries there, are leading to lower demand for unskilled workers and to higher demand for workers with scarce skills. Therefore the costs caused in Bangladesh by emigrating workers are increasing.

Fig. 8: Petroleum imports and workers' remittances to Bangladesh, and petroleum exports of major countries importing Bangladeshi labour

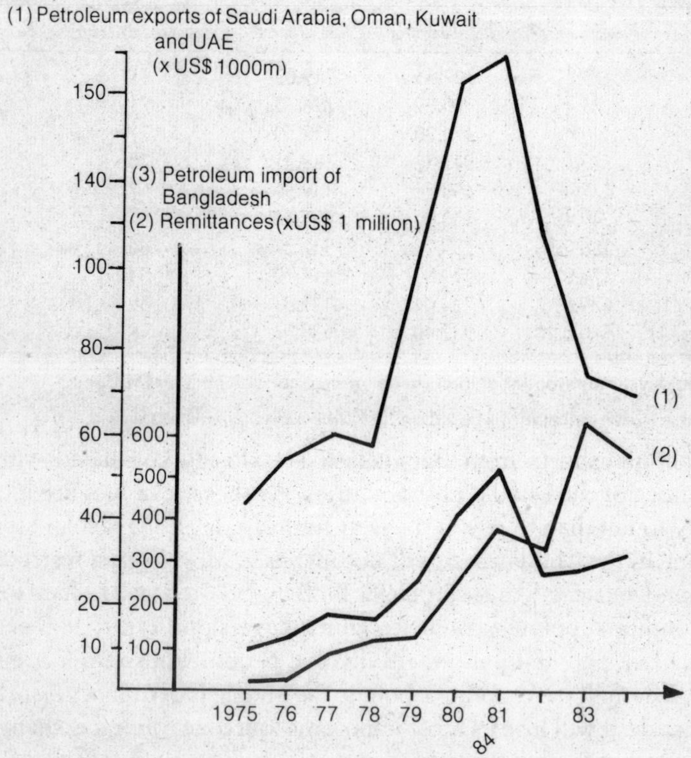

Source: Data from IMF, International financial statistics and own calculations.

These findings suggest that under the current system labour migration will have no long-term growth effects for the country as a whole. Nevertheless it might be considered positive as far as it brings with it a higher standard of living for the poor. Migrants' families are better off and the jobs they had before emigration can be filled by unemployed people. Increased demand for domestic products, especially in the construction sectors has created more employment. On the other hand some people have lost their jobs because of the import of goods which can only be imported with migrants' foreign exchange, especially in the textile sector.

TABLE 17

MAIN EXPORT PROCEEDS OF BANGLADESH
(IN MILLIONS OF US$)[1]

Year	*Remittances*	*Total exports*	*Jute exports*	*Jute exports as % of total exports*	*Remittances as % of jute exports*
1975	15.4	307.43	249.02	81	6.2
1976	23.4	400.99	296.73	74	7.9
1977	80.4	476.90	338.60	71	23.7
1978	110.3	549.52	385.21	70	28.6
1979	121.4	658.56	439.86	67	27.6
1980	49.4	758.90	496.86	66	50.2
1981	386.0	787.74	522.27	66	81.3
1982	329.0	770.82	414.70	54	79.3
1983	629.0	724.64	426.81	59	143.5
1984	550.0	932.40	538.93	58	101.9

[1] At mid-year taka-dollar market exchange rate, as indicated by IMF.

SOURCE: Own calculations based on IMF, *International financial statistics.*

Labour exports from Bangladesh are closely correlated with the oil revenues of the Middle East countries. As these revenues are much more likely to fall than to rise in the near future, at least the demand for foreign labour in the Middle East will not increase. Moreover, a restructuring of labour demand will cause problems for Bangladesh: it will be hard to compete with other supplying countries which have significantly higher levels of education, and emigration will involve people whose skills are scarce in Bangladesh. If the export of labour to the Middle East cannot go on, however, Bangladesh will lose its most important source of foreign exchange. There are no other markets in sight.

REFERENCES

Ahmad, Quazi Kholiquzaaman. 1983. 'The contribution of food aid to equitable growth in Bangladesh'. In *Report to the World Food Program*, Netherlands Government Seminar on Food Aid held at The Hague, 3–5 Oct. 1983, pp. 179–90. Rome: World Food Programme, Government of the Netherlands publication.

Ali, Syed Ashraf et al. 1981. *Labor migration from Bangladesh to the Middle East.* World Bank staff working paper no. 454. Washington.

Arab News, 12 April 1985.

Bangladesh Bureau of Statistics. 1985. *Statistical yearbook of Bangladesh 1984–85.* Dhaka.

Birks, J.S. and C.A. Sinclair. 1980. *International migration and development in the Arab region.* ILO, Geneva.

FAO. *Food aid bulletin*, no. 1/84. Rome

——— *Production yearbook* (various issues). Rome.

——— *Trade yearbook* (various issues). Rome.

Khan, Qaiser M. 1985. 'A model of endowment-constrained demand for food in an agricultural economy with empirical application to Bangladesh.' *World Development* 13, pp. 1055–66. Oxford Pergamon Press.

Kibria, M.G. and C.A. Tisdell. 'Productivity, progress and learning: The case of jute spinning in Bangladesh. '*World Development* 13, pp. 1151–62: Pergamon Press.

Leibenstein, H. 1957. *Economic backwardness and economic growth*. New York: Wiley.

Ling, L. Huan-Ming, 1984. 'East Asian migration to the Middle East: Consequences and considerations'. *International Migration Review 18*, pp. 19–36. New York: Center for Migration Studies of New York.

OECD (ed.). 1984. *Geographical distribution of financial flows*. Paris: OECD.

Reza, Sadrel. 1984. *Exchange rate incentive for home remittance in Bangladesh*. 1974–1983. Hong Kong: Asian Research Service.

Sinha, Radha. 1984. *Landlessness: A growing problem*. Rome: FAO.

Statistisches Bundesamt (ed.) 1984 and 1985. *Länderberichte Bangladesh*. 2 vols. Wiesbaden: Kohlhammer.

Stiglitz, J.E. 1976. *The efficiency wage hypothesis: Surplus labour and the distribution of income in the LDCs*. Oxford Economic Papers 28, no. 2.

——— 1982. 'The structure of labor markets and shadow prices in LDCs' in R.H. Sabot (ed.), *Migration and the labor market in developing countries*, pp. 13–64. Boulder, Colorado: West Review Press.

UN/ESCAP (ed.). 1984. *Bulletin for Asia & the Pacific*, xxxiv, 2. New York.

Vereinigung für Internationale Zusammenarbeit (ed.). 1986. *Handbuch für internationale Zusammenarbeit*, Teil I. *Die Länder: Bangladesh*. Baden-Baden: Nomos.

World Bank (ed.). 1984. *World development report 1984*. Washington.

——— 1985a. *Bangladesh: Economic and social development prospects*. 4 vols. Washington.

——— 1985b. *World development report 1985*. Washington.

Zingel, Wolfgang-Peter. 1983. 'Bangladesh' in *Handbuch der dritten Welt*, Band 7. *Südasien und Südostasien*, pp. 66–95. Hamburg: Hoffmann und Campe.

Indian Trade Unionism: The Crisis of Leadership

E.A. RAMASWAMY*

The Indian labour movement is in the throes of cataclysmic change. Even as the movement is struggling to cope with old legacies, it is being forced to reckon with major new circumstances. The perennial problem of trade union recognition continues to hang fire. There is no statute to compel recognition, nor any acceptable solution in sight for assessing the strength of competing unions. Deeply divided from within, trade unionism continues to be lost in debilitating internal squabbles. Leadership positions still vest in men who are not from the ranks of labour. The system of dispute resolution evolved during the peak of nationalist fervour remains in spite of its obvious limitations. The system has survived with no more than minor tinkering even though conciliation and adjudication have not measured up to the task. While all this may convey the impression of stagnation, the situation is one of deep ferment.

The force behind this change is the rank and file of the labour movement. The upheaval emanates from men and women who are growing conscious of their own situation as employees and trade union members, and who are more assertive towards the employer as well as the leadership. It is a situation which employers find disconcerting. Having become accustomed to managing labour through a leader whose writ ran without question, they complain that anarchic forces have taken over. The leaders are unsettled as well. The union is no longer a fief whose fruits can be taken for granted. The leaders are under constant scrutiny, and their tenure at the helm quite uncertain. These developments cannot be shown to exist across the board, nor can the process be said to have run its course. It seems nevertheless that the assertiveness of labour is so widespread that patches of quiescence are the exception.

Labour has embarked on this phase of defiance in response to significant changes in the environment. The pressures come primarily from the workplace, although problems of internal union government and the changing social background of the labour force are also of some significance. In recent times, employers have begun to perceive labour as a resource which is both expensive and difficult to manage. Traditional labour-intensive industries such as engineering, metal work and textiles have witnessed a steady escalation of labour costs. For employers who were accustomed to cheap labour, manning costs in excess of 25 or even 30 per cent of total manufacturing costs, which many labour-intensive industries are now touching, appears alarming. The deployment of labour also appears to be riddled with problems. Shifting workers from one shop or department to another, filling vacancies arising from absenteeism which may run as high as 20 to 25 per cent of the labour force, battling restrictive practices employed by workers who demarcate work finely and cussedly refuse to perform even minor tasks falling outside their domain, and coping with endemic overtime which has engulfed the production system—managers see these as the most irksome of their everyday tasks.

The strategies evolved by managements to cope with these problems are fraught with direct consequences for labour. One of the most pernicious practices from labour's point of view is the farming out of jobs to labour contractors. The contractors' men do the work on the premises of the employer, but are not deemed to be his employees. The range of tasks performed by these underpaid workers has increased steadily. Even capital-intensive process industries such as chemicals and fertilizers, whose manpower requirements are quite modest and whose labour costs are around five per cent of manufacturing costs, employ contract workers in labour-intensive sections. In fertilizers and process chemicals, where the only labour-intensive tasks are at the end of the process, it is almost axiomatic that contract labour must be employed to bag the product and stack it in the warehouse. All kinds of enterprises now employ contract labour to provide security services, man the transport fleet, run the canteen and even maintain the machinery. Although there is a law curbing the deployment of contract labour to perform tasks which are of a perennial nature and intrinsic to the operations of the firm, the practice is proliferating and extending to new areas.

Another method of shifting work from permanent labour is the putting-out system, whereby certain lines of manufacture are either scaled down or even completely scrapped and the products obtained from small manufacturers. Many multinational corporations in consumer products, electronics, and similar lines, where technology permits the farming out of manufacture to small operation get an entire range of products made this way. There are firms in the textile industry which get their fabrics woven by powerloom operators. The role of the parent corporation in this case is limited to checking quality and marketing the product under its brand name. The farming-out is so extensive in some cases that the firm's own employees have been reduced to a fraction of total employment, and the character of the firm itself transformed from a manufacturing to a trading one.

A third common practice is for enterprises in the organized sector to have on their rolls different categories of employees, who are paid differently and who enjoy vastly differing levels of security for doing the same kind of job. These categories include casual, temporary, badli, apprentice and trainee labour, apart from permanent workers who are the highest paid and most secure of them all. Although the less fortunate workers are constantly clamouring for entry into permanent employment, and have on their side a statute which requires them to be confirmed in service on completion of 240 days of continuous employment, managements are interested in denying them entry into the exalted portals for as long as possible. In practice there are numerous ways of beating the law and breaking the resistance of these workers, to keep them out of permanent employment for extended periods.

Finally, the very character of the employee force of organized industry appears to be undergoing a subtle shift away from blue-collar workers. The service sector which has been the fastest growing segment of organized industry has in any case been the preserve of white-collar employees. In recent times, manufacturing enterprises have also tended to expand employment in lower managerial positions at the expense of blue-collar workers. The expansion has been especially pronounced in such categories as junior engineer, junior manager, supervisor and foremen. The shift is sometimes achieved by a mere sleight of hand: the management may simply confer an imposing new designation on the top crust of the blue-collar force which transforms it into the bottom layer of the managerial cadre. The content of the job naturally does not change, nor do the emoluments and perquisites. What does change—adversely, from the employees' viewpoint—is these workers' ability to organize themselves, and this of course subserves management objectives. This strategy holds a special appeal to enterprises which employ process technology, as in pharmaceuticals and chemicals. With this kind of technology, the task of the operator in normal times is confined to watching instrument panels, turning valves (and where automation is advanced, pressing buttons) to control the process, and keeping a record of temperature, pressure and such other parameters. The operator needs to exert himself only when there is an emergency, as when a control system fails. Under these conditions, it is relatively simple to transfer the work to junior officers and managers, whether they are redesignated workmen or new entrants. In industries such as engineering and tyre-building, where it is a matter of actually working on the product rather than merely watching the process, it is more difficult to transfer blue-collar work to the higher categories, but even these industries have witnessed a certain expansion of the managerial force.

Whatever the strategy, the intention is unmistakable. The goal is to downgrade the blue-collar workforce by transferring work, and along with it control, away from manual workers. The steadily shrinking span of control of managers and officers, with junior managers in some enterprises controlling no more than a handful, is an indicator of the shift in the pattern of employment. All circumstances considered, the impression that organized industry conveys is that management would prefer to expand the casual, temporary and similar forms of labour at one end, and the managerial force at the other, so long as this helps to shrink the size of the permanent blue-collar force.

Cost reduction is one distinct advantage flowing from this change. Every form of labour, including even some categories of managerial manpower, is cheaper than a permanent manual force. Because of differences in the rate of neutralization of living costs, and the growing significance of dearness allowance as a proportion of gross pay, lower and middle managers sometimes earn less than the top crust of the blue-collar workforce. Nor are managers entitled to overtime payments, which make up a big chunk of blue-collar earnings.

No less important than cost is control. Permanent blue-collar workers enjoy the greatest security, and are hence the most difficult to direct and control. The various forms of casual and contract labour are by contrast highly insecure and therefore not easily organized by trade unions. Many unions also take the view that their concern is limited to the permanent force. As for managers, their associations, patterned closely on trade unions, are only now beginning to raise their head. In fact, managerial policies themselves have contributed to the collectivization of managers, for the initiative has frequently come from blue-collar workers promoted to managerial positions to nip trade unionism in the bud. A growing demand of lower and middle managers is to be recognised as workmen so that they can combine the best of both the worlds—blue-collar security and manager status. The demand is unlikely to be met soon, and the movement is likey to remain in its infancy in the foreseeable future. The perception of the top management is that managers are easier to control, and their resistance to close direction more easily overcome.

In addition to these strategies of reducing dependence on unionized labour, organized industry is also witnessing considerable labour saving automation. In labour-intensive industries, computer-controlled machine tools and other labour-saving equipment are gradually reducing manpower requirements. In capital-intensive technology, process control is being automated so that dependence on labour can be further reduced. White-collar jobs are being automated as well, with computers and new generation office equipment.

Trade unions have periodically opposed the introduction of labour-saving technology. While this opposition has been generalized among all categories of employees, white-collar workers have been especially strident in their resistance. But trade union opposition has nowhere been determined enough to prevent automation altogether. Labour has managed to slow down, rather than stop, the introduction of new generation technology. Where the management is determined, ways have been found to push through automation in spite of all the hue and cry.

Management-controlled automation has certain characteristic features. What has been eliminated through new technology is skill rather than drudgery or hazard. Typical of this is the pharmaceutical industry, where back processes are automated but not the tasks at the end of the line. The tedious tasks of packing, crating, spooling, pasting labels, arranging strips of tablets in cartons and inspecting liquids continue to be done by hand. The typical management strategy is to reduce labour requirements and increase capacity in the back processes through automation, to leave the manual tasks at the end of the process as they are, and then to bargain with the crew of the packing line to accept higher pay rather than demand additional manpower to cope with the increased flow of work. In automobile assembly, ways are found to speed up the assembly line and reduce labour requirements in fabrication with sophisticated machinery, but the paint booth is manned by masked painters because automatic spraying wastes paint.

In some cases, the unions themselves have been brought round to accepting automation after a long battle. In such cases, where decisions have been reached by agreement, labour has actually fared better: they have been able to protect manning levels, to safeguard the seniority and emoluments of redeployed workers, and to make redeployment itself less painful. In the banking industry, the All-India Bank Employees' Association, which is the leading organization of clerical staff, has signed a settlement agreeing to computerization with the Indian Banks Association, acting on behalf of the majority of commercial banks.

From labour's point of view, resistance to automation has been complicated by certain extenuating circumstances. Although there exist unions in banks, as well as in manufacturing organizations which are irreconcilably opposed to technological change, and although managements have been pushing ahead, it is hard for labour to think of automation in entirely negative terms. The experience of union leaders is that even as they battle to stop the entry of new machines, workers are vying with each other for the privilege of operating them. Individual workers look forward to better technology even though their colleagues face the risk of redundancy. Moreover the employers' failure to update technology may not always be in the interests of labour. Enterprises which have turned unprofitable and downed their shutters are usually among those which have persistently failed to modernize. When faced with the daunting prospect of closure, trade unions themselves have been forced to demand the introduction of new technology.

The choices before labour appear very limited: either they accept automation and the resulting redundancy, or they face the possible decline of the enterprise in the long run. But trade unionists themselves do not see the problem in such clear-cut terms. In normal times, when the enterprise appears to be doing reasonably well, their concern is not with the long run but with the immediate protection of their jobs, and this is why they are so implacably opposed to automation.

The employers' bag of strategies finally includes attempts at coaxing labour to take on higher workloads, or to agree to higher production norms. In sections of industry where wages are already high, the concern of management has been to devise methods of getting more out of the men rather than pursuing the conventional strategy of merely refusing to meet labour's demands. Indeed, it even seems that the demand for additional benefits at contract negotiation time does not trouble managements excessively if they can get higher production in return. The problem then is how to get workers to commit themselves, or to go beyond vague promises of cooperation which trade unions are ready to offer but which they cannot be pinned down to in practice.

At its simplest, the productivity drive takes the form of an incentive scheme, which simply means that workers are compensated for every additional unit of production above a predetermined threshold. Such schemes are common in industries where technology allows the individual worker's production to be measured, light engineering being the typical example. The overall experience is that incentive schemes do not measure up to management expectations. The primary problem is that management cannot compel labour to aspire towards incentive earnings. It is entirely up to the individual worker to pitch his production at the level of his choice so long as it reaches the threshold. For labour to aim higher, a number of preconditions have to be met. The rate of incentive per additional unit of production must first be attractive. If incentive rates are less appealing than overtime rates, and overtime itself readily available, it would make no sense for the worker to chase incentives. The threshold of production beyond which incentives become payable must be fixed reasonably, for a high base would reduce motivation. The managerial system must be geared to a high level of efficiency, so that supplies of inputs of the right quality and quantity are kept up and the plant maintained in good shape to allow continuous operation. Any lapse here immediately leads to the accusation that management is depriving labour of opportunities for additional income.

With all this, incentives can still run into problems. It becomes difficult to scale down production if the demand for the product slumps, because this has implications for incentive earnings. Redeployment of workers becomes more difficult than it already is, since the affected workers immediately figure out whether there are equal incentive opportunities in the new position. Changes in the product-mix may require renegotiation of the incentive rate, which can be problematic. What the management is looking for is greater control, whereas the incentive system leaves all the control with labour. The system allows workers to switch incentive production off and on as they wish, while the management is left powerless.

Vexed with these problems, some enterprises have gone on to negotiate revised production targets simultaneously with the agreement on additional benefits whenever the union presents a charter of wage demands. The settlement spells out the expected production as explicitly as the additional benefits, and increasingly also stipulates the penalty for non-performance, which may take the form of loss of at least a part of the additional benefits. Once again, this pattern is common where technology permits responsibility to be pinned on the individual. Where such clear attribution is not possible, the enterprise may bargain to lower manning standards, enlarge the job description of various categories of employees giving them a wider range of responsibilities, and generally strive to prune the labour force or get it to cope with the increased production capacity.

The experience with this strategy is rather mixed. While some enterprises have achieved significantly higher production, the problem generally is that the management expects the union to share responsibility for achieving production targets, on the grounds that the union was a party to the trade-off of higher production norms for better wages and benefits. The management is only secondarily concerned with enforcing punitive sanctions, the more imortant purpose being to meet production standards. It has not been easy for trade unions to live up to this expectation in a situation where workers can easily transfer their allegiance from one union and leader to another.

Employers are now veering round to the view that the most effective method of cutting down on labour costs and raising productivity may after all be to keep the entire business of work allocation as a management prerogative. What is at issue is the fixation of manpower requirement for a machine, section, department and eventually the entire plant. To put it differently, the crux is the fixing of the man-machine ratio. The allocation of work was already a part of managerial prerogative with growing union power and increasing labour costs, managers thought they should demand a *quid pro quo* by bargaining for productivity. If, as it is turning out, the union is not in a position actively to participate in meeting the agreed production norms, there may be no purpose at all in dealing with the matter bilaterally. The better strategy is seen to be to revert to unilateral fixing of manning standards and to bring down the labour requirement. Unlike the strategy of productivity bargaining, which looks at the end result, the aim here is for management to wrest control of labour and to assume responsibility for its performance.

Since it is not easy to take back into the realm of unilateral decision-making an issue which has already been dealt with bilaterally, employers have found it necessary to emphasize that manning standards would in fact be fixed not unilaterally but scientifically. The strategy is to hand over the determination of manning standards to industrial engineers who use methods of work study that hark back to F.W. Taylor. Fixing manning standards through work study is a continuous process of re-assesing labour requirements in the light of every change in technology, improvement in machinery and alteration in layout. To reinforce the claim that this is not a partisan method of settling a contentious issue, employers are sometimes willing to involve industrial engineers nominated by the trade union in fixing the norms. Employers have derived significant moral advantage from the claim that the method is scientific and therefore in the just interests of everyone. Labour has as yet no method of countering this claim.

From the employer's point of view, scientific fixing of work norms can serve yet another purpose. It supplies them with a powerful excuse for denying labour a share of the benefits which accrue from increased workloads, reduced manning levels and redeployment. The employers distinguish between labour and machine productivity, and the benefits of changes arising from work study are said to be the result of investments by the enterprise, in which labour cannot claim a share. In this view, workers can legitimately claim to share only those increases in productivity which accrue from their own effort. What the management is looking for is a trump card which would enable them to roll back labour claims for higher wages every time a contract is negotiated. Although it is impossible to distinguish in practice between benefits arising from labour and machine productivity, and on that basis to determine the just claims of the two sides, employers hope that attributing productivity to additional investment will contain labour's demands.

The inadequate trade union response to these shifts in managerial policy has been the major source of instability in the labour movement. The character of the leadership has had much to do with this inadequacy. The labour movement has been dominated since its birth by middle-class professionals, politicians, social workers, and lately even by elements from the underworld. An important attribute of all these leaders has been their unconcern for work-centred problems. The leadership has assessed itself, and believed others were assessing its performance, by the simple yardstick of additional monetary benefits. Even where the leaders have been motivated by a concern for labour's welfare, their ability to comprehend issues in the right perspective has been in doubt. Considering that many of them control a vast number of organizations from widely divergent industries, the failure to appreciate work-related problems should not come as a surprise.

Where work issues are bilaterally settled, the typical response of trade union leaders has been to put a price tag on workplace problems and to bargain for countervailing monetary benefits. A further variation of this is to trade greater managerial control over the work process for higher benefits. There is little difference between unions and union leaders of various ideological persuasions in this regard, for radicalism has often meant merely a higher price tag. In some ways, the leaders themselves have been instrumental in causing employers to step up pressure on the work front. They have aggressively bargained for higher benefits regardless of the competitive position of the enterprise, its technological base and ability to absorb additional financial burdens. When faced with mounting claims for more money and relative unconcern for how the work gets done, employers have chosen the obvious course of syphoning off work to cheap labour and stepping up pressure on the permanent force.

A second characteristic of the leadership which has influenced the course of the labour movement, is indifference to democratic forms of decision-making. The vast majority of leaders think of their members as ill-informed and incapable of deciding what is in their own best interests. One might say that they too have carried the burden of the historical stereotype of industrial workers who cannot take responsibility for themselves. As a result, even humane leaders with a deep compassion for labour arrogate to themselves the power to decide on labour's behelf. It is only a rare trade union where strike ballots are taken, issues debated in the general body or executive committee, and broad-based decisions worked out on vital questions. The more common form is where members get to know from company notice boards about commitments made in their name. While trade unions may be oligarchic everywhere, oligarchy in the Indian labour movement does not flow merely from the operation of Michels' iron law. It flows also from a stereotype, and from the moral conviction of the leaders that the members need to be guided by the hand.

A close nexus has emerged in recent times between the top layers of the trade union movement and employers in general. Employers have by and large come round to the view that trade unionism is not objectionable in itself so long as the unions operate within certain limits. They have come to realize that their own perception of the legitimate bounds of trade unionism is not far different from that of the union leaders. As Allan Fox observed, what hurts the employer is not so much the compulsion to bargain about the market price of labour as the prospect of sharing the power to determine the work process. Indian employers encounter a leadership which has no first-hand experience of work and work-related issues, and further believes that all problems can be reduced to the single common denominator of money.

Employers also expect the trade union to be structured hierarchically and bureaucratically in more or less the same manner as the business organization. What they look for is a leader who will speak with authority on behalf of his constituents and stand by agreements. The demand is really for strong leadership. They recognize that a strong leader is likely to be overbearing, but do not mind this so long as he also smothers opposition within the union and compels the members to fall in line. Democratic union government is perceived as an academic prescription which will not work in reality. Decmocratic leaders are seen to be weak, easily manipulated by conflicting pressure groups within the union, and unable to ensure that commitments are honoured. The employers find, once again, that the leadership perceives union government in much the same way. They have forged symbiotic relationships with powerful leaders who were once condemned as anarchists. The powerful leaders no doublt pressured them into favourable, even exorbitant, settlements, but they also brooked no resistance from workers sliding back from negotiated agreements.

This meeting of perceptions has produced in ironic turnabout in employer attitudes in a relatively short time. While the complaint in the fifties and sixties, when trade unionism was in its infancy, was that professional agitators were inciting gullible workers. the employers now want nothing more than that the present pattern of leadership should grow strong and continue.

Industrial workers have been rapidly growing aware of their situation in the work organization and the trade union. Although it is difficult to speak of workers in an undifferentiated manner, as it is to speak of employers and trade union leaders, there is considerable evidence of growing consciousness across the board. The changing social background of labour has contributed to this awareness. The traditional stereotype of the industrial worker as an illiterate low-caste migrant, pushed out of the village by unemployment, was dubious at the best of times. Now it is becoming more untrue with each passing day. Most enterprises in the organized sector just would not consider for employment anyone without a school leaving certificate, and the presence of graduates and postgraduates in the blue-collar workforce has long ceased to be a novelty. For the skilled trades, a technical diploma from an industrial training institute is an additional advantage. With wages so attractive and employment so scarce, the blue-collar workforce too become a polyglot mix of workers from varied caste and religious backgrounds. The situation is so vastly different from the stereotype that it is hardly worth attacking it.

The awareness has come about also because of mounting pressures at the workplace. Some of these pressures are so insidious that they are not easily perceived. The employment of causal and contract labour, and the farming out of jobs to small manufacturers, are of no concern to the individual worker so long as his own employment is secure, which it usually is because of the ubiquitous no-retrenchment clause in settlements. The declining employment of permanent workers and the scaling down of the permanent force also do not appear worrying, because permanent hands are not sent away except on voluntary retirement with a handsome parting package. Since industrial workers generally aspire to turn self-employed entrepreneurs and proprietors, the generous retirement package is seen as a step towards achieving this. Problems begin when those who quit voluntarily become destitute after squandering the money, and those left behind are redeployed. The real crunch comes when the management does not replace natural attrition caused by death and superannuation. This hurts because the firm's commitment to give preferential employment to the wards of retiring employees, incorporated increasingly in settlements, ceases to operate when the permanent force is scaled down.

The pressures are stronger when workloads are revised. If workload revision results from work study not accompanied by higher compensation, there is a sharp sense of grievance. Even if workload revision comes about through a bilateral settlement with some compensation, workers tend to react adversely. In their view, either the increased work is not accompanied by technical change, or it is disproportionate to the modification in equipment, so they have to work harder to make up for the failings of the management.

The problem is especially acute where workloads continue to be revised in successive settlements, with no more than marginal modifications in the plant. Pressures of work begin to tell on middle-aged workers, who are also the ones at whom voluntary retirement schemes are targeted. Mounting work pressure is especially visible in the private sector which is growing conscious of labour cost. Although the public sector too employs contract labour extensively, there has so far been no attempt to scale down the permanent force through voluntary retirement. Work is also easy-paced because of heavy overmanning and lax supervision. From the point of view of workers exposed to continuous revision of work norms, the problem is not merely that these revisions are disproportionate to investments in updating the plant, or even that they are strained beyond reasonable limits. The problem is equally that they are not consulted before union leaders commit them to the revision. Almost invariably zealous leaders, wanting to clinch a hefty pay increase, trade off revised work norms without bringing up the issue in any union forum. In some cases the revised norms are not even incorporated in the formal settlement, but covertly agreed between the leader and the management.

It is in the context of such arbitrary settlement of vital issues that the character of the leadership and internal union processes gain significance. The limitations of the present leadership are becoming obvious. Even the rationale for entrusting the labour movement to those leaders is evaporating. They were a historical necessity at a time when workers could not articulate their interests, but that is hardly the situation now. Worker activists who understand trade unionism and the work organization have emerged everywhere, but outside leadership still appears indispensable. There are powerful forces buttressing the present style of leadership. With the government involved in the industrial relations system as a third party, both workers and employers see political links as essential for managing the industrial relationship. Political manipulation may not be an everyday necessity, but is nevertheless a vital second string to the bow. Workers are forced to depend on the leadership for political leverage. The employers too have developed a vested interest in keeping the leadership alive. Finally, the leaders themselves seem unwilling to step aside and let worker activists take over.

The immediate remedy for this situation appears to lie in allowing the leaders to stay at the helm of the unions, but stimulating the democratic processes to make them accountable to the members. If the leaders can be made to act democratically, their acceptability to the management can be turned into an asset, ability to flex political muscle retained as an emergency back-up, and several advantages maximized simultaneously. The internal political processes of trade unions, which were for long a matter of indifference to labour, have gained a significance never before enjoyed. With shopfloor activists as the vanguard, workers have begun to hem in their leaders and constrain them act in acceptable ways. What is happening is a determined bid by the rank and file on one side, and the leader occupying the top position of president or general secretary on the other, to bring various pressures to bear on each other. The process has gone on for some time, and could presumably continue much longer before the movement reaches some kind of balance. This situation of flux finds its most dramatic manifestation in quick changes of leadership which is ultimately the most potent weapon in the hands of labour.

The frequent displacement of union leaders, increasingly visible in all major industrial centres, symbolizes the turmoil in the labour movement. It is the tip of the iceberg, beneath which lie a variety of factors which have brought about a new situation. It might appear at first sight that industrial workers are merely exercizing their normal democratic rights by periodically changing their leaders. In fact they are doing much more by giving expression to their experience at work and the trade union, they are attempting to alter the course of the labour movement.

Workers' Struggles and Indigenous Fordism in India

GÉRARD HEUZÉ

A prolonged stay in a remote Indian village deprived me of easy access to academic sources and data. A trip to Maharashtra, which I had planned in order to get a fresh view of recent controversies and events, was delayed. Nevertheless this paper contains elements for a debate if the reader would kindly consider it as a working paper.

We are dealing with the oldest, the largest and, in many respects the economically most advanced industrial concentration of India: the conurbation of Bombay, Thane and Belapur. The situation in the neighbouring town of Pune (Poona) may to some extent be related to what is observed in this metropolis. Even if this discussion were concerned with an isolated spot, and I am convinced it is not, the trends which are exposed there would assume significance.

I shall mainly discuss the problem of relationship between men and their production, mediated or not by class relations or, in other words, the connexions and interrelations between economy and society. It has been said many times that the Indian industrial worker is a poor man looking for survival and, at best, for job security. By describing the complex interrelations between deliberate working class strategies and the worker's economic situation, and refusing to give the former a passive and secondary role, I shall try to challenge this assertion. The second part of the paper consequently deals with working class autonomy. As a sociologist I have tried to describe, appreciate and understand this specific level. In the concluding section, I consider briefly—from the point of view of 'industrial relations'[1]

[1] This very commonly employed sociological term is not often used by French sociologists. A suspicion of ideological bias—of a tendency to ignore class conflict—may be the reason.

and also from other points of view—the possibilities for the emergence of a new social order, which could be as important as fordism was in the USA fifty years ago.

At the beginning of the seventies Bombay city and suburbs constituted a metropolis of more than five million people. About one million worked in secondary sector activities, a little more than half of these in the so-called 'unorganized sector' which is an aggregate of small-scale mechanized enterprises, one-man handicrafts, factories..., employing less than ten people (or twenty without use of power). The others were in the 'organized sector', mainly composed of public sector undertakings, transport, administration, and large, medium and small-scale private industries. Economic dualism was and still is an important feature of the Bombay labour situation (Holmström 1984). There was a sharp and increasing contrast between small workshops in the 'unorganized sector' and big factories of the multinational corporations, or of the biggest Indian concerns, located in the northern suburbs. It was nevertheless possible, even at this time, to question the nature of this apparent dualism, Numerous 'small-scale industries' were developing partly in the 'organized', partly in the 'unorganized' sector. Casual employment by big firms was on the rise. It seemed that, if differences between the groups of laboures in wages, living conditions and security of employment were increasing, the corresponding economic disparities were more and more tempered by a network of relationships between economic sectors and groups of firms. The development of a continuum, related to a slow process of economic integration, was then reinforced and accelerated by the growing disparities in legal status between workers. One could distinguish the following important groups of workers, with typical labour situations:

Government employees (in railways, ports and docks) were the best protected by law but not very well paid. Their working conditions were not so bad, except in some categories (locomen, leaders), and the pace of work was often slow. Their housing situation varied widely from overpopulated slums to clean and cheap municipal tenements.

Textile workers, numbering 250 000, had in the fifties been the leaders of Indian Labour in struggles for wages and social advantages. Hampered by the sluggish growth of the industry and deprived of trade union liberties in 1946 by the BIRA,[2] which effectively imposed on them on INTUC orga-

[2] The pro-Congress union RMMS took over the leadership of textile workers at Independence. This followed a long period of communist popularity and a series of general strikes between 1920 and 1940. At that time many of the Congress leaders were socialists. The Bombay Industrial Relations Act (BIRA 1946), sponsored by an employer-government alliance, aimed at stabilizing the situation. Only recognized unions had bargaining rights.

nization, their economic situation was stagnating in absolute terms but, compared to the better off segments of the working class, it was decaying: their pace of work was rapidly growing and their wages were not. Their housing conditions were bad and becoming worse.

Employees of multinational corporations, of some big Indian enterprises like Godrej and Mafatlal, and of a few Indian public sector enterprises (petrochemicals etc.) constituted a new fast growing groups located in the suburbs. Here an industrial culture might be absent but wages were better, as were working conditions, social advantages and housing. These workers resembling a white-collar class in many respects, began to be considered an example and a model by others.

The situations generally observed in *small and medium scale private* industries in the 'organized sector', mostly Indian-owned and often sub-contractors of the larger firms, were radically different. Low wages and very poor working conditions were usually associated with ignorance of the law where it protected workers. This fast growing group of enterprises was usually very profitable, and the workers, who were often those who had not been able to enter the best companies, were acutely conscious of this.

Small and very small workshops, spread all over the city, or located in industrial estates, also constituted a fast growing section of productive establishments. Casual work, deprived of any legal regulation, with very low wages and bad working conditions, was the usual lot of workers in these units. They were mostly inhabitants of slums, as were the casual labourers, construction labourers or workers employed from time to time in big factories.

Unemployment[3] was growing fast in Bombay at that time and the city had witnessed the first Shiv Sena wave, a movement led by local middle-caste

The provisions of BIRA declared that if a union was no longer representative it could be derecognized, but the law has proved to be a very strong instrument for maintaining consensus, since estimating union membership is an administrative, politically-influenced decision. When the socialists left Congress in 1948, they tried to get their followers back and to build a more independent union that the RMMS, which had become conservative. Strikes, which have occurred frequently since 1950, were mostly failures because of obstruction by the official union which is closely linked to the factory foremen. On at least three occasions, it was proved that the RMMS had lost the workers' favour, and in one case the judiciary recognized this, but the RMMS was not dislodged. Apart from its bureaucratic and paternalistic methods, the RMMS has developed its own industrial bargaining practice. This is a 'poor deal for labour' characterized by a constant policy of avoiding trouble and generally accepting the workers' present situation. It combines clientelism and a policy of gradual, moderate joint management.

[3] It seems that no labour situation can be understood without considering those who have no work and are looking for it; particularly in India where the employment situation is so bad.

Hindus with a kind of proto-fascist ideology mixed with religious revivalism and community pride, which aimed at evicting the non-Maharashtrians from Bombay. It was possible for this to happen because so many young men were disappointed after looking for a job in the 'organized sector' (men, not women: unemployment is scarcely an issue for women in India, even if women are increasingly excluded from job opportunities). Some were reluctantly joining small workshops as helpers, others were trying to do odd and casual jobs, and many others, staying idle, were waiting for a better future while subsidized by their families. The old spectre of unemployment was not as fearful as it is today but it was enough to shape everyone's strategies.

At this moment in the history of the city, it was not possible to reduce working class actions to a single principle or a set of attitudes. Offensives mostly about wages, and shy submission, related mainly to the fear of dismissal, could be observed in different units and types of factories; also, sometimes, in the same unit and among the same workers. Nevertheless it is not too much of a reduction to describe the trade union movement as attached to a socially conservative consensus having deep historical roots. Unions were mostly developed in the big industries of the 'organized sector', and they had strongholds in the public sector. They had been a historical answer to the worker's aspirations but did not really belong to the workers. Leaders of middle-class origin, acting as brokers between managements and workers, who got their growing importance from growing legislature interference, were and still are a striking feature of Indian trade unions. All organized campaigning activity was *legalistic and economistic*. Where there was no labour law, there were no union leaders, and consequently no unions. This was the case in the 'unorganized sector' and in many small enterprises in the so-called 'organized sector'. The trade union bosses were the only ones siding with labour who were able to understand English, the language of law and politics and to hold discussion with managers and ministers. They were like *fathers* and *masters* (in the way that schoolmasters are) of a restive workforce; or at least they tried to act as if they were. Notice that a 'black' side of trade union activities (rivalries and violence) was never negligible. Notwithstanding their political cleavages, most leaders agreed that the working class was feeble and uneducated and that its main problem was security. This was not false but it was also aimed at reinforcing the intermediate position of professional trade union leaders between capital and labour. They began in the 1920s to 'exchange' low wages for more security (it was a harsh time for labour) but they succeeded in achieving full consensus only after Independence. Low wages were maintained or only slowly improved 'in the national interest', and very little was said about working conditions. Greater stability of employment and a very slow pace of production were demanded as a matter of reciprocity, in the shadow of state protection. This was only partly convenient to Indian industrialists and 'industrial relations' remained tense, but it was based on a realistic appreciation of the economic situation. Workers asked for holiday facilities and got them. They tried to resist the speeding-up of their work, and they succeeded in those fairly numerous protected large-scale industries which had monopoly markets and sold their products at very high prices, and in the majority of new state-owned concerns. However, unprotected casual labourers in large factories, and workers in small subcontracting units, were working harder and harder. Union leaders were often out of step with workmen's aspirations and their reputation was bad, but the workers accepted the consensus. The equilibrium reached seems to have suited village-minded unskilled workers. In fact they had little choice. During the 1960s the labour unions got many legal provisions enacted the conditions of workers were slightly improved in the upper strata of the 'organized sector'—the big companies and now state ventures. Social change during the sixties seems to have undermined this *unwritten and usually spoken fundamental agreement.*

Workers as a whole became more city-minded and urban-based. The new waves of migrants (more than 500 people arrived in Bombay every day), including many poor families from drought-affected areas but also young graduates seeking 'good clean' jobs in the cities, were aiming more and more at staying in the metropolis for ever. Industrial workers were learning better the hard rule of city life—competition—and they tried to meet the challenge by getting a better education for their children. The school educated young industrial workers could understand the social game on a wider scale. School attendance helped to reduce the inferiority complex of manual workers in relation to white-collar workers, managerial staff and trade union leaders. The intrusion of fairly important section of high-to-middle caste people, belonging to the dominant community (middle caste Hindus from Maharashtra), into the ranks of the working class also caused some transformation. These people were not accustomed to submission and frugality as the old *mazdūr* (unskilled worker), belonging to depressed sections and low status groups, had been.

That is not to assert that society had changed deeply. Everything went slowly, in an evolutionary way. The stability of hierarchical concepts was (and still is) striking. They might be more rooted in the family pattern, left unchanged, than in the shifting caste system. Popular street life and neighbourhoods were (and are) the most important features of *workers' organization* since long before unionism, and were ruled mainly by *communalist feeling* and paternalistic client networks: little has changed today in this regard. More and more workers were realizing that their position in these networks, and in the political one which linked the state and the common people, could be better. They began trying to grasp more material advantages from local political leaders. They succeeded to some extent and consequently wanted to oblige the trade union *babu* (clerks, educated people) to listen to their claims. These were mostly about wages, as rising prices during the late sixties, especially in Bombay, were a threat to all. Education was an expensive venture and fair housing a ruinous one in Bombay. Wages were for a long time the most prominent demand of Bombay labour and the only one which brought about workers' unity. It was exacerbated by the appearance of high wage islands in the 'modernized' and 'rationalized' industries of the city. Workers were able to compare themselves with a privileged group. They hesitated less and less to ask for equality when they realized that they had become a force. Industry was no more an isolated spot in the country's economy and they were becoming numerous. Workers were nevertheless only a potential force, because as their conditions became more and more differentiated, their organizations began to split along political and non-political lines. The working class was more massive and conscious but workers were a divided lot.

These facts explain many of the reasons for the rise of independent trade union leaders like Dr Samant. Independent leaders were not a novelty in Bombay at that time. Important unionists of the fifties had already begun to act in this way. The fact is that they did not prurpose a deal any different from others, even if their organization was a one-man affair, crudely managed on paternalistic lines which were fairly well liked by the workmen.

The new brand of independent union leaders was not originally interested at helping to give birth to a new socio-economic order in Maharashtra. Some, as usual, were men apparently connected with central federations but in fact engaged in building a personal empire. Others were mavericks, completely isolated from organized union practice and ideology, who rapidly took to running their unions in the way enterprise managers do their business: for money. Among this stratum of 'industrial relations managers', only a minority felt that a new consciousness was coming and that the workers' needs and expectations were not the same as before. But it is a general fact that independent unionists were not tied, as leaders of big bureaucratic bodies are, by regulations, slow procedures and political motivations. It is no accident that some of them, unlike most of the others, were able to understand the message. Whatever their speeches and declarations, the central federation cadres had always stayed apart from the bulk of the working class. Some were respected but they were hardly popular, except during and after successful strikes. Independent leaders were usually not respected at all except by tiny groups of followers. The interesting fact is that they were weaker, occupying insecure positions and competing with each other to win the workers' favour. As they were not much protected by laws and governments, nor promoted by political parties, they felt themselves obliged to listen to the workers' demands. A big federation boss without a following is still an office-bearer. An isolated independent leader is an unemployed man. In different ways, some of them tried to get more 'extra' social advantage for labour but *money was the issue.* It was the custom at the time that independent leaders, as businessmen, got a percentage of any wage increase they could secure (the habit has not faded away). In this regard workers, like these unionists were interested in 'more money in the pocket'. This was to be the slogan of the seventies. From the very beginning there was a kind of interaction, developed in a largely unconscious way, between workmen and leaders. As the workmen became more assertive and made more demands the leaders tried to make an adequate response and sometimes became fairly creative. These two factors—workmen and independent leaders—cannot be separated.

One may ask why the workers had not created new organizations for themselves, if the conservatism and timidity of the old ones were so resented. Firstly the process was slow and irregular. Secondly, and this is the main point, the workers did not want to build organizations by themselves. A structure without a big name at its head to give a sense of unity had no future among Bombay labour at the time. Belonging to the dominant classes, independent outsider unionists also did not fear repression. They were efficient, like any professionals. Last but not least, hierarchical and paternalistic attitudes among the workers led naturally (i.e. 'culturally') to such a solution. The new leader was a *babu* (middle-class educated man), like previous ones but something had changed. He was a lone man, competing in a tense and narrow market of union leaders, and he had to succeed or to leave. *The workers were turning the old patron-client relationship to their advantage.*

The hesitations, complexities and main characteristics of the process can be illustrated by a brief look at the career of the most important, popular and successful independent union leader of the area, Datta Narayan Samant, a Maratha by caste who was born fifty years ago in a village on the Konkani coast between Bombay and Goa. Samant was not initially an 'independent' leader but an office-bearer of INTUC, the Congress Party's trade union wing, which is the largest of the central organizations and the one most attached to the old social consensus. Living at Ghatkopar in the north Bombay suburbs, this ex-medical doctor witnessed the growth of the new working class and observed the problems which faced some sections of it. He said sometimes that he was deeply moved by the life of 'unorganized sector' workers and slum dwellers he approached during his election campaigns (he was elected a

Congress member of the Maharashtra Assembly in 1967, and is now—since 1985—a Member of Parliament in New Delhi). This may be true, and indeed the 'INTUC leader turned independent' became more and more 'radical' at the end of the sixties. This approach brought him several immediate successes; he became increasingly popular among workers in the engineering industry, where his union had begun, and then in the chemical industry. He led hectic struggles and was quickly recognized as the workers' champion and the terror of managements. He failed in one long strike, at the Godrej company where the union is controlled by the management. He was jailed during the Emergency; but this emerging union leader did not spare the Janata government which released him. By then he had the support of the Congress Party, which had been driven into opposition by its electoral defeat, and he began to direct and represent what is now commonly known as the 'Samant wave'. It was not a general strike but a three-year-long process of strikes, lockouts and counter-strikes in large, medium and small-scale modern and less modern industries in the northern suburbs. The radical 'Doctor' was put out of INTUC in 1980 when the Congress Party came back to power.

Some years earlier, Samant had given up two main ideas of the consensus age. The first was the legalistic approach, and the second was moderation in demands. Workers wanted more money, in the quickest way. They resented being considered 'second-class citizens'. Taking his inspiration from the voice of the workers, he said that legal procedures, which could (and can) last for years and were aimed at preventing autonomous action by labour, should be scrapped. Wage demands had previously amounted to Rs 10–20 a month (the 1979 textile strike won a princely increase of Rs 4 month). The demands rose to one, two, even five hundred rupees a month. After a movement led by Samant, the Indian-owned Mukand Steel company paid a minimum wage of Rs 1058 in its Bombay factory. This firm, which radically modernized its production process as a result, was the only Indian one at the time to stay among the 'top ten': all the others were multinationals. Many other Indian and foreign-owned firms were to join the good payers in the following two years.

The new form of struggle was effective because of a new kind of contract between workers and the leader. They had to obey him, but he promised never to give up the struggle until all demands were met. Strikes went on for months, sometimes years. Private owners of middle-sized industrial enterprises, who were the leader's main target and were also the main exploiters according to the workers, were afraid, and the success of strikes was impressive. In a few years the standard of living of a large section of the working class, mostly employed in the middle and lower strata of the 'organised sector', improved greatly. The aim which inspired the workers to greater militancy was parity with the better-off section, who themselves did not disdain Samant's methods or personality.

In 1983 he had more than a million committed followers and his union was the largest in Maharashtra.[4] Two years before, textile workers at 63 large factories had asked, or rather demanded, that Samant should lead their historic strike. Samant was faithful, paternalistic and adamant as usual, but he could not bring success to the workers. He realized at this moment that the state was the most powerful and determined watchdog of the old-style 'moderation' in 'industrial relations'. He and the militant workers also met with considerable opposition from the traditional left and more generally from the bulk of the politicians. At a mass meeting in May 1982, Bhosale (Congress), Dange (CPI) and Thackeray (Shiv Sena), who usually oppose each other, agreed to condemn the Doctor's inflexibility. This was a great moment in the history of the social consensus. The leader moved towards a more radical and global political view, and started to think of a 'Labour Party' which would be the first in Indian history. After some time, workers in small scale industries and even tiny workshops were demanding and obtaining his help.

The kind of independent unionism which the great leader built up was not a common one. Most independent leaders did not combine worker radicalism and business-like unionism in the way Samant did. They might have some problems with legal procedures but they did not oppose them outright as he did. Like Samant they had paternalistic and authoritarian relations with the workers but they did not give the members the kind of autonomy they enjoyed in the great leader's union, barring two or three exceptions (A.G. Mehta, Khanolkar). This is not a paradox. Many sections of the Maharashtra General Kamgar Union, the Samant (disaffiliated) union founded in 1980, are in fact largely managed by the workers themselves. Their day-to-day life is in the hands of rank and file leaders, mostly educated skilled workers and white-collar employees. One-man leadership is made for struggle. The usual independent unions have no efficient organization at the grassroots. Their bosses grasp opportunities to lead struggles and make money and go elsewhere when the 'job' is done. They are not interested in the workers' movement. Their following consists of this vast shapeless mass of workers who developed the habit of joining many unions, independent or not, without trusting any of them.

It is clear that the tremendous success of Samant's methods has induced other unionists, even those who stay in central federations—party-affiliated

[4] All membership figures are bogus. Many workers join several unions, and union leaders are never afraid of exaggerating. The official figures are strongly based in favour of INTUC. Nevertheless Samant's union was clearly the most popular at the time.

or not—to copy the 'new star' and adapt to follow his example. More and more employees were asking their leaders, whatever their political affiliations and philosophies, to follow Samant's way; and if they did not, the workers began to desert the leaders.

Samant was not different from other independent leaders in giving more and more attention to economic matters in the conduct of union struggles. He was even a little late in doing so. The previous aim of trade union leaders was to negotiate for as long as possible, in order to get wage increases more or less equivalent to inflation. Their main strategy in accordance with government policy, was to get more fringe benefits (leave, social security, provident fund, housing etc.) and to emphasize the legal aspects of the matter. Pressed by the impetuous demands of labour, the new generation of unionists—both independent and affiliated—was compelled to change its ways. Unionists began to ask themselves *how much each kind of employer, or each individual employer, would be able to give.* They started to work out rates of profit and wage/capital ratios in order to determine the possible gains in each specific situation. Samant did this, but sometimes he failed, forcing a unit to close after an exhausting struggle. Mehta and Dastur, other well-known union leaders in the city, had long been known for their understanding of that side of the problem. The new union practices were not isolated from considerations of politics and power: many entrepreneurs would rather starve than satisfy the demands of workers and independent leaders, as they did not want to share their power in the factory. The new emphasis on economic matters, *putting aside legal procedures and ideological considerations*, has nevertheless been striking. For example, during the first lockout at Premier Automobiles, the manufacturers of Padmini cars, Samant calculated that the share of wages in the factory's costs did not exceed 5%. As 12% was common in other parts of the world, he asked for, and won, a Rs 400 increase for 4000 metal-workers. After this event the workers bought the 'Doctor' a car. As pressure from workers increased, as it did continuously over the five years between 1977 and 1982, the unions paid more attention to matters of this sort.

The reaction of the managers and owners of industry was not united. A strong section, centred on the Textile Millowners' Association and organizations of middling entrepreneurs, took a firm stand against the Samant tide and the accompanying waves. Many of the smaller industrialists and a fair member of the big ones were attached to management practices connected with the industrial relations consensus. They sold expensive products to a small and protected market and did not want to change anything in this profitable situation. Some were also under financial stress. *Big corporations*, which owned most of the textile mills, reacted in the same way, since they considered the textile industry as a place for getting *capital without making any investment*. Labour must remain cheap and submissive. Some big industrialists declared nevertheless that Samant and others were waking up Indian industry, which had been much too attached to old techniques, state protection, and commercial rather than industrial attitudes—a kind of 'Malthusian' entrepreneurship.[5] 'Labour should be more expensive but more efficient,' they added, 'that is the only way to build up competitive industries'.

Those who had given wage rises to the city's working class, during Samant's movement, were soon thinking about ways to get their precious money back. Their main proposal, after months or years of conflict,[6] was to link wages with productivity. It was an age-old controversy, and historical experience had shown the workmen that it usually meant a sharp intensification of work, badly compensated by small monetary advantages. The situation was very different at the end of the seventies. For the first time, workers had real money, and it was a question of getting more. In January 1983 the lowest-paid workers at Premier Automobiles earned Rs 1100 a month. This rose to Rs 1850 by the end of the year, after another strike and an agreement between the management and the MGKU: an agreement which included a productivity deal.

It is not possible to say whether it was the workers themselves who overcame their old fears of this kind of 'bandage', or whether it was the independent leaders—growing increasingly popular as they won more wage rises—who persuaded workers to change their minds. The fact is that this was a turning point. The independent unions, especially the MGKU, promised to act as watchdogs during the implementation of the agreements. They would take care that the result would not be sheer exploitation. At the same time they promised the managements that they would hold workers to their side of the deal and they began to do so, usually with some success. The workers earned much more money, and the factory aften increased production on a large-scale, to meet the rising cost of labour. Does this not remind you of Henry Ford's policy in the USA?

The transformation may be recent and local, but we should understand its significance. This is the first time in India that a large group of industrial workers have broken through the framework of laws and regulations, and succeeded in getting wages which may make possible—to a limited extent—a consumer society for workers. This has been achieved through a renewal

[5] This description of entrepreneurs' attitudes has nothing to do with demography. It is just an analogy between Malthus' proposals to limit population and the employers' reluctance to produce more and pay more. It is commonly employed in French labour studies.

[6] Lock-outs have always been a major feature of industrial conflict. Indian millowners are more ready to strike than workers are.

of the old leadership, and it has been—at least to some extent—an expression of the genuine mind and will of Bombay workers. It has led to the end of the old preference for a slow pace of work, which was strongest where workers were protected by law. This does not mean that workers have changed their minds radically: they do not enjoy boring machine work, but they are more ready to tolerate it. They are at least willing to consider linking wages to productivity. The consequences of this development are not yet fully in evidence. First, it has brought about large-scale modernization leading to a reduction of the work force and the workers are divided over the issue. Some agreements accepted it on a moderate scale. Others were ended for this reason when new conflicts arose.

This movement with independent leadership has not only been able to secure good wage rises for the workers. It has also helped to promote a general, although uneven, renewal of important sections of industry. If tomorrow more goods at a cheaper price are produced by industrial methods for a mass market, then the 'industrial community'—workers and managements—the wider society and the government could give some credit for it to workers' radicalism and to the new leaders' social creativity. These people are building an indigenous 'fordism'. They are now fully conscious of what they are doing: 'We are bringing economic progress', as Dr Samant said to a journalist in 1982.

The 'Samant phenomenon' has its equivalents in other parts of India. I suggest that the promulgation of the 'New Economic Policy' in 1985 would have been more difficult if there had not already been pressure from these living social 'agents of modernization'. They are certainly very different from what it usually meant by the term, and they seem less 'rational' than the many speeches by those who uphold the consensus, but htey have proved their efficacy, or rather their socio-economic relevance. One interesting feature of the situation is that the move towards a kind of fordism was nto prompted by the conscious planning of modern managers, but by the 'uncontrolled' demands of workers mediated by a system of competing union leaders. *It seems that economic competition, which has been weak because of state protection and 'Malthusian' management, has been partly replaced—as a force for socio-economic change—by acute competition among trade unions, and on a wider scale, by political competition.*

This is not to assert that every change came from the workers' side. We have to consider that economic and social facts are not separated but in constant and deep interaction. A first impulse was given by multinational corporations during the sixties. The innovations of some industrialists, especially those who introduced taylorist methods in large factories made it possible for them to impose—at first by compulsion—work norms which the workers gradually came to consider inevitable. The introduction of productivity awards, strongly appreciated by young permanent workers who got the best wages in their own factories, was also an early manifestation of management pressure for gradual change. The presence of high-wage islands in some sections of industry, due partly to early successful union action and partly to deliberate management strategies adjusting to the scarcity of skilled labour, has been also a factor which pushed the workers forward. The argument is that industrial workers, far from being a timid lot of protected and downtrodden people, have shown that they can seize opportunities when motivated, and that they are also builders of history, artisans of economic and social change. The question whether they have been fully 'class-conscious' may be irrelevant and we shall not discuss it here.

Recent events suggest some conclusions to the arguments developed in this paper. Millowners and small entrepreneurs are reacting to the deal which has been imposed on them. Victimization of union activists is rampant. A slow process of dismissal, on obscure and hidden grounds, is taking place to discourage the worker's militancy. The owners' main argument, backed in this by the state, is that the new union practices were illegal. The owners seemed ready to welcome increased competition between firms, but they are less willing to accept high wages and union control which are the main targets of union action in many factories. Increased competition seems to be a factor which drives them, first to reduce labour costs, and then to modernize, following the entrenched tradition of the past thirty years. A race to increase production per head, using the same machinery but without new investment, is taking place at the expense of the worker's health and sometimes his life. The accident rate is increasing in all branches of industry, especially in chemicals, and the permanent workforce is stagnating once more. The use of labour contractors, on the other hand, is increasing.

One of the means the owners employ to win this class struggle is to divide the unions. There are plenty of unions in Bombay, and on the whole this did not prove a hindrance but a help to workers' militancy in the seventies. This was clear especially when labour was able to choose the 'best' leaders and to reject others, a situation which occurred for example among engineering and related workers of medium and large factories. In the textile industry, where a big union was forced upon workers, they could make no progress. Fully aware of this, the industrialists' organization FICCI has argued continuously in favour of 'one factory, one union'. What is in question now is the management's ability to split well-entrenched, popular and radical unions, especially the MGKU sections. There is often no need for management intervention, as the workers are divided along may lines and are better at fighting the management than at exploiting the kind of joint management their victory has led to. Many sections have also cut their ties with the independent federations and are becoming plant-based unions. This kind of union has been common in the multinational-owned modern factories of north Bombay since 1965. This has been an early reaction of workers to political union rivalries and an adaptation to a kind of collective bargaining favoured by progressive managements. Old and new plant-based unions are still controlled by the workers, but they try to avoid the long and exhausting struggles of the past decade. Facing automation and an end to recruitment, some of them are trying new and less harmful forms of pressure (work to rule, mass casual leave). Many think of placing a renewed emphasis on legal regulation and protection, and all are moderating their demands concerning wages. Some formerly successful unions are also becoming more and more corrupt, indulging in rackets and selling social peace to the managements. This is a well entrenched tradition of strong minorities in India's unionism but the growing tide of unemployed youths ready to pay or to do anything to get jobs, and the rise of Shiv Sena, which is rapidly spreading clientelism in the places where it did not exist, are giving a new impetus to the process.

Many plant-based unions are quickly coming back to independent leaders after a period of isolation. They seem to prefer moderate ones like Khanolkar, Mehta and Dastur, and it is striking to observe how each union *chooses* the style of independent leadership it needs according to the factory situation. Samant was the best for taking the offensive. The others are used, more or less crudely, to secure the gains. The decay of the workers' movement has not put an end to the popularity of the main independent leaders. Samant is still the greatest, even if his political career seems to be failure.[7] His increasing involvement in the 'unorganized sector' could be a major breakthrough for the union movement. In this connection, it seems that paternalistic pattern of independent organizations is more adaptable, and easier for people in small units to use, than the large-scale bureaucratic organization of central or local federations led by highly-educated outsiders.

The biggest shadow threatening the recent historic movement of workers, and even industrialists, is the growing nightmare of unemployment. Today more people are registered in the employment agencies (how many unemployed are not?) than as employees in the 'organized sector', in Bombay as in the rest of India. People are asking for jobs and the elected politicians, the local and central governments, are forced to react. They did so in one case by giving subsidies to the textile industry and preventing it from going

[7] To be elected a Member of Parliament is a measure of great popularity, especially if we consider that the 'Doctor' opposes both Congress and Shiv Sena, the dominant organizations in Bombay. His failure relates to his founding of a Labour Party. Samant is alone.

elsewhere after the textile strike. Thirteen more old Bombay mills have been nationalized, and the city's textile industry has become primarily a public sector one. Small industries are helped if only by the lack of any control over working conditions and wages. Labour-intensive processes condemned by the New Economic Policy may be revived, even if they produce more problems than they solve. Short term views and electoral considerations are important once again. Industry may have to go back to the old habits of protected small-scale markets. In this situation the consensus is reviving, at least partly, and workers' autonomy, which has recently been more limited by law, could suffer badly. The workers have to adjust to the 'black laws' as they did in the Emergency.[8]

The question which arises here is not whether people feel that better paid and protected workers 'exploit' the others unemployed, casual and unorganized workers who have not got many of the newly acquired benefits. They have in fact got some money through family networks, because there is large scale redistribution in some sections of the working class which even cuts across sectoral boundaries. Local politicians and some national leaders are saying these things in their speeches just to please the affluent sections of the modernized peasantry. In fact, in the city, those who can better their lot do so and no one objects. The main problem is that, in the new conditions of life and culture, unemployment become more and more unbearable. The development of communalist, chauvinist and localist feelings, which are very common among the middle and lower sections of the working class and may spread into the whole society, could be the most powerful and destructive answer to the achievements that workers have won for themselves and for their country in past years. A complete regression is quite possible. This is not an expanding industrial country like the USA in the twenties, but a previously colonized and now over-populated and weakly industrialized young nation.

Let me conclude provisionally that it is not only techniques which mould human behaviour patterns but also men's thoughts and acts which affect the shape and the pace of technical evolution. I hope this will lead to more discussion.

(Author's English Text revised for publication by Anton Pinschof and Mark Holmström)

[8] The most important of the recent 'black laws' are the National Security Act (1980), the Essential Services Maintenance Act (1981) and the Anti-Terrorist Act (1984), which can be used to curb labour activities. There are also state Acts (e.g. in Tamil Nadu, Maharashtra and Bihar).

REFERENCES

Abraham, A. 1981. 'Textile industry, cotton prices and Datta Samant'. *Econ. & Pol. Weekly* XVI, 52, 2119–21.

Batra, V.K., Kalra, N.K. and Mediratta, S.K. 1985. *Illegal strikes in India*. Delhi: Triveni.

Basu, T. 1982. 'Textile strikes and Datta Samant.' *Frontier*.

Breman, J. 1976. 'A dualistic labour system? A critique of the "informal sector" concept'. *Econ. & Pol. Weekly* XI, 48, 1870–6; XI, 49, 1905–8; XI, 50, 1939–44.

Chhachhi, A. and Kurian, P. 1982. 'New phase in textile unionism?' *Econ. & Pol. Weekly* XVII, 8, 267–72.

Chandavarkar, R. 1981. 'Workers' politics and the mill districts in Bombay between the wars'. *Mod. Asian Studies* XV, 3, 603–47.

Chatterjee, R. 1980. *Union politics and the state: A study of Indian labour politics*. New Delhi: South Asian Publishers.

'Correspondent' 1978. 'Working class women and working class families in Bombay'. *Econ. & Pol. Weekly* XIII, 29, 1169–73.

Dadi, M.M. 1973. *Income share of factory labour in India*. New Delhi: Sri Ram Centre for Industrial Relations and Human Resources.

Das, A.N., Rojas, F. and Waterman, P. 1981. 'The labour movement and labouring people: Notes towards a research proposal'. *Human futures* (New Delhi) 4, 4, 3–24.

Economic & Political Weekly 1975. 'Productivity deals: Case of Lube India'. *Econ. & Pol. Weekly* X, 3, 57–60.

——— 1975b. 'Tamil Nadu: Decline of trade union bosses'. *Econ. & Pol. Weekly* X, 19, 747–8.

——— 1981. Special number on the Indian working class. *Econ. & Pol. Weekly* XVI, 44–6, 1717–1868.

——— 1983. 'An example of a "production incentive" system'. *Econ. & Pol. Weekly* XVIII, 23, 999–1000.

Indian Express. 1983. 'Break-away group scores over Samant'. *Indian Express*, 21 March 1983.

India Today. 1982. 'Datta Samant, the striking terror'. *India Today*, 28 Feb. 1982.

——— 1983. 'Datta Samant at the crossroads'. *India Today*, 31 July 1983.

Clarity. 1981. 'Samant for workers' control over unions'. *Clarity* VII, no. 39.

Bombay. 1980. 'The taming of Datta Samant'. *Bombay*, 22 Sept. 1980.

Factsheet Collective. 1983. *The ten-month Bombay historic textile strike*. Bombay: Centre for Education and Documentation.

Ghosh, A. 1980. 'The working class'. *Seminar*.

Gupta, D. 1977. *The Shiv Sena movement, 1960–1974*. Ph.D. thesis, JNU, New Delhi.

Heuzé, G. 1985. 'La sécurité ou la liberté? Reflexions sur les nouvelles formes d'action syndicale en Inde contemporaine.' *Esprit*.

——— 1987. *Travail et travailleurs en Inde*. Nantes: Lersco.

Holmström, M. 1984. *Industry and inequality: The social anthropology of Indian labour*. Cambridge Univ. Press and Hyderabad: Orient Longman: 1986.

Iyer, R. 1980. 'The Datta Samant factor'. *Business Standard*, 15 Sept. 1980.

Joshi, H. and V. 1976. *Surplus labour and the city: A study of Bombay*. Delhi: OUP.

Kothari, R. 1984. 'The non-party political process'. *Econ. & Pol. Weekly* XIX, 5, 216–24.

Labour Bureau. 1971. *Survey as to how workers support themselves during retrenchment, lay-off, closure and strikes and collection of data regarding indebtedness*. Simla: Labour Bureau. Summarized in Labour Bureau, *Third digest of labour research (1968–1972)*. Chandigarh and Simla: Labour Bureau.

Mathur, A.S. 1965. *Trade union elite in India*. Agra.

Patankar, B. 1981. 'Textile workers and Datta Samant'. *Econ. & Pol. Weekly* XVI, 49, 1981–2.

Pendse, S. 1981. 'The Datta Samant phenomenon'. *Econ. & Pol. Weekly* XVI, 16, 695–7; XVI, 17, 745–9.

——— 1984. 'Politics and organisation of urban workers'. *Econ. & Pol. Weekly* XIX, 8, 340–56.

Rao, P.K. 1983. *Industrial wages in India*. Lyon: Colloque 'Economie et Humanisme'.

Ramaswamy, E.A. (ed.). 1978. *Industrial relations in India: A sociological perspective*. Delhi: Macmillan.

Ramaswamy, U. 1983. *Work, union and community*. Delhi: OUP.

Revri, C. 1972. *The Indian trade union movement*. New Delhi: Orient Longman.

Sengupta, A. 1979. 'Workers' needs and expectations and strategies of motivations'. *Econ. & Pol. Weekly*, Review of Management, Aug. 1979, pp. M–83–90.

Singh, J. 1980. *India's trade union leaders*. New Delhi: National.

'Special Correspondent' 1982. 'Orgy of violence and arson in Bombay'. *Indian Warrior*, 23 Aug. 1982.

Tellis, O. 1980. 'Bombay's trade union wars' and 'Many uses of the Doctor: Pawar uses Dr Samant as a pawn'. *Sunday*, 14 Sept. 1980.

Tulpule, B. 1982. 'Bombay textile workers' strike: A different view'. *Econ. & Pol. Weekly* XVII, 17–18, 719–21.

Vaid, K.K. 1972. *Gheraos and labour unrest in West Bengal*. New Delhi: Sri Ram Centre for Industrial Relations and Human Resources.

Index

o